ESSAYS IN
EIGHTEENTH-CENTURY
ENGLISH LITERATURE

PRINCETON SERIES OF COLLECTED ESSAYS

This series was initiated in response to requests from students and teachers who want the best essays of leading scholars available in a convenient and relatively inexpensive form. Each book in this series serves scholarship by gathering in one place previously published articles representing the valuable contribution of a noted authority to his field. The format allows for the addition of a preface or introduction and an index to enhance the collection's usefulness. Photoreproduction of most or all of the essays keeps costs to a minimum, preserving resources for the publication of new manuscripts.

ESSAYS IN EIGHTEENTH-CENTURY ENGLISH LITERATURE

Louis A. Landa

PRINCETON UNIVERSITY PRESS
PRINCETON, NEW JERSEY

To
HAZEL AND EVELYN
AND
THE MEMORY OF MAYNARD

ACKNOWLEDGMENTS

The following is a list of the places and dates of the original publication of the essays in this volume. I am grateful to the various editors and presses for permission to reprint.

"Swift's Economic Views and Mercantilism," *ELH, A Journal of English Literary History*, X (1943), 310-35. Reprinted by permission of The Johns Hopkins University Press.

"*A Modest Proposal* and Populousness," *Modern Philology*, XL (1942), 161-70. Reprinted by permission of the University of Chicago Press.

"Jonathan Swift and Charity," *Journal of English and Germanic Philology*, XLIV (1945), 337-50. Reprinted by permission of the University of Illinois Press.

"Jonathan Swift: 'Not the Gravest of Divines'," in *Jonathan Swift, 1667-1967: A Dublin Tercentenary Tribute*, eds. Roger McHugh and Philip Edwards (Dublin: Dolmen Press, 1967), pp. 38-60.

"Swift, the Mysteries, and Deism," in *Studies in English, Department of English, The University of Texas 1944* (Austin: University of Texas Press, 1945), pp. 239-56. Reprinted by permission of the University of Texas Press.

"Swift's Deanery Income," in *Pope and His Contemporaries: Essays presented to George Sherburn*, eds. James L. Clifford and Louis A. Landa (Oxford: Clarendon Press, 1949), pp. 159-70. Reprinted by permission of Clarendon Press.

"Jonathan Swift," in *English Institute Essays 1946: The Critical Significance of Biographical Evidence; The Methods of Literary Studies* (New York: Columbia University Press, 1947), pp. 20-40. Reprinted by permission of Columbia University Press.

"The Shandean Homunculus: The Background of Sterne's 'Little Gentleman'," in *Restoration & Eighteenth-Century Literature: Essays in Honor of Alan Dugald McKillop*, ed. Carroll Camden (Chicago: University of Chicago Press, 1963), pp. 49-68. Reprinted by permission of the Trustees of William Marsh Rice University.

"Johnson's Feathered Man: 'A Dissertation on the Art of Flying' Considered," in *Eighteenth-Century Studies in Honor of Donald F. Hyde*, ed. W. H. Bond (New York: Grolier Club, 1970), pp. 161-78. Reprinted by permission of the Grolier Club.

"Pope's Belinda, the General Emporie of the World, and the Wondrous Worm," *South Atlantic Quarterly: Essays in Eighteenth-Century Literature in Honor of Benjamin Boyce*, LXX (1971), 215-35. Reprinted by permission of Duke University Press.

"Of Silkworms and Farthingales and the Will of God," in *Studies in the Eighteenth Century II: Papers presented at the Second David Nichol Smith Seminar*, ed. R. F. Brissenden (Canberra: Australian National University Press, 1973), pp. 259-77. Reprinted by permission of the Australian National University Press.

"London Observed: The Progress of a Simile," *Philological Quarterly: From Chaucer to Gibbon, Essays in Memory of Curt A. Zimansky*, LIV (1975), 275-88. Reprinted by permission of the University of Iowa Press.

CONTENTS

ESSAYS IN
EIGHTEENTH-CENTURY
ENGLISH LITERATURE

INTRODUCTION

The essays in this volume were originally published in various scholarly journals and collections over a period of roughly three decades ranging in time from 1942 to 1975. Of the authors who are the main focus of the discussions Jonathan Swift has received by far the most extensive treatment. Seven of the essays are concerned with him; Alexander Pope, Samuel Johnson, and Laurence Sterne are central figures in single essays. Of the two remaining essays one is devoted to the great metropolis, London, as Englishmen of the seventeenth and eighteenth centuries viewed it; the other is a study of a pervasive and influential idea or concept in the mercantilist economic thought of the times, a rationalistic concept that awed men of all persuasions and found its way reverentially into the works of theologians, scientists, and ethical writers as well as literary men. I wish to suggest that it will be misleading to consider an essay in this volume which bears the name of an author in the title as the sole domain of that particular author. The approach I have used permits—in fact, it demands—that a host of writers be used to build up the background or climate of opinion which intellectually nourished the writer under discussion. Such a climate of opinion, drawn from both major and minor authors past and present and from various fields, represents a body of ideas, presuppositions, and assumptions the writer shared with others of his day and to which they would respond. Logically this approach ought to prepare a twentieth-century reader to read the eighteenth-century authors, to an extent at least, as contemporaries sharing a common heritage. In most of the essays reprinted here works of the several authors have been placed in this cultural matrix and examined not from the vantage point of literary merit but as the authors assimilated and adapted for their own purposes certain concepts and ideas from both traditional and contemporary culture, specifically as these concepts and ideas had been formulated in the seventeenth and eighteenth centuries by many thinkers in the fields of economics, religion, and science.

I have, it will soon be apparent, given more attention to the climate of economic opinion, appropriately in view of the Englishman's article of faith that his country had become the greatest of all trading nations. The English merchant (i.e., the man engaged in foreign trade) was justly celebrated as a national benefactor. Yet there was dissent: though one segment of the nation proclaimed that commerce was the true basis of a nation's flourishing, an equally convinced group maintained that a flourishing agriculture was more valuable. This latter view derives from the biblical and classical tradition of the importance of an agrarian culture. It was eloquently supported, about the time Swift published *Gulliver's Travels* (1726), by Richard Bradley, Professor of Botany in the University of Cambridge and a Fellow of the Royal Society, who maintained that one learns from the Holy Scriptures themselves that the science of husbandry was "appointed by God himself."

In the clash of opinion between the trading and the landed interests Swift was a vocal supporter of the landed class. He was particularly indignant that England should rule Ireland by the harsh colonial principles prescribed by the mercantilist economic philosophy, and it is in his various Irish tracts that one finds instances of his reaction to these principles both explicitly and implicitly as England unjustly and arbitrarily applied them to a hapless Ireland. This is the crux: some of the mercantile principles he thought valid, but an England bent on oppression did not permit them to operate normally in Ireland. It is striking how frequently Swift's writings can be interpreted in economic terms, in many of his miscellaneous tracts, in *The Drapier's Letters* (1724), in *Gulliver's Travels* (1726), in his correspondence, and even in one of his sermons, "Causes of the Wretched Condition of Ireland" (1715 or later). Like his contemporaries Swift was the inheritor of an amorphous body of economic ideas formulated by miscellaneous thinkers of the seventeenth and eighteenth centuries, ideas generally accepted as embodying the true nature of an economic society and the principles that should guide a nation's foreign trade.

In the essay entitled "Swift's Economic Views and Mercantilism," I have cited instances which reveal his strategy in using commonly accepted mercantilist principles as a basis for his indictment of England. His logic is that in natural resources Ireland had the potentialities of becoming a flourishing nation by means of commerce had England left if free to operate according to those mercantilist principles which had assured England's maritime greatness. Any balanced assessment of Swift's economic views would recognize that despite his preference for the landed interest he understood well the importance of trade, of what he called the moneyed interest.

In 1729 Swift published the most brilliant of his tracts, the ironic comment on the economic conditions of Ireland, then enduring a famine of three years' duration. "A Modest Proposal for Preventing the Children of poor People in Ireland from being a Burden to their Parents or Country; and for making them Beneficial to the Publick" is political in its intention but economic in its substance. For his purpose

Swift uses one of the most cherished economic principles among the mercantilist writers, the "undisputed maxim" that people are the wealth of a nation. In 1698 Sir Josiah Child, a widely respected propounder of mercantilist doctrine, had written: "Most Nations in the Civilized Parts of the World are more or less Rich or Poor proportionably to the Paucity or Plenty of their People, and not to the Sterility or Fruitfulness of their Lands." A like-minded mercantilist, Sir Francis Brewster, four years later maintained that "Nothing makes Kingdoms and Commonwealths, Mighty, Opulent and Rich, but Multitudes of People; 'tis Crowds bring in Industry." Daniel Defoe, the laureate of trade, agreed: ". . . the glory, the strength, the riches, the trade, and all that is valuable in a nation as to its figure in the world, depends upon the number of its people, be they never so mean and poor. . . ." As Swift observed the people of Ireland, the increase in beggary, thievery, undernourishment, and unemployment—and utterly despaired that any future generation of Irishmen could possibly fare better—he realized the cruel irony inherent in the unqualified doctrine as applied to Ireland, that people are "in truth the chiefest, most fundamental, and precious commodity." In the guise of a public-spirited citizen seeking a solution, Swift noted the "prodigious Number of Children" in Ireland doomed to grow up to a life of misery and uselessness. But they too were people, and in mercantile theory counted as potential units of the wealth of the nation. Though a grievance to the nation at that moment, they could become actual units of wealth: the modest proposal is to turn them into delectable and tender meat, some to be used as a new dish for the Irish palate, others to be exported for the Englishman's table, to the improvement of Ireland's foreign trade. Thus by the simple expedient of cannibalism Ireland too might operate under the universally valid mercantile principle that people are the wealth of a nation, a principle that English restrictions on Irish trade negated.

The essay "Swift and Charity," although it has some affinity with the more purely economic essays, is primarily biographical. The problems created by poverty were overwhelming in Ireland, and Swift as a clergyman and Dean of a great cathedral was inevitably involved. The essay details his various charitable activities, relates him to the flourishing charity-school movement of the times, and examines the traditional Christian theory of charity as he and his contemporaries, both clergymen and laymen, understood it. The man of wealth must consider himself not the *owner* of his wealth but its steward. He held his wealth in trust, and the distribution of it as charity was an obligation not to be scanted. As a parallel to his examination of the meaning of riches in the Christian scheme of things, Swift examines as well the significance of poverty. He accepts the prevailing view that the division of men into rich and poor is providential. The disparity in the condition of men is agreeable to the will of God, and thus the poor should accept their state without repining. Nevertheless, though they have no legal demand upon the rich, they do have a right or claim under God antecedent and superior to any merely mundane or human rules for the dispensing of charity. However sensitive Swift was to the sufferings of the poor and the injustices in the social order, he was conservative, not inclined to argue in his sermons for radical changes in the structure of society. In those sermons where he examines the meaning of riches and poverty in the Christian scheme of things, we find him accepting the commonplaces and rationalizations which had come down to his day and were pervasive in homiletic literature.

Even Swift's enemies, those who attacked him on both political and religious grounds, granted that he was a dedicated churchman and an effective Dean of St. Patrick's Cathedral in Dublin. In the essay titled "Jonathan Swift: 'Not the Gravest of Divines' " I have sketched his troubled career from its beginnings, his rise from an obscure parish priest to the dignity of a Dean, his relationship with the canons in his cathedral chapter, and his workaday world as the Dean of the most important cathedral in the Irish Anglican establishment. As a bemused observer of himself as a clergyman Swift described himself as "not the gravest of Divines." Elsewhere he had asserted that

> Humour, and Mirth, had Place in all he Writ:
> He reconcil'd Divinity and Wit

Such casual remarks should not obscure his long and dedicated service to the Church of Ireland as an institution. Indeed, Swift was not a theologian. He rarely entered into the heated controversies that agitated the contemporary clergymen: the respective claims of reason and faith in religion, the validity of the Christian miracles, doctrinal differences between Catholicism and Protestantism. It is possible that in some of his lost sermons he "reconcil'd Divinity and Wit," but in the eleven extant sermons he is little concerned with divinity or doctrinal matters. There is one interesting exception, "On the Trinity," in which his views are lucidly set forth. The sermon is one of scores in the Trinitarian Controversy of the seventeenth and eighteenth centuries and is directed against the extreme rationalists then attacking the orthodox view of the Trinity—the deists and the Socinians. The deists particularly were the most feared of those asserting heterodox views of the Trinity and the other mysteries and miracles of Christianity. It was the deists who insisted on the primacy of reason over faith, who maintained that the Trinity could not be accepted as a valid article of faith unless it was intelligible to human reason. To Swift they exemplified the old heresy, the prying intellect with its subtleties and quibbles which were the source of contention in the Christian, world, and he ridiculed their excessive claim that weak human reason could penetrate the grand mysteries of revealed religion. Human reason might indeed arrive at the conclusion that such a mystery as the doctrine of the Trinity was a true revelation of the deity, but once it reached this conclusion it then must resign itself to faith and accept the doctrine even though it might be in many aspects beyond human comprehension. In the essay "Swift, the Mysteries, and Deism," I have examined Swift's sermon on the Trinity, a remarkably complex document, in the context of the relevant religious thought of the times, both orthodox and heterodox.

The essay "Swift's Deanery Income" is restricted in scope, but it bears interestingly on the temporal as contrasted to the spiritual aspect of Swift's life. It prints for the first time a recently discovered manuscript which sets forth in detail the sources—rents, tithes, fees—from which Swift's annual income was derived. The Anglican clergymen of eighteenth-century Ireland were firmly convinced that only flourishing church temporalities could keep the Anglican faith vibrant and strong in its struggles to keep pace with a vigorous Presbyterianism. Swift and the clergy generally were in controversy with laymen about the divine tenth—the tithe due the priesthood from the produce of the land. Resistance to the payment of tithes by dissenters, Anglican landlords, and others was much resented by the clergy, who argued that tithes were due them by divine right, by immemorial custom, and as a legally defensible property right. Over the years Swift had much to say on the subject, including his amusing remark to Alexander Pope in a letter, February 26, 1729/30: ". . . although tithes be of divine institution, they are of diabolical execution." Since tithes were roughly half of his income, Swift frequently grumbled over being deprived of his due, and increasingly in his later years his sense of doom was intensified as he wrote about both his personal fortune and the impoverished state of the Church of Ireland. The newly discovered document, which is a list of his possessions and income about 1742, was in all probability drawn up for the Commission of Lunacy preparatory to the verdict which found him to be of unsound mind and memory. As a result Swift's property and person were placed in the hands of trustees. The document is highly personal: it reveals that his income was ample for his personal expenses and his extensive charities. The essay entitled "Jonathan Swift" was first delivered as an address in 1946 in a session at the English Institute devoted to the critical significance of biographical evidence. Swift is an appropriate subject for this

theme since his biographers, both past and present, have relied so
heavily on biographical fact—and fiction—to interpret his writings.
The biographical approach to literary interpretation is of course a valid
one, but Swift has suffered more than most authors from commentators who have made their interpretations of the works by unwarranted emphasis on selected facts of his life, finding it convenient to
ignore the facts which would give a different or more balanced interpretation. It should be mentioned that the twentieth-century critics
of Swift have done much to correct the distortions and misapprehen-
sions of the eighteenth and the nineteenth centuries.

Two of the essays exemplify the impact of contemporary science on
authors of widely different temperaments and intentions, Sterne and
Johnson. In "The Shandean Homunculus: The Background of
Sterne's 'Little Gentleman' " I have examined the opening passages of
Tristram Shandy in the light of the prevailing embryological theories
which resulted from the microscopic investigation of such respected
biologists of the late seventeenth century as Harvey, Leeuwenhoeck,
de Graaf, and others. The microscope revealed, it was maintained, that
the sperm is in fact a fully formed, or preformed, animalculum, a
homunculus, or manikin, so exceedingly small that, according to John
Keill, a scientist lecturing at Oxford in 1700, it exemplifies the dream
of some philosophers concerning angels: "many thousands of them
may dance on the Point of a small Needle." Inevitably a controversy
divided the scientists: the animalculist contended that the male sperm,
already a preformed human being, needed the ovum or the womb—a
resting-place—to develop, but that the woman is not the true agency
in the process of conception and generation. Hers is the passive
agency. The ovists or ovarians derived their view from the famous dictum of Harvey, *ex ovo omnium*, enunciated in 1651. The two schools
of thought agreed that the very moment of conception had great importance, a topic which had been discussed from ancient times. Sterne,
alive to the risible aspects of the preformation theory and certain of its
implications, introduces in the opening chapters of the novel the
homunculus who is to burgeon into Tristram, the little gentleman, so
young a traveler, arriving in a "sad disordered state of nerves"—the
result of Mrs. Shandy's untimely question to her husband at the
critical moment of conception. Tristram's "misfortunes began nine
months before ever he came into the world." Unconventional in his
ideas of time and structure in the novel, Sterne introduces his hero not
at birth or later, as was customary, but as a little man already at the
moment of conception "a Being guarded and circumscribed with
rights . . . a Being of as much activity . . . and as truly our fellow-
creature as my Lord Chancellor." The witty context of the Shandean

homunculus and the humorous tone are achieved at the expense of the prevailing embryological views but with little or no distortion of what the scientists and others were maintaining. Some of the implications of embryological science Sterne found useful at least for passing treatment, such old subjects as infant salvation, the relationship of the child to the parent (of significance for the establishment of property rights), indivisibility of matter, and the "numerosity" of animalcula when only an occasional one functioned in the act of generation. This last topic implied wastefulness in a universe that the rationalist considered to be the handiwork of a deity who created nothing in vain. It is unlikely that any admirer of Sterne would disagree with the judgment that Sterne's learned wit is surpassingly illustrated in the opening chapters of *Tristram Shandy*.

The other essay which reflects prevailing scientific thought is concerned with one of the most important chapters in Samuel Johnson's philosophic tale, *Rasselas*. This is chapter 6, to which Johnson gave the title "A Dissertation on the Art of Flying." The substance of the chapter derives from the controversy between the defenders of modern learning and those who maintained the superiority of the ancients in most fields of human knowledge. One of the chief claims by the Moderns was that they had far surpassed the Ancients in various fields of science, and particularly in the mathematical sciences. The quarrel, to state it in eighteenth-century phraseology, was actually between the natural philosophers (the scientists) and the moral philosophers (the humanists). The former, pointing to the great advances made by The Royal Society, optimistically proclaimed that man would some day master the art of flight, using the established principles of contemporary mathematics and physics. The dangerous heterodox implications of this view for the nature of man and his relationship to God and the divine scheme of things disturbed the ethical writers. These stoutly asserted that the deity had not given man wings, that human attributes were precisely designed to adapt man to his mundane existence and to his proper status in the animal hierarchy. As Rasselas remarks: "every animal has his element assigned him: the birds have the air and man and beasts the earth." Man's aspiration to flight is therefore an affront to the deity, obliviousness to the limitations of human nature, and the sin of pride. Johnson's reaction to the absurdities of the natural scientists of his day and their excessive claims for man's accomplishments emerges from the conversation between Rasselas and an artisan engaged in building a flying-machine. The artisan, eminent for his knowledge of Modernist mechanical principles, speaks the language of the natural philosophers and expresses their optimism that the science of the day has opened the way for human flight. Rasselas, whose curiosity destines him to travel throughout the world seeking knowledge of the true state and nature of man, is mildly skeptical and not surprised when the artisan attempts to fly and ignominiously fails. The incident takes its meaning from the controversy between the Ancients and the Moderns, and the chapter itself is Johnson's affirmation that the best knowledge is man's knowledge of himself, that is, moral knowledge, not knowledge of nature, the domain of the scientist.

The religious coloration of the dissertation on human flight rises out of a heterodoxy that reached back in time as early as the third century A.D. when "a subtle philosopher" questioned the justice of the deity's distribution of qualities among created beings. Why was the small gnat created with six legs and wings whereas the greatest of beasts, the elephant, was given only four legs and no wings? An answer to this cavil, which had been given renewed vitality by the experiments in human flight, had come in the fourth century A.D. from Eusebius, Bishop of Caesarea in Palestine. The answer was current and easily available in the seventeenth and eighteenth centuries in the writings of another bishop, John Wilkins, the Anglican Bishop of Chester, who among others wrote copiously on the subject of human flight. Eusebius had maintained that by "necessity every thing is confined by the Laws of Nature and the Decrees of Providence, so that nothing can go out of that way unto which naturally it is designed; as a Fish cannot reside on Land, nor a Man in the Water, or aloft in the Air. . . ." This is essentially the response implicit in *Rasselas*, chapter 6.

"Pope's Belinda, the General Emporie of the World, and the Wondrous Worm" is concerned with a literary work whose rich implications are most fully understood in an economic context. The emphasis in mercantilist economic thought and practice on foreign trade was not something merely theoretical. It derived from what the English were witnessing: a small island in the process of becoming a colonial and imperial power by virtue of a vast expansion of its foreign trade. The flow of luxuries into England, particularly into the busy port of London, generated pleasing visions of maritime splendor and wealth previously beyond the dreams of man. Practical businessmen, ethical writers, clergymen, and poets, among others, joined with the mercantile writers to envisage England as the mart of nations, the emporium of the entire world, its merchants and ships tirelessly seeking exotic products in remote corners of the earth: spices from Arabia, silks from Persia, gems from India, ivory from Africa, drugs from America, pottery and decorative articles from China and Japan. A heightened rhetoric appropriate to this extensive commerce emerged in literary and subliterary works, the eulogies often displaying tolerance of exotic luxuries ordinarily the subject of indictment in mercantilist theory. What we observe is the acceptance, more or less, of luxury, of

England as a nation of consumers, of conspicuous expenditure. If not acceptance, at least recognition that the woman of quality, the fine lady of the times, was of special interest not only in economic theory but as well in poetry, the drama, the essay, even in homiletic works. Pope's charming heroine, Belinda, in "The Rape of the Lock," bedecked in jewels and silks and brocades, with—in Pope's words—"all that Land and Sea afford," is just such a consumer, a stimulus to the adventurous merchant whose ships traversed the boundless seas from Lapland to the equator to gather exotic luxuries for the Belindas of the day. Pope's literate contemporaries, sensitive to the economic implications in his depiction of Belinda, may well have viewed her as testimony to England's maritime splendor, as evidence that England was in fact a world emporium, the anointed empress of the deep.

"Of Silkworms and Farthingales and the Will of God" is a companion-piece to the essay on Pope's Belinda. The fine lady of the eighteenth century is more extensively analyzed in her dual role, first as the austere mercantilist viewed her, a creature of indulgence and an emblem of ruinous economic consumption, one for whom the whole machinery of foreign trade functions wastefully to satisfy her demands; then, second, as a positive and significant image or symbol in belles-lettres and mercantilist economic doctrine. The doctrine itself is a subtle rationalization of man's basically materialistic and acquisitive nature by claiming a divine sanction for commerce and the merchant. A benign deity, it was asserted, had built into the universe all the elements needed for navigation and trade: seas, rivers, harbors, winds, and the principle of flotation. He had, moreover, provided regional diversity, dispersion throughout the world of varied products so that what one nation lacked another could supply. "Nature," Joseph Addison declared, "seems to have taken a particular Care to disseminate her Blessings among the different Regions of the World, with an Eye to this mutual Intercourse and Traffick among Mankind, that the Natives of the several Parts of the Globe might have a kind of Dependance upon one another, and be united together by their common Interest" (*The Spectator*, no. 169, 1711). The doctrine envisaged a universal economy and a universal mercantile amity both providentially arranged. The merchant engaged in international commerce is thus divinely sanctioned. He "promotes humanity" and diffuses "Mutual Love from Pole to Pole," so wrote George Lillo in his popular play, *The London Merchant* (Act III, sc. 1), 1731. By the same token, the fine lady demanding silks, brocades, gems, and other exotic objects becomes more than a pleasing mercantile image. As depicted in the context of the eulogies of international commerce, she too is a facet of the universal economy and a pleasing mercantile symbol in the grandiose apotheosis of the merchant and trade.

"London Observed: The Progress of a Simile" explores the intrusion into eighteenth-century literature of a significant demographic attitude inherited from the preceding century. To Englishmen generally London seemed to be emerging as the equal of the great cities of the world past and present. As the seat of the government and the center of the nation's finance, commerce, and cultural life, it was often the subject of eulogy. But amidst the eulogies one finds mounting concern that the city's "monstrous Growth" had certain adverse effects. As early as the reigns of Elizabeth and James I, the authorities expressed fear that London's vast expansion was at the expense of "other places abroad in the Realm." The king himself encapsulated this view in his assertion that London is like "the head of a rickety child in which an extensive flux of humour drained and impoverished the extremities. . . ." The simile, depicting England as the human body and London as the head, reappears in 1641, in a speech (later printed) by a distinguished member of Parliament, Sir Thomas Roe. Here London was visualized as a fat head and the rest of the nation as resembling "thin guts and lean members." As the figurative expression moved down the cultural stream, the diction varied slightly at times but the idea remained unchanged. For Peter Heylin, in *Cosmography* (1652), London became the spleen: as the diseased spleen swells, the body wastes. As London increases, the rest of the country dwindles. For the mercantilist writers and the political arithmeticians, such as John Graunt, Charles Davenant, and Sir William Petty, the simile, brief as it is, embodied the political, social, and economic distortions resulting from London's disproportionate size and importance. In the eighteenth century Defoe, whose fascination with London was unbounded, rejected the simile, vigorously denying that London could aptly be described in the language of morbidity by an image of a diseased and swollen organ unwholesomely fattening at the expense of the rest of the body. To Smollett, a harsh critic of the metropolis, the simile expressed in medical terms was appropriate. A physician himself, he has his mouthpiece, Matt Bramble in *Humphry Clinker* (1771), describe London as an overgrown monster and like a dropsical head that will leave the body without nourishment. A few years earlier Smollett's contemporary, Laurence Sterne, had introduced the simile into *Tristram Shandy* (1759-67) with characteristic comic playfulness; and in 1775, a century and a half after James I had voiced the similitude, we find Johnson and Boswell, both of whom had—in Johnson's phrase—"a gust" for London, discussing its vast size. Boswell remarked on the "immensity of London," to which Johnson, assuming his magisterial tone, replied: "It is nonsense to say the head is too big for the body. . . ." London, he said, "has no similarity to a head connected with a body."

SWIFT'S ECONOMIC VIEWS
AND MERCANTILISM

Commentators on Swift have traditionally, and quite properly, called attention to his preference for the landed interest of Great Britain, an attitude, it is usually pointed out, that stems from his Toryism. This view of Swift was, of course, current in his own day. Witness the words of one of his contemporaries, the anonymous author of *Torism and Trade Can Never Agree* (*ca.* 1713), who attacked *The Examiner*—i. e., Swift—as a "Daemon of Torism" who "never fail'd to maul" the trading interest or eulogize the landed interest.

> Can we imagine that Persons who have two such Interests on their side, as a *Church Interest* and a *Land Interest* will be mindful of so Paltry an interest as Trade. The *Examiner*, who was possess'd more than any Man with the *Daemon* of *Torism*, was always launching out in his Panegyricks on the *Land Interest* and *Church Interest*, and tho he had not quite Front enough to stand by what his old Friend Castlemain said, that we should have no *Trade at all*, yet he never fail'd to maul it when ever it fell in his way.[1]

The purely partisan intention in this pamphlet—it is a violent attack on the French trade and the Tory sponsored commercial treaty with France at the Treaty of Utrecht—discredits the author's words; yet the equations set up, in which Toryism and land or Whiggism and trade become interchangeable terms, have often been accepted in modern scholarship, to the obscuration of the many individual differences that prevailed in the eighteenth century. Tories who defended the primacy of trade were not by any means as numerous as Whigs, but they did exist—for example, Sir Dudley North, Sir Josiah Child, and Charles Davenant, to mention three obvious instances. There

---

[1] P. 16. "Trade" is used in this pamphlet—and throughout this article—in one of the usual eighteenth-century acceptations: foreign trade. Although I have been unable to trace the remark of Swift's "Old Friend Castlemain," the allusion must be to the husband of the mistress of Charles II. Roger Palmer, Earl of Castlemain (1634-1705), an ardent apologist for Catholicism and a member of a secret council to James II, was tried for complicity in the Popish Plot. By linking Swift with him (there is not, so far as I am aware, any evidence that the two were acquainted), the author of the pamphlet was making the usual implication that Tories and Papists are one and the same.

is no reason to believe that these staunch Tories assumed in the eyes of their contemporaries a particulay anomalous or heterodox position, such as would logically be imposed on them by the oversimplified distinctions and formulae of scholars who are tempted to accept at face value the Whiggish insistence of our anonymous author, that " the *Tories* will, upon all Occasions, be Enemies to Trade." [2]

Swift, too, has suffered from the obscuration of individual differences. By insisting that he was a Tory in Church and a Whig in politics,[3] he himself protested against being enclosed within the confines of a term, a formula, a single group, although no one was more culpable in utilizing this device against opponents, as witness his persistent identification of Whigs with dissenters and Presbyterians with antimonarchists. In any case, the traditional view of Swift as a supporter of the Tory landed interest, true as it is and deserving of emphasis, need not preclude some emphasis on the importance with which he viewed trade. Indeed, Swift has not been given sufficient credit for his very strong realization of the importance of trade in the economy of a nation. This realization, it is true, came only belatedly out of his residence in Ireland after 1714; still he was no less wholehearted in his acceptance of certain principles of trade as necessary to Ireland or England's welfare than the most ardent Whig. These principles and the assumptions underlying them are constantly iterated in his Irish tracts; and on their application to Ireland's economy, as well as on the utili-

---

[2] *Torism and Trade Can Never Agree* (London, n. d.), p. 1. Cf. Swift's attributing to the Whigs a maxim " dangerous to the constitution ": ". . . that of preferring, on all occasions, the moneyed interest before the landed" (*The Prose Works of Jonathan Swift, D. D.*, ed. Temple Scott, 12 vols. [London, 1897-1908], 9. 231, hereafter referred to as *Works*). There were, of course, Whigs as well as Tories among the landed gentry; and from this group came frequent pleas that trading restrictions on wool be lifted for the welfare of the nation. They were not, in their capacity as landed gentlemen, opposed to trade as such; they were opposed to restrictions on trade that penalized the landed interest and favored the manufacturer and the merchant who exported finished goods. The Tories who favored trade with France were accused of being hostile to the trading interest; and we get the spectacle of Daniel Defoe being called an enemy to trade and the trading interest by the author of *Torism and Trade Can Never Agree*. It will be recalled, too, that the East India Company in Swift's day received strong Tory support. Here is a flagrant instance in which " Torism and Trade " did agree.

[3] *Works*, 3. 314; 5. 65. Cf. also *The Correspondence of Jonathan Swift, D. D.*, ed. F. Elrington Ball (London, 1910-14), 2. 279, 354.

zation of the land, Swift believed the welfare of the country depended. It will serve as a corrective to the conception of Swift as wholly of the landed Tory interest to examine his major ideas about trade, so often casual and unelaborated, and to relate them to the dominant economic theory of his day, that complex of ideas which Adam Smith attacked under the name of the commercial or mercantile system.[4]

2.

Swift viewed problems of trade from the vantage of a small country lacking freedom of action and occupying, more or less, the status of a colony subject to restrictive colonial measures. It was this fact that stimulated him to concern himself with economic problems at all and to seek a sound economic solution consistent with the harsh realities of Ireland's dependency; and from this fact is, of course, derived the emotional tone of his tracts on trade. From 1720, when the first of these tracts appeared, to the end of his active writing career, he tirelessly, though rather hopelessly, protested England's restrictions on Ireland's trade. A passage from *A Short View of the State of Ireland* (1728) is typical:

Ireland is the only Kingdom I ever heard or read of, either in ancient or modern story, which was denied the liberty of exporting

[4] There has been little attempt by scholars to relate Swift's economic views to contemporary economic theories. In "A Modest Proposal and Populousness," *Modern Philology*, 40 (1942). 161-70, the present writer has related *A Modest Proposal* to prevailing theories of population. The same tract was related to the economic background by George Wittkowsky in his article, "Swift's *Modest Proposal*," *Journal of the History of Ideas*, 4 (1943). 75-104. An article by J. M. Hone, "Berkeley and Swift as National Economists," *Studies*, 23 (1934). 420-32, is almost wholly devoted to the views of Berkeley. The few casual remarks about Swift are primarily to contrast him with Berkeley. Without elaboration or proof Hone writes that "Swift had learned his economics from his patron, Sir William Temple, a doctrinaire of that mercantilist school which Berkeley wished to refute."
The historian of ideas who wishes to trace the ramifications of mercantilist thought will find the following secondary sources, which I have listed in chronological order, of great value: E. S. Furniss, *The Position of the Laborer in a System of Nationalism* (Boston and New York, 1920); Br. Suviranta, *The Theory of the Balance of Trade* (Helsingfors, 1923); E. Lipson, *The Economic History of England* (London, 1931); Eli F. Heckscher, *Mercantilism*, tr. Mendel Shapiro (London, 1935); E. A. V. Johnson, *Predecessors of Adam Smith* (New York, 1937); Jacob Viner, *Studies in the Theory of International Trade* (New York and London, 1937); Philip W. Buck, *The Politics of Mercantilism* (New York, 1942).

their native commodities and manufactures wherever they pleased, except to countries at war with their own Prince or State, yet this by the superiority of mere power is refused us in the most moment-ous parts of commerce, besides an Act of Navigation to which we never consented, pinned down upon us, and rigorously executed, and a thousand other unexampled circumstances as grievous as they are invidious to mention.[5]

These protests were not limited to works intended for publi-cation. They appear in his private correspondence,[6] and he even issued them from the pulpit. One of his few sermons to come down to us, *On the Causes of the Wretched Condition of Ireland*, is devoted to an analysis of Ireland's economic diffi-culties, in which he complains bitterly that " The first cause of our misery is the intolerable hardships we lie under in every branch of trade, by which we are become as hewers of wood, and drawers of water, to our rigorous neighbours." [7]

The discriminatory acts against which Swift wrote began after the Restoration and were part of the vigorous protectionist policy for home industries. Ireland was simply one of many victims. The Navigation Acts to which he often refers dated from 1663.[8] They constituted a series of enactments designed to make more difficult and expensive the importation into Ireland of commodities from the colonies and exportation from Ireland to the colonies. The Cattle Acts of the same period reduced drastically a thriving trade between England and Ireland in cattle and animal products, to the detriment of Irish raisers of cattle, sheep, and swine.[9] At the end of the

[5] *Works*, 7. 85-86; for similar complaints see also *Works*, 6. 201; 7. 66, 100, 138, 157 ff., 195, 198, 220.

[6] For example, *Correspondence*, 3. 311.

[7] *Works*, 4. 212.

[8] The chief Navigation Acts which crippled the Irish trade were 15 Charles II, c. 7; 22 & 23 Charles II, c. 26; 7 & 8 William III, c. 22. For a contemporary dis-cussion of the early navigation laws and other Acts affecting Ireland, see *Britannia Languens* (1680), sec. xi, generally credited to William Petyt, reprinted in *A Select Collection of Early English Tracts on Commerce*, ed. J. R. McCulloch (London, 1856), pp. 275-504. See also John Hely Hutchinson, *The Commercial Restraints of Ireland*, ed. W. G. Carroll (London, 1888), pp. 118 ff.; George O'Brien, *The Economic History of Ireland in the Eighteenth Century* (Dublin and London, 1918), pp. 173 ff.; Lawrence A. Harper, *The English Navigation Laws* (New York, 1939), pp. 162-63, 397.

[9] The Cattle Acts were 15 Charles II, c. 8; 18 Charles II, c. 23; 20 Charles II, c. 7; 22 & 23 Charles II, c. 2; 32 Charles II, c. 2. See A. E. Murray, *A History*

seventeenth century came the restriction which Swift terms
"this fatal act," 10 & 11 Wm. III, c. 10, designed to prevent
the Irish woolen industry from competing with English growers
and manufacturers by prohibiting the exportation of woolen
goods from Ireland to any country except England. These discriminatory acts, which seemed so unjust to Swift and other
Irishmen, were viewed in a different light by the English, who
merely had been putting into effect the prevailing mercantilist
principle that a colony or dependent nation is intended to serve
the national economic interest of the mother country.

The colonial relationship between England and Ireland by
which English mercantilists justified their treatment of Ireland
was expounded at length at the end of the seventeenth century
by John Cary, famous merchant of Bristol and a correspondent
of John Locke:

We come now to speak of *Ireland*; which of all the Plantations
setled by the *English* hath proved most injurious to the Trade of
this Kingdom, and so far from answering the ends of a Colony,
that it doth wholly violate them; for if People be the Wealth of a
Nation, then 'tis certain that a bare parting with any of them
cannot be its Advantage, unless accompanied with Circumstances
whereby they may be rendered more useful both to themselves,
and also to those they left behind them, else so far as you deprive
it of such who should consume its Product and improve its Manufactures you lessen its true Interest, especially when that Colony
sets up a Separate, and not only provides sufficient of both for its
self, but by the Overplus supplys other Markets, and thereby lessens
its Sales abroad. . . .

Nor is there any reason to be offered why *Ireland* should have
greater Liberty than *our other Plantations* [italics mine], the
inhabitants whereof have an equal Desire to a free Trade, for-
getting that the first design of their Settlement was to advance the
Interest of England, against whom no Arguments can be used
which will not equally hold good against *Ireland*.

1. As it was settled by Colonies spared from *England*.

2. As it hath been still supported and defended at the Charge
of *England*.

3. As it hath received equal Advantages with the other Plantations from the Expence *England* hath been at in carrying on Wars
Abroad and Revolutions at Home . . . so that 'twould be a piece
of great Ingratitude for the Free-holders of *Ireland* unwillingly to

*of the Commercial and Financial Relations between England and Ireland from the
Restoration* (London, 1903), pp. 23 ff.

submit to any thing whereby the Interest of England may be advanced. . . .[10]

Cary's words are echoed by Charles Davenant, who maintained that Ireland is England's colony " by the Interpretation both of Law and Reason " and that " it seems the Right of *England*, and as well for the Benefit of *Ireland* its best and noblest Colony, that the Legislative Authority here should . . . make such Regulations and Restrictions, relating to Trade especially, as shall be thought for the Weal-Publick of both Countries." [11]

These are merely statements of the old colonial policy as it was also being applied to the American colonies, and thus the English had accepted economic dogma as their support when they restricted or abolished those branches of Irish trade and industry which operated to the disadvantage of English trade and industry. Even those who were moved by a genuine consideration for the ills of Ireland did not question the rightness of this principle, for example, Swift's patron, Sir William Temple, whose *Essay upon the Advancement of Trade in Ireland* appeared in 1673:

. . . one Thing must be taken notice of as peculiar to this Country [Ireland], which is, That as it is the Nature of its Government, so in the very improvement of its Trade and Riches, it ought to be considered not only in its own proper Interest, but likewise in its Relation to *England*, to which it is subordinate, and upon whose Weal in the main that of this Kingdom depends, and therefore a Regard must be had of those Points wherein the Trade of *Ireland* comes to interfere with any main Branches of the Trade of *England*; in which Cases the Encouragement of such Trade ought to be either declined or moderated, and so give way to the Interest of Trade in *England*, upon the Health and Vigour whereof the

[10] *An Essay on the State of England, in Relation to Its Trade, Its Poor, and Its Taxes* (Bristol, 1695), pp. 89, 105-6. In *The Case of Ireland's Being Bound by Acts of Parliament in England, Stated* (1698), William Molyneux, whose arguments for Ireland's independence impressed Swift, denied that Ireland " is to be look'd upon only as a *Colony* from *England* "—a view without the " least *Foundation* or *Colour* from *Reason* or *Record* (1720 ed., p. 125). Cary answered Molyneux on this point in *A Vindication of the Parliament of England, in Answer to a Book, Written by William Molyneux of Dublin, Esq.* (London, 1698), pp. 123-24; see also *An Answer to Mr. Molyneux* (London, 1698), pp. 140 ff., a work credited to Cary.

[11] *An Essay upon the Probable Methods of Making a People Gainers in the Ballance of Trade* (London, 1699), pp. 106, 120.

Strength, Riches and Glory of his Majesty's Crown seems chiefly to depend.[12]

After the turn of the century the same view was set forth by Sir Francis Brewster, who argued for a union between Ireland and England, yet insisted in the same breath that even from union Ireland could not expect equality in matters economic: ". . . I do not mean, nor would insinuate, that all the Priviledges and Immunities *England* hath in Trade and Manufactures, should be allow'd to *Ireland*; but only encouraged in such a way as will advance *England* in theirs . . . ." [13] Among the Irish expounders of mercantilism in Swift's day was Arthur Dobbs, who pleaded for the removal of restrictive measures not so much on the grounds that such action would be right but that it would be more profitable: the people of Ireland " in the Possession of their Properties, Rights, and Privileges, *consistent with the good of its Mother Country* [italics mine] . . . will be of the greatest Moment to them, in contributing to support the Honour and Dignity of the Crown, and the Power, Wealth, and Naval Strength of Britain." [14]

Swift does not challenge the rightness of the mercantilist attitude toward a dependent kingdom or the justice of restricting a dependency in the interests of the mother country. To have done so, as he must have realized, would have been to run counter to widely accepted views. Instead he bases his arguments on another level—a constitutional one. Whatever his real interpretation of the constitutional relation between England and Ireland or his views of the respective rights of native Irish and Anglo-Irish,[15] he saw the necessity and per-

---

[12] *The Works of Sir William Temple* (London, 1731), 1.112-13.

[13] *New Essays on Trade* (London, 1702), pp. 75-76; cf. also p. 71.

[14] *An Essay on the Trade and Improvement of Ireland* (Dublin, 1729), p. 66. See also *Works*, 6.188, where Swift uses a similar argument: "I conceive this poor unhappy island to have a title to some indulgence from England; not only upon the score of Christianity, natural equity, and the general rights of mankind; but chiefly on account of that immense profit they receive from us; without which, that kingdom would make a very different figure in Europe, from what it doth at present." A similar attitude is expressed by the author of *Reflections upon the Present Unhappy Circumstances of Ireland; in a Letter to His Grace the Lord Arch Bishop of Cashel* (Dublin, 1731), pp. 4-5.

[15] In *The Intelligencer*, No. 19, he wrote: ". . . what is lawful for a subject of Ireland, I profess I cannot determine . . ." (*Works*, 9.327). Cf. also *The Drapier's Letters*: "Then I desire, for the satisfaction of the public, that you will please

suasiveness of arguing from the premise that the people of Ireland are in no way distinct from the people of England, that they are fellow subjects, citizens entitled to the same rights. His reliance upon this position is presented most elaborately in *The Drapier's Letters,* for example in his comment on the Report of the Committee of the Privy Council at that point where the Report refers to the " liberty or privilege of the King's subjects of Ireland." Swift challenges the implication that the liberty or privilege of the Irish subject is different from the liberty or privilege of the English subject:

... in specifying the word *Ireland,* instead of saying ' His Majesty's subjects,' it would seem to insinuate that we are not upon the same foot with our fellow-subjects in *England*; which, however, the practice may have been, I hope will never be directly asserted, for I do not understand that Poining's act deprived us of our liberty, but only changed the manner of passing laws here . . . by leaving the negative to the two Houses of Parliament. But, waiving all controversies relating to the legislature, no person, I believe, was ever yet so bold as to affirm that the people of Ireland have not the same title to the benefits of the common law, with the rest of His Majesty's subjects, and therefore whatever liberties or privileges the people of England enjoy by common law, we of Ireland have the same; so that in my humble opinion, the word *Ireland* standing in that proposition, was, in the mildest interpretation, *a lapse of the pen.*[16]

In another of the *Drapier's Letters* he protests against ignorant and weak people who refer to Ireland as a " ' depending kingdom,' as if they would seem, by this phrase, to intend that the people of Ireland is in some state of slavery or dependence different from those of England." [17] There is no statute, Swift insists, that " makes Ireland depend upon England, any more than England does upon Ireland." All that can be said is that the two have the same king: " We have indeed obliged our-

to inform me why this country is treated in so very different a manner, in a point of such high importance; whether it be on account of Poining's act; of subordination; dependence; or any other term of art; which I shall not contest, but am too dull to understand " (*Works,* 6. 149). On the problem of Swift's attitude toward the native Irish and the Anglo-Irish, see Daniel Corkery, " Ourselves and Dean Swift," *Studies,* 23 (1934). 203-18. It is not altogether clear whether Swift wanted independence (that is, independence of action) for the " Whole People of Ireland " or merely for the English in Ireland.

[16] *Works,* 6. 77-78.
[17] *Ibid.,* p. 113.

selves to have the same king with them, and consequently they are obliged to have the same king with us." [18]

It was doubtless Swift's intention that these passages should be read as a challenge to the recent act of the English parliament which had affirmed in no uncertain terms the political dependency of Ireland.[19] If he had accepted this subordinate status for Ireland, he could not have made, given the prevalent mercantilist view that a dependency has only inferior economic rights, as strong a case against England's treatment of Ireland. The restrictive measures under such a relationship were both legal and conformable to economic dogma. Swift prefers, therefore, to blacken England by showing, not merely that the restrictive policies are short-sighted and unprofitable, but that they are constitutionally invalid because they are based upon force and upon an illegal denial of Irish rights as fellow-subjects. Thus we find him complaining, as a prelude to his analysis of Ireland's economic difficulties in his sermon *On the Causes of the Wretched Condition of Ireland,* that these difficulties " are not to be remedied, until God shall put it in the hearts of those who are stronger to allow us the common rights and privileges of brethren, fellow-subjects, and even of mankind." [20] In *A Short View of the State of Ireland* he writes that Ireland is prevented from exporting freely " by the superiority of mere power," and he adds: " It is too well known that we are forced to obey some laws we never consented to," a point he repeats

---

[18] *Ibid.* See also p. 126 and *The Answer to the Injured Lady,* where Swift writes: " That your family and tenants [Ireland] have no dependence upon the said gentleman [England], further than by the old agreement, which obligeth you to have the same steward, and to regulate your household by such methods as you should both agree to " (*Works,* 7.105).

[19] The Act was 6 George I, c. 5. Its language affirming the dependency of *Ireland* is unequivocal: " That the said kingdom of Ireland hath been, is, and of right ought to be subordinate unto and dependent upon the imperial crown of *Great Britain,* as being inseparably united and annexed thereunto; and that the King's majesty, by and with the advice and consent of the lords spiritual and temporal and commons of *Great Britain* in parliament assembled, had, hath, and of right ought to have full power and authority to make laws and statutes of sufficient force and validity, to bind the kingdom and people of Ireland " (*Statutes at Large* [Cambridge, 1765], 14.205).

[20] *Works,* 4.212. Swift adopts some of the language of William Molyneux, who had argued that Ireland's being bound " *by Acts of Parliament made in* England, *is against Reason, and the Common Rights of all Mankind* " (*op. cit.,* p. 127).

in *The Story of an Injured Lady.*[21] It was necessary to exercise caution in presenting this theme, as Swift well knew from the fate of the Drapier's *Fourth Letter*[22] and his first pamphlet on Irish economic matters, *A Proposal for the Universal Use of Irish Manufacture,*[23] both of which had been charged with sedition. Possibly here is the reason that Swift used the idea of independence with restraint; but he left little doubt that he believed, as he wrote to the Earl of Peterborough after an interview with Sir Robert Walpole in 1726, that Irishmen were being denied " a natural right of enjoying the privileges of subjects." [24]

3.

Much of Swift's comment on Ireland's economic condition is predicated on his belief that Ireland is potentially a great trading nation. In *The Drapier's Letters* he wrote that " we are denied the benefits which God and Nature intended to us; as manifestly appears by our happy situation for commerce, and the great number of our excellent ports." [25] In a later Irish tract he remarked on " the conveniency of ports and havens which Nature bestowed us so liberally," with the complaint that they are " of no more use to us, than a beautiful prospect to a man shut up in a dungeon." [26] Thus the onus is on England for not permitting the utilization of these natural resources. He also affirmed that Ireland possessed another requisite of a great trading nation, potential richness in native products. Ireland " is capable of producing all things necessary . . . sufficient for the support of four times the number of its inhabitants." [27] At another point he wrote: " As to the first cause of a Nation's riches, being the fertility of its soil, as well as the temperature of climate, we have no reason to complain . . . ." [28] And again: " Thus Ireland is the poorest of all

[21] *Works*, 7.86; cf. also pp. 84, 103; *Correspondence*, 3.311. Molyneux discusses "consent" at length (*op. cit.*, pp. 127-30).

[22] Cf. *The Drapier's Letters*, ed. Herbert Davis (Oxford, 1935), pp. xli ff.

[23] Cf. Swift's letter to Pope, Jan. 10, 1721-22, in *Correspondence*, 3.113-16.

[24] *Ibid.*, p. 309.

[25] *Works*, 6.202. For the importance with which mercantilists viewed shipping, see Heckscher, *op. cit.*, 2.34 ff.

[26] *Works*, 7.85.   [27] *Works*, 4.211.   [28] *Works*, 7.85.

civilized countries in Europe, with every natural advantage to make it one of the richest." [29] In the expression of these views he was echoing sentiments expressed by such English observers as Sir William Temple, Sir William Petty, Sir Francis Brewster, as well as many Irishmen, among whom were John Browne and Bishop Berkeley.[30] One passage from *The Dublin Society's Weekly Observations* may be taken as representative:

The natural soil of this Island, and the number and Ingenuity of its Inhabitants, would under proper management, make it as remarkable for Wealth as it now is for Poverty. There is no Country in the Northern Parts of *Europe* which it does not equal in Fertility, and most of them it remarkably excels. . . . No Kind of Growth, that can be rear'd under a Northern Sun, has miscarried in this Climate. . . .[31]

Although mercantilists stressed the primacy of manufactures and foreign trade, they had a definite realization of the importance of the land.[32] There was due recognition that land, linked with labor, constituted a significant factor in the wealth of a nation. As one writer on trade expressed it at the end of the seventeenth century: " Land is the Foundation, and regular Labour is the greatest Raiser of Riches." [33] The concern of the mercantilist for the land and its products was expounded at length by Charles Davenant, who prefaced his remarks with the statement: " *That Gold and Silver are indeed the Measure of Trade, but that the Spring and Original of it, in all Nations, is the Natural or Artifical Product of the Country; that is to say, what their Land, or what their Labour and Industry produces.*" [34] The fertility of soil was important, among other reasons, because a country could thereby provide for its in-

[29] *Ibid.*, p. 148.

[30] See *The Works of Sir William Temple* (London, 1731), 2.111; Sir William Petty, *Political Arithmetic*, in *Later Stuart Tracts*, ed. G. A. Aitken (Westminster, 1903), p. 30; Sir Francis Brewster, *op. cit.*, p. 66; John Browne, *An Essay on Trade in General; and, on That of Ireland in Particular* (Dublin, 1728), pp. 38-39; George Berkeley, *The Querist* (1735), ed. J. M. Hone (Dublin and Cork, n. d.), Part 1, Nos. 130-33; Part 2, Nos. 2-3; Part 3, No. 2.

[31] (Dublin, 1739), 1. 10-15.

[32] Cf. Buck, *op. cit.*, p. 48.

[33] John Bellers, *Essays about the Poor, Manufactures, Trade, Plantations, and Immorality* (London, 1699), Preface.

[34] Davenant, *op. cit.*, p. 12.

habitants and at the same time have a surplus to be exported, particularly in manufactured form. Thus John Bellers declared: "Without we increase our Husbandry (by improving our land) we cannot increase our Manufactures, by which we should increase our Trade." [35] The great emphasis in mercantilist literature is on exportations; natural resources are viewed mainly with an eye to what they will contribute to foreign trade. That Swift could think and write like his mercantilist contemporaries is evident from a list of rules he set forth as "the true causes of any country's flourishing and growing rich." The first of these rules is relevant at this point: "The first cause of a Kingdon's thriving is the fruitfulness of the soil, to produce the necessaries and conveniences of life, not only sufficient for the inhabitants, but for exportation into other countries." [36]

It is particularly in his attitude toward exports and imports that Swift manifests his acceptance of prevalent English mercantilist theory. To a great extent his solutions for Ireland's economic problems are based on a fundamental mercantilist assumption, that importations are, economically speaking, an evil, that an excess of exports over imports—a favorable balance of trade—is the means by which a nation may be enriched. The expressions of this principle in the seventeenth and eighteenth centuries are numerous. "The ordinary means," wrote Thomas Mun in *England's Treasure by Forraign Trade* (1664), "to increase our wealth and treasure is by *Forraign trade*, wherein wee must ever observe this rule; to sell more to strangers yearly than we consume of theirs in value." [37] By the turn of the century the principle had been so widely enunciated that Sir Francis Brewster could write: "The Maxim is thread bare, *that no place can be Rich, where their Imports exceed their Exports.*" [38] In Ireland Bishop Berkeley posed the question: "Whether that trade should not be accounted most pernicious wherein the Balance is most against us?" [39] The emphasis on exports and a favorable balance of trade is obvious; and the

[35] Bellers, *op. cit.*, p. 9.
[36] *Works*, 7. 83.
[37] Reprinted in *A Select Collection* . . . , ed. McCulloch, p. 125.
[38] Brewster, *op. cit.*, p. 40.
[39] Berkeley, *op. cit.*, Part 1, No. 167.

reasoning back of these general statements was as follows: if the imports from a foreign country to England exceed in value the exports to that country, an overbalance is created against England and in favor of that country, a situation which results in a flow of treasure into that country and the impoverishment of England; if, however, England's exports to that country exceed the imports, the balance is favorable and treasure flows in to enrich England. The concern of the mercantilist was in "the balance of payments" in the sense that one nation in its commercial relation with another incurs a net balance of indebtedness, an obligation to pay in specie. This flow of specie from one nation to another was signficant because of the importance attached to the national stock of money. Obviously the favorable balance of trade was a means of increasing that stock.[40] A succinct statement of this fundamental mercantilist attitude was set forth in *The British Merchant*, a repository of orthodox mercantilism, under the heading of "Propositions":

1. That the Prosperity and Happiness of this Kingdom depend very much upon our foreign Trade.

. . . .

3. That we gain Gold and Silver from those Countries which do not sell us so great a value of Manufactures as they take from us; for in this case the Balance must be paid in Money.

4. That we must pay a Balance in Money to such Countries as sell more Manufactures than they take from us; and that the capital Stock of Bullion is diminished by such a Commerce, unless the Goods we import from an over-balancing Country shall be re-exported.

5. That we are most enriched by those Countries which pay us the greatest Sums upon the Balance; and most impoverish'd by those which carry off the greatest Balance from us.[41]

[40] For discussions of the doctrine of the favorable balance of trade, see Suviranta, *op. cit.*, pp. 9 ff. and *passim*; Viner, *op. cit.*, pp. 6 ff.; Buck, *op. cit.*, pp. 22 ff. These works quote copiously from seventeenth- and eighteenth-century economic literature.

[41] [Charles King], *The British Merchant* (London, 1713; 3d ed., 1748), 1.18. This work has been called "the most unimpeachable exposition of mercantilist thought" (Lipson, *op. cit.*, 3.89-90). It was a collaborative Whig effort in answer to Defoe's *Mercator: or Commerce Retrieved*. Defoe was hired by Bolingbroke to defend the commercial treaty with France at the Treaty of Utrecht, and the Whigs countered with *The British Merchant*. The three-volume edition of 1721 was compiled by Charles King, London merchant and chamber-keeper to the Treasury. For a discussion of *The British Merchant*, see Johnson, *op. cit.*, pp. 141 ff.

This reasoning Swift accepted. It is to be found both implicit and explicit in his Irish tracts, not elaborated, of course, because he has no desire to theorize—and no need to justify theory that so widely prevailed. He could merely apply the balance of trade theory to a particular situation and expect his reader to see its logic. Thus he wrote in *The Present Miserable State of Ireland*: "Our exportations to England are very much overbalanced by our importations; so that the course of exchange is generally too high, and people choose rather to make their remittance in specie, than by a bill, and our nation is perpetually drained of its little running cash."[42] In the *Answer to the Craftsman* he proposed ironically that Irish trade be operated for the benefit of England because the English "have a just claim to the balance of trade on their side with the whole world."[43] And at various other points Ireland's trade with England is commented on with reference to its unfavorable balance.[44] The trade with France, on the contrary, received his approval, though hardly an enthusiastic one. ". . . If an original extract of the exports and imports be true, we have been gainers, upon the balance, by our trade with France, for several years past; and, although our gain amounts to no great sum, we ought to be satisfied, since we are no losers . . . ."[45] In *A Proposal for the Universal Use of Irish Manufacture* he credited the woolen trade with France with bringing in "the little money we have to pay our rents and go to market"; but he was disturbed, obviously thinking of Ireland's depleted stock of money, that the country was paying for French wines in specie.[46] By the same token he disapproved of Ireland's trade with "the northern nations" because with them the Irish are "obliged, instead of carrying woollen goods to their markets, and bringing home money, to purchase their commodities," whereas he approved the trades with France, Spain, and Portugal since they bring to Ireland "moydores, pistoles, and louis-

[42] *Works*, 7.162. Mr. Herbert Davis gave me convincing arguments that this tract is not by Swift, but they came too late for revision of my article. I have quoted from it only twice, and no point is dependent on these quotations. In any case, the tract reflects Swift's views as accurately as any he unquestionably wrote.

[43] *Ibid.*, p. 223.

[44] For example, *ibid.*, pp. 112, 140.

[45] *Ibid.*, p. 197.

[46] *Ibid.*, p. 18; cf. also p. 88.

dores." [47] Like many of the mercantile writers of the seventeenth and early eighteenth centuries, Swift appeared to accept the view that profit or loss to a nation engaged in foreign trade should be judged by particular balances resulting from trade with separate countries rather than by the general balance accruing to the nation. Thus he judges the trade with England bad, with France good, and so on, though it is not altogether evident that he thought seriously about the matter. The validity of judging by particular or general balance was being vigorously debated in his day, the proponents of the East India Company defending the Indian trade, despite its unfavorable balance, on the ground that it contributed in the long run to a favorable general balance for the nation at large.[48]

Swift accepts without qualification the prevalent mercantilist distinction between importations of manufactured and of raw materials. Although importations of any kind were ordinarily looked at askance as being economically disadvantageous, there were degrees of badness. Importation of manufactured articles was worse than importation of raw materials. Raw material at least provided employment for the native worker, thereby circulating money and increasing internal trade, whereas the importation of the finished product tended to draw bullion from the nation, thus decreasing its wealth. Particularly bad were those imported manufactured articles which competed with the domestic product. Thus John Cary wrote: ". . . 'tis a certain Rule, that so far as any Nation furnishes us with things already manufactured . . . so much less is our Advantage by the Trade we drive with them; especially if those Manufactures interfere with our own, and are purchased with Bullion." [49] He applies this rule specifically to England's trade

[47] *Ibid.*, pp. 161-62. Swift's complaints about the scarcity of money need fuller investigation. His primary concern was the influence of such a condition on domestic trade. The mercantilists, too, complained frequently about the scarcity of money (see Heckscher, *op. cit.*, 2. 221 ff.; Lipson, *op. cit.*, 3. 68-69), which they related to rents, prices, employment, and, of course, to the effect on foreign trade. The problems involved receive full treatment in Arthur Eli Monroe, *Monetary Theory before Adam Smith* (Cambridge, Mass., 1923), Parts 4 and 5.

[48] See P. J. Thomas, *Mercantilism and the East India Trade* (London, 1926), pp. 8 ff.; cf. also on the matter of general and particular balances, Suviranta, *op. cit.*, pp. 25 ff., and Viner, *op. cit.*, pp. 10 ff.

[49] *Discourse on Trade, and Other Matters Relative to It* (London, 1745), p. 78. This is a rewriting of a work published in 1695.

with Spain, Turkey, and Portugal, which " are very advantagious, as they vend great Quantities of our Manufactures, and
furnish us with Materials to be wrought up here " and to the
African and West Indian trades, which are "most profitable to
the Nation, as they imploy more of our People at Home." [50] In
the widely circulated *British Merchant*, among the " general
Maxims in Trade which are assented to by everybody," appeared the following:

Foreign Materials, wrought up here into such Goods as would
otherwise be imported ready manufactured, is a means of saving
Money to the Nation; and if saving is getting, that Trade which
procures such Materials ought to be look'd upon as profitable. . . .[51]

That Trade is eminently bad, which supplies the same Goods as
we manufacture our selves, especially if we can make enough for
our Consumption. . . .[52]

In *The British Merchant* stress was laid on what was later
called " the balance of employment." The argument was that
those foreign countries which imported goods manufactured in
England bought not merely these goods but also the labor
engaged in making them. These foreign consumers thus contributed to the "Employment and Subsistence of our People." [53] On the other hand, when the English imported manufactured goods, England paid for the labor in the country which
produced and manufactured these goods.

If his [the laborer's or manufacturer's] whole Time is taken up in
working for the Consumption of the *Portuguese*; for instance, if
his whole Wages are paid him by that Nation, he gains from
Portugal the whole Value of his yearly Labour. And the same
thing must be said of the *Portuguese* Manufacturer that works for
the Consumption of the *English* Nation; he clears his whole Wages
from this Kingdom.[54]

[50] *Ibid.*, pp. 78-79.

[51] 1.2. This and the following quotation were first printed in the 1721 edition
of *The British Merchant*. They were originally published in Sir Theodore Janssen's
General Maxims of Trade (London, 1713), pp. 6, 8.

[52] 1.4. These are essentially the rules of trade set forth by William Wood in his
Survey of Trade (London, 1718), pp. 224 ff. It is pleasant to observe that Swift
and the man he attacked so violently in *The Drapier's Letters* are in fundamental
agreement about foreign trade.

[53] 1.18.

[54] 1.29.

Thus, the writer argues, " It is certain, that all that the Con-sumption of *Portugal* pays to the English Labourers, more than is paid by the Consumption of *England* to the Labourers of *Portugal*, is clear Gain to England, and so much Loss to *Portugal*." [55]

Among the contemporary Irishmen who advanced these views was John Browne, whom Swift attacked violently in *The Drapier's Letters* and later forgave and praised for his public spirit.[56] As a preliminary to his discussion of Ireland's trade Browne laid down certain general maxims, among which were the following:

That Trade is the least beneficial, which takes of the primums of Manufactures, and not the Manufactures themselves, because it deprives the People of matter to work upon, and gives it to Strangers, *et Vice Versa*, that Trade is more advantagious which takes off our Manufactures, than that which takes primum only, because it pays not only for the Produce of our Lands, but for the Art and Labour of our People also.

It is better to buy the primums of Manufactures from abroad, than the Manufacture itself, because in the first Case, Value issues only for the Materials, but in the last, we must not only pay for the Materials, but for the Labour and Art also which brought them to perfection.[57]

The viewpoints expressed by these writers find unqualified acceptance in Swift. His most direct statement of the impor-tant distinction between manufactured and raw materials is presented in *A Short View of the State of Ireland,* where he lays down a set of maxims much in the manner of economic writers of the day. These are the " rules generally known, and never contradicted . . . of any country's flourishing and grow-ing rich," three of which have an application to the point under discussion:

The second, is the industry of the people in working up all their native commodities to the last degree of manufacture.

The third, is the conveniency of safe ports and havens, to carry out their own goods, as much manufactured, and bring in those

[55] *Ibid.*

[56] See *Correspondence,* 4. 24 ff.; *The Drapier's Letters,* ed. Herbert Davis (Oxford, 1935), pp. 226-28.

[57] *An Essay on Trade in General; and, on That of Ireland in Particular* (Dublin, 1728), p. 29.

of others, as little manufactured as the nature of mutual commerce will allow.

. . . .

The fourteenth, is a disposition of the people of a country to wear their own manufactures, and import as few incitements to luxury, either in clothes, furniture, food or drink as they possibly can live conveniently without.[58]

The same principles are pervasive in the Irish tracts, applied particularly to manufactured goods shipped in from England. With the Irish parliament powerless, where England was concerned, to impose duties or prohibit importations, Swift realized that appeals had to be made to the Irish people. Accordingly, with the publication of *A Proposal for the Universal Use of Irish Manufactures* in 1720, he began a campaign to persuade the Irish that their economic welfare depended upon a drastic reduction in their use of foreign commodities. He made shrewd use of patriotic feelings and resentment against England's restrictive policies to enforce his economic plea. In this first tract is also evident an appeal to readers who recognize the validity of the common mercantilist view that importation of manufactured articles hinders home industry whereas the substitution of a native product encourages domestic manufacturers, increases employment, stimulates internal trade, and reduces the flow of money abroad. Thus he pleaded with the Irish to wear only cloths of Irish growth and manufacture. The women are told that they will look as handsome in Irish " stuffs " as in imported brocades. The wearers of silks, velvets, calicoes—all imported and finished materials—ought to be considered enemies of the nation. Here, too, is the first of several appeals to the Irish clergy to utilize only native cloths in their habits. The economic disadvantage of sending out raw materials to be manufactured and then imported in the finished product is clearly implied in his ironic treatment of the grievances that " poor England suffers by impositions from Ireland." One project on foot to relieve the distress of England is the shipment of Ireland's " best wheaten straw " to Dunstable, to be made up into straw hats which the Irish will be obliged by law to import.[59]

[58] *Works,* 7. 83, 84.   [59] *Ibid.,* p. 23.

The mercantilist bias was persistent thereafter. In the Drapier's *Seventh Letter* Swift complained that the importation of " Indian stuffs, and calicoes " has been profitable to England and " an unconceivable loss to us; forcing the weavers to beg in our streets," [60] an obvious bias against importations on the ground that they do not provide employment for home laborers. The same principle is involved in his remark on wool: " Our own wool returned upon us, in English manufactures, to our infinite shame and damage; and the great advantage of England." [61] He was particularly urgent in 1728 and 1729, when a succession of bad harvests aggravated Ireland's difficulties, that the " ruinous importation of foreign luxury and vanity " be stopped and that the Irish " utterly discard all importations which are not absolutely necessary for health or life." [62] In *A Proposal That All Ladies Should Appear in Irish Manufacturers* he stressed the economic evil of imported manufactured products in which foreign labor is embodied. He computed that Ireland imports annually " ninety thousand pounds worth of silk, whereof the greater part is manufactured." " I allow," he added, " that the thrown and raw silk is less pernicious, because we have some share in the manufacture." [63] The principle is given ironic statement in the *Answer to the Craftsman*, where he wrote that England " may very reasonably demand the benefit of all our commodities in their natural growth, to be manufactured by their people, and a sufficient quantity of them for our use to be returned hither fully manufactured." [64]

In mercantilist literature the economic prejudice against importations in general is intensified in the case of importations of luxuries. Although there was some dissent or qualification, it was commonly believed that imported luxuries were economically indefensible. Sir Josiah Child wrote that " *Luxury* and *Prodigality* are as well prejudicial to *Kingdoms* as to Private *Families;* and that the expense of Foreign Commodities . . . is the worst expence a Nation can be inclinable to." [65]

[60] *Works*, 6.189.
[61] *Ibid.*
[62] *Works*, 7.138, 124.
[63] *Ibid.*, p. 199.
[64] *Ibid.*, p. 223; cf. also p. 222.
[65] *A Discourse of Trade* (London, 1698), Preface, p. [vi].

Much criticism of England's trade with France was based on the supposedly harmful economic effects of importing luxuries. Thus John Cary wrote: " . . . the *French* Trade is certainly our Loss, *France* being like a Tavern, with whom we spend what we get by other Nations and 'tis strange, we should be so bewitcht to that People, as to take off their Growth, which consists chiefly of things for Luxury, and receive a Value only for the Esteem we pùt on them." [66] Both Sir Theodore Janssen and William Wood assented to the general maxim, " That the importing *Commodities* of *mere Luxury*, is so much *real Loss* to the Nation as they amount to." [67] To these writers and others, luxuries were economic evils because they were usually manufactured products and thus embodied foreign labor. Similar attacks appeared in Irish journals and tracts. " The next thing I shall mention, highly prejudicial to Trade," wrote Arthur Dobbs, " is, our Luxury and Extravagance in Food, Dress, Furniture and Equipage." " What is spent in Luxury," he adds, " is just so much lost to the Nation in the way of Trade: For if it be in foreign commodities, it increases our imports; and if in the things of our own Country . . . it lessens our Exports." [68] The author of *An Inquiry into Some of the Causes of the Ill Situation of Ireland* (1732) complained bitterly that the Irish send to foreign markets " the Necessaries of Life, and bring home Trifles; for Instance we send to *France Butter* and *Beef.* . . . In Return of these Necessaries, what do we import from *France* of any Value, but *Vanities for our Backs, Diseases for our Bodies, and Poverty and Idleness for our Manufacturers and Husbandmen?* " [69] In Bishop Berkeley's *The Querist,* the attack on imported luxuries is a persistent note. Two queries may be taken as representative. " Whether an Irish lady, set out with French silks and Flanders lace, may not be said to consume more beef and butter than a hundred of our laboring peasants? " " Whether it be possible for this country to grow rich, so long as what is made by domestic industry is spent in foreign luxury? " [70]

[66] *A Discourse on Trade, and Other Matters,* pp. 79-80. Cf. also John Pollexfen, *A Discourse of Trade and Coyn* (London, 1697; 2d ed., 1700), pp. 92 ff.

[67] *The British Merchant,* 1.3; Wood, *op. cit.,* pp. 224, 225.

[68] *An Essay on the Trade of Ireland* (London, 1731), Part 2, pp. 41-42.

[69] P. 52.

[70] Part I, No. 150; Part II, No. 226. For additional attacks on luxury by Irish

To these voices Swift added his. Among the rules he laid down to make a country rich is the " disposition of the people . . . to wear their own manufactures, and import as few incitements to luxury, either in clothes, furniture, food or drink as they possibly can live conveniently without." [71] In his sermon on Ireland's economic condition he referred to the importation of luxuries as " another cause of our low condition," [72] and he wrote with animus, in the *Letter to the Archbishop of Dublin Concerning the Weavers*, against the " vanity and luxury " of Irish women who deplete the nation's stock of money by their purchases of such importations as tea, coffee, chocolate, laces, silks, and calicoes—all " unwholesome drugs, and unnecessary finery." [73] In another tract he catalogued and computed the value of the "ruinous importations of foreign luxury and vanity," [74] but pleaded for the continued importation of wine without duties on the ground that the people of no other nation are "more in want of some cordial to keep up their spirits, than in this of ours." [75] Swift did not elaborate his objection to the importations of luxuries as distinct from other importations. Actually he tended to identify all importations as luxuries since Ireland could afford none; with the case against importations of any kind so strong, the case against imported luxuries was too obvious to need elaborated argument. It is of interest that Swift kept his argument against luxuries wholly on the economic level. Moral considerations did not enter the discussion.[76] He called for frugality and consumption of native products in the interests of native industries, without emphasizing that prodigality and high living were, as many mercantilists believed, in some special way corrupting and thus conducive to national weakness. Yet he did not align himself with

writers, see *The Dublin Journal*, No. 37, Dec. 11, 1725; *The Tribune*, Nos. 5 and 12, 1729; *The Present State of Ireland Consider'd* (Dublin and London, 1730), pp. 21-23; Samuel Madden, *Reflections and Resolutions Proper for the Gentlemen of Ireland* (Dublin, 1738; 1816), Resolutions VIII, IX, X, XXX.

[71] *Works*, 7.84.
[72] *Works*, 4.213.
[73] *Works*, 7.140.
[74] *Ibid.*, p. 199.
[75] *Ibid.*, p. 197.
[76] But see *Works*, 7.124, where he seems to combine the moral and economic arguments. The intention is economic.

those writers on trade who maintained that " 'tis no wrong to the Commonwealth, if men of estates drink, drab, live profusely, and dye beggars, as long as every penny comes to the natives. . . . The mischief only is, when forraigners are the better for this disorder, for that does insensibly ruine the Commonwealth." [77]

In the Drapier's *Seventh Letter* Swift listed among the " wishes of the nation " that the Irish parliament would declare " by some unanimous and hearty votes, against wearing any silk or woollen manufactures, imported from abroad." [78] He expressed the same hope in the first of the Irish economic tracts and at least twice in tracts written in 1729. [79] As a matter of fact, the Irish parliament had passed resolutions against importation in 1703, 1705, and 1707, the wording of the first of which gives the impression that Swift had taken it as the theme of his *Proposal for the Universal Use of Irish Manufacture*:

Resolved, Nemine Contradicente. That by Reason of the Great Decay of Trade and Discouragement of Exportation of the Manufactures of this Kingdom, many poor Tradesmen are reduced to extream Want and Beggary. Resolved, Nemine Contradicente, That it will greatly conduce to the Relief of said Poor, and to the Good of the Kingdom, that the Inhabitants thereof should use more of the Manufactures of this Kingdom in their Apparel, and the Furniture of their Homes. [80]

What effect these resolutions had may easily be inferred. Swift may or may not have known of them; in any case it is difficult to believe that he had any faith in the efficacy of such resolutions. His was, of course, anything but a lone voice pleading for wider use of native products and for decreased importations, as an examination of the pages of *The Dublin Journal* and *The Tribune* and of the tracts of such public-spirited Irishmen as Berkeley and Madden will reveal. [81]

---

[77] Thomas Manley, *Usury at Six Per Cent. Examined* (London, 1669), Preface, p. [9].

[78] *Works*, 4.199.

[79] *Works*, 7.19, 143, 199.

[80] *Journal of the House of Commons of Ireland*, 2.407. See also Hutchinson, *op. cit.*, p. 143.

[81] See *The Dublin Journal*, No. 25, Dec. 11, 1725; *The Tribune*, No. 12, 1729; *The Present State of Ireland Consider'd* (Dublin and London, 1730), pp. 27 ff.; Madden, *op. cit.*, Resolution VIII.

In his pleas for reduced importations Swift used, in support of his arguments, an analogy from personal finance. This analogy, of long standing in mercantilist theory, assumed the resemblance between the income of an individual and that of a nation. Just as an individual spending in excess of his income threatens himself with debt, poverty, and eventual ruin, so does a nation whose importations exceed exportations tend toward the same condition by virtue of the decrease in its treasure. The analogy was widely used, and in Swift's own library it was to be found in the economic writings of Sir William Temple and John Locke.[82] The statement of it by John Pollexfen, one of the Commissioners of Trade and Plantations, is representative:

It is with Nations as with Families: Those Masters that are careful and good Husbands themselves, and keep their Servants to their Labour, and frugal in their Expences, generally thrive most; so with Nations, those that have the most Industrious People, and are most Parsimonious, will be the Richest. . . .

A Gentleman that hath but 500 l per Annum, that is Industrious with his Servants in Husbandry, and content with his own, for Food and Apparel, and careful to avoid unnecessary Outgoings and Expences, may bring Money into his House and keep it too; but a Gentleman that hath 1000 l per Annum, that keeps Idle Servants, despises his own Food and Cloathing, and instead thereof takes in Silks, Wines, and dear bought Commodities from Abroad in the room of them, at the end of the Year either cannot bring Money into his House, or not keep it long because of his Debts: The same with Nations that . . . despise their own Commodities, and are fond of those that are far fetcht, and dear bought. That undeniable Maxim, *That the way to be Rich is to be careful in Saving, as well as industrious in Getting,* hath the same reference to Nations as to particular Persons, or Families.[83]

Swift uses the analogy several times. In the *Letter to the Archbishop of Dublin Concerning the Weavers* he wrote:

If a private gentelman's income be sunk irretrievably for ever from a hundred pounds to fifty, and that he hath no other method

---

[82] See *The Works of Sir William Temple* (London, 1731), 1.65; John Locke, *Some Consideration of the Consequences of the Lowering of Interest, and the Raising of the Value of Money,* in *Works* (1824), 4.19-20. Cf. also Charles Davenant, *An Essay on Ways and Means of Supplying the War,* in *Political and Commercial Works* (1771), 1.13; Sir Francis Brewster, *Essay on Trade and Navigation* (London, 1695), p. 51.

[83] Pollexfen, *op. cit.,* pp. 80-81.

to supply the deficiency, I desire to know . . . whether such a person hath any other course to take than to sink half his expenses in every article of economy, to save himself from ruin and the gaol. Is not this more than doubly the case of Ireland . . . ? Therefore instead of dreams and projects for the advancing of trade, we have nothing left but to find out some expedient whereby we may reduce our expenses to our incomes.[84]

Even on occasion where he does not make overt use of the analogy, Swift appears to think of the economy of a nation as being that of a family or individual writ large.

From the assembled evidence it is reasonable to conclude that Swift was fully aware of the importance of both the trading and the landed interests in the economy of a nation. His awareness of their relationship is evident throughout the Irish tracts, where he frequently mingles proposals for both. There is a sense of urgency in his discussion of the problems of trade, significantly not less strong than in his discussions of the problems of agriculture. Of the extent of his reading in economic literature and of his knowledge, there is not much to be said. His library, with only a few works in the field,[85] suggests that his reading was in no way extended, though we need not assume that his reading was limited to books he owned or preserved. It would be utter folly to make serious claims for Swift as an economic thinker. He utilized the same pleas and arguments to be found in such Irish contemporaries as Berkeley, Prior, Dobbs, Browne, and in the Irish journals. The atmosphere was thick with the assumptions of mercantilism, and these he accepted without criticism, applying them to Ireland. It was not part of his purpose to be either systematic or independent; he was simply adapting the commonly accepted principles of the day to an instance of special pleading, using invective, irony, cajolery—all the arts of attack and persuasion so manifest in his political and religious writings—to mitigate Ireland's plight.

---

[84] *Works*, 7. 139; cf. also pp. 124-25, 195.
[85] Cf. Harold Williams, *Dean Swift's Library* (Cambridge, Eng., 1932), Sales Catalogue, Nos. 276, 288, 296, 300, 412, 435, 444.

The reader of the Irish tracts is likely to suffer from the delusion—perhaps intentionally created by Swift—that Ireland's case was unique, that Ireland was an isolated instance, a country singled out by England for oppression and restrictive measures. It is important to correct this impression by viewing the economic legislation as part of the trend toward protectionism which became increasingly a dominant aspect of mercantilism in the last part of the seventeenth century. " All the Nations of *Europe* . . . concur in this *Maxim*," wrote an author in *The British Merchant*, " That the less they consume of foreign Commodities, the better it is for them." [86] The logic of this position necessitated the discouragement of imports, and England applied this logic to India, to France, to its colonies in America, as well as to Ireland, " its best and noblest Colony," to use the words of Charles Davenant. The English woolen industry that acted as a pressure group to force the Act against Ireland in 1699 is not to be distinguished from the woolen industry that fought violently against the East India trade and achieved the protection for home industries enacted in 1700. The conceptions of national self-interest and self-sufficiency rooted deeply in mercantilist thought dictated a policy towards Ireland's competitive industries not to be distinguished from the policies toward the competitive industries of Turkey or Spain. Religious and political issues cut athwart English economic policies in the treatment of Ireland; but the fundamental fact is that the English, in their desire to secure the national welfare by vigorous protection of home industries, looked upon Ireland as a dependency which must not be permitted to become a trade rival. It was the situation created by this attitude that gives meaning to almost everything Swift wrote concerning the trade of Ireland.

In the last analysis Swift, it may be freely admitted, was an ardent defender of the landed interest. " I ever abominated," he wrote to Pope in 1722, " that scheme of politics . . . of setting up a moneyed interest in opposition to the landed: for I conceived, there could not be a truer maxim in our government than this, that the possessors of the soil are the best judges of what is for the advantage of the kingdom." [87] These words

[86] 1.14.   [87] *Correspondence*, 3.121.

echo what he had written a decade earlier in his reference to an "acknowledged maxim" of the Whig party "as dangerous to the constitution as any I have mentioned; I mean, that of preferring, on all occasions, the moneyed interest before the landed." [88] Nor can the reader of the Irish tracts ignore the persistent emphasis embodied in the statement that "There is not an older or more uncontroverted maxim in the politics of all wise nations, than that of encouraging agriculture." [89] What must be guarded against, in the interest of a better balanced conception of Swift, is permitting these statements to obscure the fact that he recognized the importance of trade, particularly after 1714. The Swift of *The Examiner* who "never fail'd to maul" trade was transformed into a person who realized that great benefits would accrue to Ireland if she were permitted liberty of trade.

[88] *Works,* 9. 231.
[89] *Works,* 7. 134.

A MODEST PROPOSAL AND
POPULOUSNESS

IN 1724, five years before the publication of *A modest proposal*, Swift wrote a tract entitled *Maxims controlled in Ireland*, in which he examined "certain maxims of state, founded upon long observation and experience, drawn from the constant practice of the wisest nations, and from the very principles of government."[1] His purpose was to demonstrate that however much these maxims applied to other countries they had no application to Ireland. Among the maxims examined and confuted is one that was cherished by the mercantilist economic writers of the last half of the seventeenth and the first half of the eighteenth centuries: that people are the riches of a nation. The passage in which this maxim is presented would seem to be the germ of *A modest proposal:*

It is another undisputed maxim in government, 'That people are the riches of a nation'; which is so universally granted, that it will be hardly pardonable to bring it in doubt. And I will grant it to be so far true, even in this island, that if we had the African custom, or privilege, of selling our useless bodies for slaves to foreigners, it would be the most useful branch of our trade, by ridding us of a most unsupportable burthen, and bringing us money in the stead. But, in our present situation, at least five children in six who are born, lie a dead weight upon us, for want of employment. And a very skilful computer assured me, that above one half of the souls in this kingdom supported themselves by begging and thievery; whereof two thirds would be able to get their bread in any other country upon earth. Trade is the only incitement to labour; where that fails the poor native must either beg, steal, or starve, or be forced to quit his country. This hath made me often wish, for some years past, that instead of discouraging our people from seeking foreign soil, the public would rather pay for transporting all our unnecessary mortals. . . . .[2]

The parallelism in ideas between this passage and *A modest proposal* is striking. In each there is the complaint that the people, for want of employment, must turn to begging and thievery, that a portion of the population is a useless burden, and that under certain conditions these

[1] *The prose works of Jonathan Swift, D.D.,* ed. Temple Scott (London, 1897–1908), VII, 65. This edition will hereafter be referred to as *Works.*

[2] *Ibid.,* p. 70.

useless people could become a source of wealth to the nation. The ironic solution for Ireland's economic difficulties in each instance is the selling-off of human bodies, as slaves in the one case and as food in the other. In effect, Swift is maintaining that the maxim—people are the riches of a nation—applies to Ireland only if Ireland is permitted slavery or cannibalism. In both the *Maxims controlled in Ireland* and *A modest proposal* populousness is overtly and impliedly made a vicious economic condition for Ireland. The methods are, of course, different in the two, with *A modest proposal* gaining its effects through broad and sustained irony; but for fear that the reader may miss his telling point, that people are not the riches of Ireland whatever they may be in other countries, Swift inserts at the close of *A modest proposal* a more direct statement of his purpose:

I can think of no one objection, that will possibly be raised against this proposal, unless it should be urged that the number of people will be thereby much lessened in the kingdom. This I freely own, and was indeed one principal design in offering it to the world. I desire the reader will observe, that I calculate my remedy *for this one individual Kingdom of Ireland, and for no other that ever was, is, or, I think, ever can be upon earth.*[3]

The satirical point of *A modest proposal* would have been sharpened for Swift's contemporaries to the extent to which they believed the maxim it refuted. How much more damaging to England that her drastic policies had forced Ireland outside the pale in which universally valid economic laws could operate!

An examination of economic tracts in the second half of the seventeenth century reveals constant iteration of the principle that people are the riches of a nation. Sir William Petty, whose views on Ireland were widely quoted in Swift's day, wrote that "Fewness of people is real poverty; and a Nation wherein are Eight Millions of People, are more than twice as rich as the same scope of Land wherein are but Four."[4] People, wrote William Petyt, the supposed author of *Britannia languens* (1680), are "in truth the chiefest, most fundamental, and precious commodity."[5] Sir Josiah Child, great merchant and expound-

---

[3] *Ibid.*, pp. 214–15.

[4] *A treatise of taxes and contributions*, in *The economic writings of Sir William Petty*, ed. Charles H. Hull (Cambridge, 1899), I, 34.

[5] Reprinted in *A select collection of early English tracts on commerce*, ed. J. R. McCulloch (London, 1856), p. 458.

er of mercantilist ideas, maintained that "most Nations in the Civilized Parts of the World, are more or less Rich or Poor proportionably to the Paucity or Plenty of their People, and not to the Sterility or Fruitfulness of their Lands."[6] These statements are frequently repeated in the early eighteenth century. In *New essays on trade* (1702), Sir Francis Brewster wrote: "Nothing makes Kingdoms and Commonwealths, Mighty, Opulent and Rich, but multitudes of People; 'tis Crowds bring in Industry."[7] From Defoe came a similar expression: ". . . . the glory, the strength, the riches, the trade, and all that is valuable in a nation as to its figure in the world, depends upon the number of its people, be they never so mean and poor. . . . ."[8] These are typical expressions and could be multiplied. In their context and with their supporting arguments, these expressions, it is true, are not tantamount to an unqualified assertion that people are the riches of a nation. People are conceived of as a source of riches; their labor is potential wealth but it must be utilized. As one writer expressed it, the people are *"capital material . . . . raw* and indigested."[9]

Yet often the maxim was stated without qualification or without any attempt to equate the number of people and the employment available to them, although there was likely to be an assumption that employment could be provided.[10] The mercantilist wanted a large or dense population in order to keep wages low[11] and manufactures cheap, a condition by which a country gained an advantage in export trade, the great desideratum of the mercantilist. As William Petyt wrote: "The *odds in Populacy* must also produce the like odds in Manufac-

---

[6] *A new discourse of trade* (London, 1698), p. 179.

[7] P. 51.

[8] *Giving alms no charity* (1704); reprinted in *A collection of pamphlets concerning the poor*, ed. Thomas Gilbert (London, 1787), p. 71.

[9] William Petyt, *Britannia languens*, in *A select collection* . . . . , ed. McCulloch, p. 458.

[10] See the discussion on this point in Eli F. Heckscher, *Mercantilism*, trans. Mendel Shapiro (London, 1935), II, 159 ff. Heckscher writes: "It is natural to wonder how the notion that there could never be too great a population could ever be reconciled with the anxiety concerning the insufficiency of employment. In actual fact, this contradiction was never resolved."

[11] See Jacob Viner, *Studies in the theory of international trade* (New York and London, 1937), pp. 56–57, where it is pointed out that commentators on mercantilism have neglected to take sufficiently into account dissent—on economic and humanitarian grounds—from the dominant doctrine that low wages are desirable. Viner's first two chapters, with their clear exposition of seventeenth- and eighteenth-century economic theory and their rich documentation from writers in the period, are of great value to the student of the history of ideas.

ture; plenty of people must also cause *cheapnesse of wages:* which will cause cheapnesse of the Manufacture; in a scarcity of people wages must be dearer, which must cause the dearnesse of the Manufacture. . . . ."[12] Mandeville was thinking in the same terms when he declared that "in a free Nation where Slaves are not allow'd of, the surest Wealth consists in a Multitude of laborious Poor."[13] Though the insistence on populousness received support from serious economic writers by serious arguments, the maxim was as likely as not to be set down in nontechnical and popular writings without consideration of the implications and assumptions involved, as it was, for example, in the *Weekly journal, or Saturday's post,* April 11, 1724, and in the Irish weekly, the *Tribune,* No. 17 (1729).

Against the uncritical enunciation of the maxim there were sporadic protests. In an *Essay upon the probable methods of making a people gainer in the ballance of trade* (1699), Charles Davenant declared: "Their's is a wrong Opinion who think all Mouths profit a Country that consume its Product; And it may more truthfully be affirmed, That he who does not some way serve the Commonwealth, either by being employed, or by employing Others, is not only a useless, but a hurtful member to it."[14] A similar protest came from Laurence Braddon in 1723:

But tho' *Populousness be designed as the greatest Blessing to a Nation, yet,* in fact, *it proves a Blessing only to that Kingdom and State,* where due care is taken . . . . *that* none, who are willing to work, shall be forced to be Idle for want of Employment. . . . . And where none who are able are permitted to live idle, by begging, or other more Vicious Practices. . . . .[15]

Swift, too, made a protest of the same nature. In *The history of the four last years of the queen,* which he was writing in the trying days near the end of Anne's reign, he complained that "The maxim, 'That people are the riches of a nation,' hath been crudely understood by many writers and reasoners upon that subject." At the moment his animus was directed against the Palatines, whose numbers immigrating into England had increased the population by just so many dissenters; yet he was also establishing a general point: that populousness per se is

[12] *Britannia languens,* in *A select collection* . . . . , p. 349.

[13] *The fable of the bees,* ed. F. B. Kaye (Oxford, 1924), I, 287.

[14] P. 51.

[15] *To pay old debts without new taxes* (London, 1723), p. xi.

not a blessing; that a person who does not function productively in economic or political society makes the nation poorer, not richer; and that such a person is comparable, to use Swift's own figure, to a wen, which, although it makes a man fatter, is "unsightly and troublesome, at best, and intercepts that nourishment, which would otherwise diffuse itself through the whole body."[16]

Viewed against this background, *A modest proposal* is seen to be another protest, in Swift's unique manner, against the unqualified maxim that people are the riches of a nation. The tract was written for a public in whose consciousness the maxim was firmly implanted, in the expectation that the ironic impact would thus be greater. The terrible irony in the bare maxim, divested of its supporting arguments, was even more apparent at this time than usual because of the famine conditions which prevailed in Ireland after three successive failures in harvests; and Swift takes occasion in two other tracts, one written in 1728 and one in 1729, to insist that "the uncontrolled maxim, 'That people are the riches of a Nation,' is no maxim here under our circumstances."[17] Here, at least, was one country where populousness was not a virtue. Swift seemed to be aware—the evidence was before his eyes—of the contradiction in the mercantilist attitude that the wealth of a country was based on the poverty of the majority of its subjects. However, we must guard against endowing Swift with unusual knowledge of or insight into economic matters,[18] or even seeing him as moving against the trend of mercantilist thought. His purpose was not primarily to expose an economic fallacy; it was purely propagandistic: to put the onus on England of vitiating the working of natural economic law in Ireland by denying Irishmen "the same natural rights common to the rest of mankind."

It would seem, on merely logical grounds, that Swift should have favored a reduction of the population to achieve a higher level of sub-

---

[16] *Works*, X, 114–15.   [17] *Ibid.*, VII, 114, 139.

[18] There is no evidence that Swift did any extended or systematic reading in economic theory. His library contained the following: Josiah Child, *Discourse on trade* (1693); Charles Davenant, *Picture of a modern whig: with other tracts* (1701); John Browne, *Essays on the trade and coin of Ireland* (1729); John Locke, *Tracts relating to money, interest and trade* (1696); William Petty, *Essays in political arithmetick* (1699); Samuel Madden, *Reflections and resolutions for the gentlemen of Ireland* (1738). I have listed these in the order in which they appear in the Sales Catalogue reprinted by Harold Williams in *Dean Swift's library* (Cambridge, 1932), Nos. 276, 288, 300, 412, 435, 444. To these may be added the economic tracts of Sir William Temple.

sistence, that he should have defended, for example, the emigration of the Irish people to the American colonies; and he did pretend to see in emigration a partial solution. In *Maxims controlled in Ireland* he wrote that he has often wished "for some years past, that instead of discouraging our people from seeking foreign soil, the public would rather pay for transporting all our unnecessary mortals, whether Papists or Protestants, to America."[19] He repeats the view in the *Intelligencer*, No. 19: "It must needs be a very comfortable circumstance, in the present juncture, that some thousand families are gone, or going, or preparing to go, from hence, and settle themselves in America."[20] But these statements, viewed in their context, are seen to be ironic, their function being to emphasize the dire position of a country which must resort to emigration. In the light of contemporary economic theory, with its insistence on an increasing population, emigration could not be viewed with complacency; it was not acceptable as a solution. There was much concern that England's population was declining or was not increasing at a sufficiently rapid rate; and many mercantilists advocated encouragements to marriage, to achieve a higher birth rate,[21] and laws to facilitate immigration.[22] There were complaints that emigration to the colonies has been detrimental to the nation. "The peopling of the American Plantations subject to the Crown of England," wrote Roger Coke, "hath diminished the strength of Eng-

---

[19] *Works*, VII, 70.   [20] *Ibid.*, IX, 328.

[21] In *A modest proposal* Swift lists among the ironical advantages of his proposal that it "would be a great inducement to marriage, which all wise nations have either encouraged by rewards, or enforced by laws and penalties" (*Works*, VII, 214). Charles Davenant complained that the duties imposed on marriages and birth were detrimental: "a very grievous Burthen upon the poorer Sort, whose Numbers compose the Strength and Wealth of any Nation." He adds: "In order to have Hands to carry on Labour and Manufactures, which must make us Gainers in the Ballance of Trade, we ought not to deterr but rather invite Men to marry . . . ." (*An essay upon the probable methods of making a people gainers in the ballance of trade* [London, 1699], p. 33). Contrast Swift's statement in *A proposal for giving badges to the beggars of Dublin* (1737): "As this is the only Christian country where people contrary to the old maxim, are the poverty and not the riches of the nation, so, the blessing of increase and multiply is by us converted into a curse: and, as marriage hath been ever countenanced in all free countries, so we should be less miserable if it were discouraged in ours, as far as can be consistent with Christianity" (*Works*, VII, 330).

[22] In *The history of the four last years of the queen*, Swift makes an interesting application of the maxim, that people are the riches of a nation, to the problem of immigration (*Works*, IX, 114–15). On the immigration and naturalization of foreigners see Slingsby Bethel, *An account of the French usurpation upon the trade of England* (London, 1679), p. 15; Charles Davenant, *Discourses on the public revenues and trade of England* (London, 1698), II, 199; William Wood, *A survey of trade* (London, 1718), pp. 299 ff.

land."[23] It is not, Slingsby Bethel maintained, in "the interest of State, to suffer such multitudes of people to pass out of his Majesties Kingdoms into other Princes Dominions, or the Western Plantations, thereby to disfurnish our selves of people; the sad consequences and effects whereof, are too visible in the misfortunes of *Spain*."[24] The author of *Britannia languens* argued in the same vein: ". . . . our *Plantation-Trade* hath robbed and prevented us of some Millions of our People, amongst which very many being, or might have been Manufacturers, the Nation hath also lost more Millions of Pounds in the loss of their Manufactures."[25] Those Irishmen, Swift among them,[26] who had observed the losses to Ireland resulting from the emigration of workers in the Irish woolen industry to France, Spain, Germany, and the Low Countries—an exodus caused by the restrictive acts passed by the English Parliament at the close of the seventeenth century—would have read such complaints understandingly.

Many mercantilists found, however, that they could reconcile emigration to colonies with the desire for an increasing population and the fear of loss of numbers. It could not be denied that by reducing the number of laborers in the nation emigration tended to raise the costs of labor and manufactures and thus to put the country in a less favorable position for advantageous foreign trade; yet it could be and was argued that colonies compensated for the disadvantages created by providing raw materials to be manufactured in the mother-country and a market for the finished products. Emigration to colonies whose trade was carefully controlled by navigation acts was justifiable, therefore, if such colonies created employment at home and swelled the exports to a value greater than that lost by the numbers who emigrated. Thus Sir Josiah Child wrote: "That all Colonies and foreign Plantations do endamage their Mother-Kingdom, whereof the Trades (of such Plantations) are not confined to their said Mother-Kingdom, by good Laws and severe Execution of those Laws."[27] He continued:

[23] *A treatise wherein is demonstrated that the church and state of England are in equal danger with the trade of it* (London, 1671), p. 26.

[24] *An account of the French usurpation upon the trade of England* (London, 1679), p. 16.

[25] P. 370.

[26] Any reader of the Irish tracts will recall examples of Swift's laments about the Irish woolen industry. See, as typical, *The present miserable state of Ireland*, in *Works*, VII, 160 ff.

[27] P. 194.

Plantations being at first furnished, and afterwards successively supplied with People from their Mother-Kingdoms, and People being Riches, that loss of People to the Mother-Kingdoms, be it more or less, is certainly a damage, except the employment of those People abroad, do cause the employment of so many more at home in their Mother-Kingdoms. . . . .[28]

The argument is more fully expressed by John Cary:

. . . . it having been a great question among many thoughtful Men whether our Foreign Plantations have been an advantage to this Nation, the reasons they give against them are, that they have drained us of Multitudes of our People who might have been serviceable at home and advanced Improvements in Husbandry and Manufacture; That the Kingdom of *England* is worse Peopled by so much as they are increased; and that Inhabitants being the Wealth of a Nation, by how much they are lessened, by so much we are poorer than when we first began to settle our Foreign Colonies; Though I allow the last Proposition to be true, that People are or may be made the Wealth of a Nation . . . . Its my Opinion that our Plantations are an Advantage . . . . every one more or less, as they take off our Product and Manufactures, supply us with Commodities which may be either wrought up here, or Exported again, or prevent fetching things of the same Nature from other Princes for our home Consumption, imploy our Poor, and encourage our Navigation. . . . .[29]

Such justifications, as Swift was aware, had no application to Ireland, which was itself treated as a colony, with its trade strictly controlled by the Navigation Acts in the interests of England. An emigrant from England, Holland, or France might be looked upon as a unit of economic value who would eventually return his value to the mother-country; but one could hardly apply the same economic logic to the Irish emigrant, whose country was peculiarly removed from the operations of economic law. "I have often taken notice," Swift wrote, "both in print and in discourse, that there is no topic so fallacious . . . . as to argue how we ought to act in Ireland, from the example of England, Holland, France, or any other country, whose inhabitants are allowed the common rights and liberties of humankind."[30] Public-spirited Irishmen were concerned at the numbers who were departing. Even Lord Primate Boulter, whose first thought was for the welfare of England rather than for Ireland, was disturbed in 1728, when

[28] *Ibid.*, p. 195.

[29] *An essay on the state of England, in relation to its trade, its poor, and its taxes* (Bristol, 1695), pp. 65–66.

[30] *Works*, VII, 196; see also VII, 66, 123, 339.

famine was widespread, at the size of the emigration. In a letter written to the Duke of Newcastle, then Secretary of State, Boulter brought the problem before the English Cabinet for possible parliamentary action:

I am very sorry I am obliged to give your Grace so melancholy an account of the state of this kingdom. . . . . For we have had three bad harvests together there [in the north], which has made oatmeal, which is their great subsistence, much dearer than ordinary. . . . . We have had for several years some agents from the colonies in *America*, and several masters of ships that have gone about the country, and deluded the people with stories of great plenty and estates to be had for going for in those parts of the world: and they have been better able to seduce people, by reason of the necessities of the poor so late. . . . . But whatever occasions their going, it is certain that above 4,200 men, women, and children have been shipped off from hence for the *West Indies* within three years, and of these above 3,100 this last summer. . . . . The whole north is in a ferment at present, and people every day engaging one another to go next year to the *West Indies*. The humour has spread like a contagious distemper, and the people will hardly hear any body that tries to cure them of their madness.[31]

Swift, too, was genuinely perturbed. In 1728 and 1729 he refers several times to the subject of emigrating Irishmen, particularly to those who are leaving for America, which for several reasons he thinks no better than Ireland. Like Boulter, he believed that they had been given false representations and that they were doomed to disappointment; yet he is not at a loss to understand their motives for going, since "men in the extremest degree of misery, and want, will naturally fly to the first appearance of relief, let it be ever so vain, or visionary."[32] It was at this time that Swift wrote *A modest proposal* and its lesser known companion piece, *An answer to the craftsman*. This last tract was occasioned by the license given to France to recruit Irishmen for military service in the French army; and it too is a bitter and ironic commentary, among other matters, on the subject of Ireland's depopulation by England. As he had done in *A modest proposal*, Swift makes in this tract an ironical computation of the monetary profit to Ireland from the reduction and destruction of its people. And he adds this recommendation: ". . . . for fear of increasing the natives in this

[31] *Letters written by His Excellency Hugh Boulter . . . . to several ministers of state in England* (Dublin, 1770), I, 209–10.

[32] *Works*, IX, 330; see also VII, 120, 123.

island, that an annual draught, according to the number born every year, be exported to whatever prince will bear the carriage, or transplanted to the English dominions on the American continent, as a screen between his Majesty's English subjects and the savage Indians."[33]

What Swift wanted for Ireland was not fewer people but more opportunities—opportunities that would present themselves if England adopted a less restrictive policy, if the Irish absentees were regulated, and if the Irish people could be made to see wherein their welfare lay. He maintained, as did many contemporary Irishmen,[34] that Ireland possessed the potentialities of a rich country and could, under proper conditions, easily support its population. Ireland, he wrote, "is the poorest of all civilized countries in Europe, with every natural advantage to make it one of the richest."

[33] *Ibid.*, VII, 222. Compare this passage with what Swift has to say in the *Intelligencer*, No. 19, on the conditions which confront the Irish emigrant to America: "The English established in those colonies, are in great want of men to inhabit that tract of ground, which lies between them, and the wild Indians who are not reduced under their dominion. We read of some barbarous people, whom the Romans placed in their armies, for no other service, than to blunt their enemies' swords, and afterward to fill up trenches with their dead bodies. And thus our people who transport themselves, are settled in those interjacent tracts, as a screen against the insults of the savages, and may have as much land, as they can clear from the woods, at a very reasonable rate, if they can afford to pay about a hundred years' purchase by their labour" (*Works*, IX, 329–30).

[34] Cf. John Browne, *An essay on trade in general, and on that of Ireland in particular* (Dublin, 1728), pp. 38–39; George Berkeley, *The querist* (1735), Nos. 123–24, 132–34, 272–73; *Some thoughts on the tillage of Ireland* (Dublin, 1738), pp. 52 f.

JONATHAN SWIFT AND CHARITY

THAT SWIFT WAS a charitable person his biographers have agreed with surprising unanimity, although their accounts of his charitable activities, for the most part cursory and anecdotal, have left much to be desired. Nor have commentators troubled to examine closely his utterances on the subject of charity, some of which are of special interest as an aspect of his social and religious thought. The story related by George Faulkner, the Dublin bookseller, that Swift divided his income into three parts—one for living expenses, one to be disposed in present charities, one to be saved for posthumous charity[1]—has been quoted as evidence that his charity was "splendid relatively to his means."[2] Even his detractors have been forced to admit, as Dr. Johnson grudgingly did, that Swift was "liberal by principle"; but the great Cham hastened to add that the Dean's "beneficence was not graced with tenderness or civility; he relieved without pity, and assisted without kindness."[3] Dr. Delany, who had only high praise for Swift's "very distinguished generosity," seems unwittingly to have provided a clue to later biographers by drawing Swift's character in a sharp antithesis of avarice and generosity.[4] The temptation to exploit this apparent paradox has been too great to resist. The conception of a misanthropic Swift "almost a monomaniac upon the question of money,"[5] yet whose charity can not be questioned, has afforded commentators interested in the "mazy turnings of his character" an opportunity to speculate on this strange psychological twist. At best the seeming contradiction has been useful in building up the familiar theatrical conception of Swift. If we grant the value of probing for the impulses out of which his charity sprung, does some recondite explanation appear satisfactory? Was his charity, as a recent interpretation has it, "a way of showing his power, an expression of his egotism"?[6] Was the bequest of his fortune for an insane asylum an instance of eccentric

[1] *A Supplement to Dr. Swift's Works*, ed. John Nichols (London, 1779), p. 760. Faulkner, who is referring to the later period of Swift's deanship, says that Swift did not spend upon himself the third set aside for that purpose, that he actually used about half of his income for "pensions and charitable uses." This figure is supported by a remark Mrs. Pilkington attributes to Swift's housekeeper, Mrs. Brent: that Swift's "income is not above six-hundred pounds a year, and every year he gives above the half of it in private pensions to decayed families." See *Memoirs of Mrs. Laetitia Pilkington, 1712–1750*, ed. J. Isaacs (London, 1928), p. 64. Mrs. Pilkington's report of conversation is open to suspicion.

[2] Leslie Stephen, *Swift* ("English Men of Letters"; London, 1931), p. 142.

[3] *Lives of the English Poets* ("World Classics": Oxford and London, 1929), II, 223. Johnson probably took his cue from Hawkesworth, who granted that Swift "abounded in charity" but added: "It must be confessed that these acts of bounty did not appear to be the effects of compassion, for of the soft sympathy with distress that sometimes sparkles in the eyes, and sometimes glows upon the cheek, he shewed no sign." Swift's charity, Hawkesworth thought, was "a *Christian* duty, a reasonable service." See *The Works of Jonathan Swift, D.D.*, ed. J. Hawkesworth (London, 1755), I, 35–36. Dr. Lyon, the prebendary of St. Patrick's who took care of Swift in his last days, answered Hawkesworth, insisting that Swift merely concealed the "tenderness and natural affection, which he really felt most sensibly for the poor and miserable." Nichols, *op. cit.*, p. 755.

[4] [Patrick Delany], *Observations upon Lord Orrery's Remarks on the Life and Writings of Dr. Jonathan Swift* (London, 1754), pp. 5–6, 145, 259–260. The Earl of Orrery is also responsible. See his *Remarks on the Life and Writings of Dr. Jonathan Swift* (London, 1752), p. 4: Swift "was a mixture of avarice and generosity: the former, was frequently present, the latter, seldom appeared, unless excited by compassion."

[5] Leslie Stephen, *op. cit.*, p. 141. Cf. also Robert Wyse Jackson, *Jonathan Swift: Dean and Pastor* (London, 1939), p. 168: "Swift combined a rather exaggerated meanness with a wonderful generosity."

[6] Mario M. Rossi and Joseph M. Hone, *Swift; or, the Egotist* (London, 1934), p. 134.

behavior, or was it, as the citizens of eighteenth-century Dublin realized, a sensible recognition of the city's eleemosynary needs? I suggest that a simple humanitarian desire to aid his fellowmen is a sufficient explanation and one consistent with his character. Nevertheless, with Swift as a dispenser of charity, as in so many other aspects, biographers have found it pleasant to dwell on the bewildering contradictions and on the eccentric or the whimsical. The story of his seraglio of old women in distress, to whom he gave such names as Pullagowna, Stumpha-nympha, and Friterilla, has been delightedly repeated by commentators who have played down his more sober activities.[7]

In the interests of a more accurate conception of Swift's character the anecdotes, occasional eccentricities, and concealed motives should be seen in their proper perspective; at the very least these should be balanced by certain instances of his charitable activities which have been hitherto ignored or under-emphasized. Observing him more completely, we find a person eminently practical in his philanthropy, with well formulated views reflecting traditional Christian sentiments on the subject of charity and the proper relationship between rich and poor in a Christian society. It is not evident that he differed in any respect from his contemporaries who engaged in individual and organized charities, except possibly in being more active and more vocal as befitted one of his clerical position. He was sensible, of course, that the problems of the poor were part of a larger context of social and economic maladjustment in Ireland as a whole; and his valiant but unsuccessful attempts to solve these national difficulties are well known. These problems of large scope and a full-length study of Swift's charities must wait another occasion. As a preliminary I wish, first of all, to record here some little known instances of Swift's charitable activities and, second, to examine in the light of contemporary opinion certain of his utterances on the subject of charity—in particular, his views concerning the charity schools of his day and his explanation, as a Christian divine, of wealth and poverty.

Since institutional relief could not be provided for all of the needy, begging in the eighteenth century, despite statutory penalties, received tacit public sanction. A fundamental difficulty in both England and Ireland was to prevent the sturdy beggars from usurping the alms that belonged to the deserving poor. Concerning those who "choose to live lazily by a Trade of Begging," a contemporary, expressing the general sentiment, remarked, " 'tis so far from being Charity, or a Duty to relieve them, that, on the contrary, 'tis a Sin . . . A Sin against the truly Poor and Necessitous, who suffer by our misplacing our Charity upon Undeserving Objects."[8] But there was also an economic reason for refusing aid to the sturdy beggars: to force them into labor. In mercantilist theory the labor of each person was a commodity of stated value and constituted part of the national wealth. Thus Arthur Dobbs, Irish economic writer contemporary with Swift, endeavoring to bring home to the Irish public the great loss from unproduc-

---

[7] Apparently Delany was the first to record an account of the old women, *op. cit.*, pp. 131–134; see also *The Correspondence of Jonathan Swift*, ed. F. Elrington Ball (London, 1910–1914), IV, 410, hereafter referred to as *Corres.*

[8] William Talbott, "A Sermon Preach'd in the Parish-Church of St. Sepulchre, June 13, 1717," in *Twenty Five Sermons Preached at the Anniversary Meetings of the Children Educated in the Charity-Schools in and about the Cities of London and Westminster . . . from the Year 1704, to 1728 inclusive* (London, 1729), pp. 306–307. This work is hereafter referred to as *Twenty Five Sermons.*

tive beggars, multiplied the estimated number in the country (30,000 sturdy beggars) by the computed value of the daily labor of each (4d) and arrived at an annual figure of 142,000 pounds, "which is," he wrote, "just so much Money lost to the Kingdom in the way of Trade."[9] With both humanitarian and economic grounds for distinguishing between the deserving and undeserving poor, public-spirited Irishmen sought to control indiscriminate almsgiving. As a palliative measure designed primarily for the aggravated situation in Dublin, though he hoped its salutary effects would spread, Swift urged the adoption of the long established principle of parochial responsibility, under which each parish provided for its own indigent.

Swift obviously had his eyes on England, where parochial relief had been a matter of statutory enactment since the reign of Elizabeth; and it was apparently with the Elizabethan poor law (43 Elizabeth, c. 2) in mind that he wrote, in reference to Ireland, "by the ancient law of this realm, still in force, every parish is obliged to maintain its own poor."[10] Actually there was no such law for Ireland; nor did Swift's plan call for parliamentary action. His was a plea for organizing and controlling charity by voluntarily distributing the burden among the parishes. Unquestionably he felt that his first obligation was to the small tradesmen and weavers who lived in the vicinity of the Cathedral and in the adjacent liberties. These people, who suffered periodically from reduced trade and unemployment, were under his constant observation, and he felt qualified to pass on their deserts. They represented a stable population—the deserving poor—for whom the problems of administering charity were comparatively simple. The difficulties lay in another quarter, from the strolling beggars who came in from other parishes, and in particular from the mendicants and vagrants who gravitated to Dublin from other parts of Ireland, especially in the spring and summer months. Swift had a special animus against these "perpetual swarms of foreign beggars," understandably so in the light of their practice as it was vividly described by Arthur Dobbs:

... it is very well known that great Numbers of the Native *Irish* in the Mountainous parts of the Kingdom, that have Houses and small Farms, by which they might very well Maintain themselves, when they have sown their Corn, planted their Potatoes and cut their Turf for Firing, do either hire out their Cows or send them to the Mountains, then shut up their Doors and go a begging the whole Summer until Harvest, with their Wives and Children, in the most tatter'd and moving Condition they can appear in, and disperse themselves over all the richest parts of the Kingdom. This practice has been so much incourag'd of late by the success these Strolers have met with, that in several places many who pay at least 4 pounds *per annum* Rent, Hire 3 or 4 Servants and give to each of them 3 pounds for their chance of the Summers begging.[11]

To prevent charitably inclined persons from wasting alms on these undeserving vagabonds and sturdy beggars, Swift proposed that the authorities in each parish, who by virtue of their position would best know the deserving poor, provide badges to identify the wearers as valid objects of charity, licensed to beg within the confines of their own parishes. If the giver of alms refused aid to badgeless beggars or to those soliciting outside

---

[9] *An Essay on the Trade of Ireland* (Dublin, 1731), Part II, pp. 46–47.

[10] *The Prose Works of Jonathan Swift, D.D.*, ed. Temple Scott (London, 1897–1908), IV, 219. This edition is hereafter referred to as *Works*. See *Works*, VII, 328, where Swift is less certain that the English poor law applied to Ireland. Sir George Nicholls (*A History of the Irish Poor Law* [London, 1856], p. 31) writes that the principle of parochial responsibility appears to have been operative to a certain extent in Ireland.

[11] *Op. cit.*, p. 47.

their own parishes, strolling beggars would eventually disappear and each parish could provide more adequately and equitably for its own destitute.[12]

This is the proposal which Dr. Delany declared enthusiastically to be "the wisest, the best judged, the most practicable, and the most christian scheme, for relieving all those who were proper objects of charity." It would, he asserted, banish "vagrant beggary from the earth, with all its attendant abominations."[13] The idea was by no means original with Swift, as Delany implies. The practice of badging beggars had existed in Tudor England, and was the subject of discussion and statute (8 & 9 Wm. III, c. 30) in the last part of the seventeenth century.[14] For some time before 1725, the year in which the plan was instituted in Dublin,[15] Swift appears to have urged its adoption on the incumbent Lord Mayors and on William King, Archbishop of Dublin, who finally put it into effect.[16] But Swift's high hopes were not realized, as we learn from his sermon "On the Causes of the Wretched Condition of Ireland," preached in 1725 or thereafter, and from a tract of 1737, *A Proposal for giving Badges to the Beggars in all the Parishes of Dublin*, in which he pleads once again for its strict enforcement. In these works he complains bitterly that the poor are too proud to wear the badges and the officials responsible for enforcing the regulation are either lax or corrupt.[17]

We are not concerned here with Swift's many private benefactions, although they deserve a word in passing. His early account books, in which he meticulously recorded his expenditures, are sprinkled with such entries as "Charity 2s 8d" (Nov. 3, 1702); "poor woman 2s 8d" (May 18, 1703); "G[ave] poor 4d" (April 1, 1709); "G[ave] poor mad girl 3d" (Aug. 16, 1709); "G[ave] D[ean] Stearn for a poor Clergyman 0—5—5" (Jan. 9, 1709/10); "deaf girl 6d" (Oct. 22, 1713).[18] These earlier entries suggest a philanthropy both modest and casual; it is the later account books and other relevant documents not now available, covering the years of increased income, that should show why Swift gained a reputation as a man of charity. That his benefactions grew in proportion to his income is indicated by certain known instances, for example, his subscription in 1732 of thirty-six pounds to Dr. Steevens' Hospital,[19] his gift—recorded in the *Dublin Journal*, Jan. 22, 1739/40—of ten pounds to the poor, and his erecting at his own expense an alms house near the Cathedral for "ancient and orderly wid-

---

[12] *Works*, IV, 219; VII, 326 ff.   [13] *Op. cit.*, pp. 8–9.

[14] Sir George Nicholls, *A History of the English Poor Law* (London, 1854), I, 145, 155; Thomas Firmin, *Some Proposals for the Employment of the Poor*, 1681, reprinted in *A Collection of Pamphlets concerning the Poor*, ed. Thomas Gilbert (London, 1787), pp. 35–36; Danby Pickering, *The Statutes at Large* (Cambridge, 1764), x, 106–107.

[15] See Sir W[illiam] F[ownes], *Methods proposed for Regulating the Poor* (Dublin, 1725), p. [3]. Fownes was an ex-Lord Mayor, friendly with Swift, whose pamphlet gives an elaborate statement of a plan to badge beggars. I suspect that Fownes came under Swift's persuasive influence and wrote this pamphlet at Swift's instigation.

[16] *Works*, VII, 326–327 n.

[17] *Works*, IV, 220; VII, 329, 332. It is possible that under Swift's watchful eye the plan was not wholly ineffective in the precincts of the Cathedral. Delany writes that the poor there were "badged and never begged out of their district" and that "there was no such thing as a vagrant or unbadged beggar seen about [the] cathedral." *Op. cit.*, pp. 8, 9.

[18] The account books are in the Forster Collection, Victoria and Albert Museum, South Kensington, London. I am greatly indebted to Mr. Arthur Case of Northwestern University for permitting me to examine his photostatic copies, which cover seven years of Swift's expenditures.

[19] See Percy C. Kirkpatrick, *The History of Doctor Steevens' Hospital, Dublin, 1720–1920* (Dublin, 1924), p. 56.

ows."[20] These substantial outlays support the remark of Dr. Lyon, who served as his almoner for a time, that "his charities made always a considerable part of his expences."[21]

Swift himself declared on one occasion that a Dean of St. Patrick's is as a matter of course placed on committees and boards;[22] and this fact in itself accounts partly for his activity in organized and institutional charities. He served, for example, as a member of the Board of the Dublin Workhouse and Foundling Hospital, an institution established in 1702.[23] The design of the Workhouse, so Swift informs us, was to maintain "the poor and orphans of the city, where the parishes are not able to do it; and clearing the streets from all strollers, foreigners, and sturdy beggars."[24] Since the fulfilment of this last purpose was so much a part of his own efforts, he was vigorous in his criticism of the Governors of the Workhouse for their failure to achieve it.[25] He also played a prominent part in two medical charities established in Dublin in his day. The first of these was a hospital founded by a bequest in the will of a Dublin physician, Dr. Richard Steevens. In 1721, at the instigation of Dr. Steevens' sister, who held the funds in trust, Swift became a trustee and was immediately placed on a committee to arrange for the erection of the hospital, serving with his friends, Thomas Proby, the Surgeon-General of Ireland, and Richard Helsham, Regius Professor of Physic in the University of Dublin.[26] He also had an active part, perhaps chief responsibility, in obtaining the charter for incorporating the Governors of the hospital as a prelude to its formal opening in 1733[27]—a charter which provided among other things that the Dean of St. Patrick's serve *ex officio* as a Governor. There is no doubt that Swift was kindly disposed toward this particular charity. Not only did he subscribe funds;[28] he seriously considered leaving his fortune at the disposal of the Governors for the erection of the asylum provided for in his will.[29] And it is further evidence of his good will that Stella left a bequest, very likely at his suggestion and certainly with his knowledge and approval,[30] for the maintenance of a chaplain for the Hospital. The other medical charity in which Swift had a part was reported in the *Dublin Journal*, March 11, 1734/35, where it was announced that Mrs. Mary Mercer had bequeathed six thousand pounds to charity, with Swift as chief trustee of her will. Before her death Mrs. Mercer had made plans to provide a hospital "for the reception and accommodation of such poor, sick, and diseased persons, as might happen to labour under diseases of tedious and hazardous cure, such as the

---

[20] Delany, *op. cit.*, p. 8; William Monck Mason, *The History and Antiquities of the Collegiate and Cathedral Church of St. Patrick* (Dublin, 1819), p. 296, note c.

[21] Nichols, *op. cit.*, p. 755.   [22] *Works*, VII, 325.

[23] See William Dudley Wodsworth, *A Brief History of the Ancient Foundling Hospital of Dublin, from the Year 1702* (Dublin, 1876).

[24] *Works*, VII, 326; cf. also Wodsworth, *op. cit.*, p. 3.

[25] *Works*, VII, 326.   [26] See Percy C. Kirkpatrick, *op. cit.*, p. 34.

[27] *Ibid.*, p. 43; *Corres.*, III, 418.   [28] Percy C. Kirkpatrick, *op. cit.*, p. 56.

[29] *Ibid.*, p. 67: "On June 24, 1737, Dr. Helsham informed his fellow-Governors at Steevens' that the Dean intended to vest his fortune in them 'for erecting and supporting a convenient building for the reception of madmen and idiots.' The Governors at once appointed a small committee of their number 'to fix upon the most convenient place for the said building,' and Dr. Helsham was asked 'to acquaint the Dean of St. Patrick's therewith.' There is no further reference in the minutes of the Governors to this proposal, and it is probable that the death of Helsham, which took place in August, 1738, induced the Dean to alter his plans once more."

[30] See *Corres.*, III, 318; W. R. Wilde, *The Closing Years of Dean Swift's Life* (Dublin, 1849), p. 98. Wilde reprints Stella's will.

falling sickness, lunacy, leprosy, and the like." To carry out her intentions she enlisted the aid of Swift, who became a Governor of the Hospital, along with his friend, William Jackson and—an appointment that could not have been pleasant to him—Archbishop Boulter.[31]

Swift's part in the most striking manifestation of institutional and organized charity in the period, the charity-school movement, has been almost wholly ignored. In 1716 he helped to found a charity school in the liberty of St. Patrick's for children of the poor inhabitants, and in that year preached a sermon for their benefit.[32] More notably, he served as a member of the Board of the King's Hospital, also known as the Blue Coat School, established in 1670 for the care and education of the sons of "reduced freemen" or "decayed citizens."[33] This was Dublin's most famous and firmly established charity school. Swift took an active part in its affairs for a period of twelve years, from his appointment—at the instigation of Archbishop King—until 1737, at which time he began withdrawing from such activities because of his health.[34] In addition to exercising his prerogative of nominating boys to the Blue Coat School—two letters are extant in which he makes recommendations[35]—he served on several committees, one of which is of special interest in revealing the cooperation, heartily approved by Swift, between Irish manufacturers and the charity school authorities to make the well endowed schools a source of apprentices for the various branches of trade.[36]

The full extent of Swift's participation in the charity school movement is a matter for further inquiry; but we have evidence that he did not stand aside when this vigorous humanitarian spirit was manifesting itself in Ireland. A contemporary account indicates that the schools multiplied rapidly between 1710 and 1720:

From that time [1710] *Charity-Schools* began to spread both in *Dublin* and the *Country;* so that in 1716, their Number spread to about Thirty wherein were upwards of Seven Hundred *Children:* The Year following the *Schools* rose to One Hundred and the Children to Two Thou-

---

[31] I have relied on the brief account of Mercer's Hospital in the *Irish Builder*, Jan. 15, 1897, pp. 15–18.

[32] In a report of charity schools in Ireland in 1719 is the following statement concerning the liberty of St. Patrick's: "A Charity-School of *Boys*, belonging to the Cathedral, hitherto clothed out of a *Collection* at a Charity-Sermon, preached in 1716, by the *Dean of St. Patrick's*." See *Methods of Erecting, Supporting & Governing Charity-Schools: with an Account of the Charity-Schools in Ireland* (3rd ed.; Dublin, 1721), p. 24. In this report are also listed two other charity schools in the liberty, the children of which attended daily services in the Cathedral. It is a reasonable surmise that Swift interested himself in these schools.

[33] For a history of this school see Sir Frederick R. Falkiner, *The Foundation of the Hospital and Free School of King Charles II* (Dublin, 1906).

[34] *Ibid.*, pp. 159, 162, 185.

[35] *Corres.*, v, 131; vi, 36–37; see also vi, 46. One of these letters throws more light on Swift's failing memory. In July, 1737, he wrote to Sir James Somerville, then Lord Mayor of Dublin and chairman of the Board of the Hospital, recommending a pupil (*Corres.*, vi, 36). In his letter he writes: "I have not for several years recommended one boy to this Hospital . . . ." Actually he had made such a recommendation, which had been accepted, in December of 1736. See Falkiner, *op. cit.*, p. 185.

[36] In 1734, George Vaughan of the linen trade proposed to the Governors of the Blue Coat School that he be allotted twenty-four apprentices from among the pupils. Swift and Archbishop Boulter served on the committee to consider the proposal, which was accepted. Unfortunately, Vaughan's experience with the Blue Coat apprentices was not a happy one. See Falkiner, *op. cit.*, pp. 185–187. Swift also served on committees for the infirmary, for the reform of the house and government, for the restoration of the chapel, for the inspection and direction of the diet of the pupils, and for preparing a petition to Parliament for rebuilding the Hospital. *Ibid.*, pp. 162, 186.

sand; In 1719, the *former* was computed at One Hundred and thirty, and the *latter* reckoned to be near Three Thousand; and by the Information *since* received, there is an Addition of about Thirty new *Schools* actually opened, (besides several that are erecting) with a proportionable encrease of the *Children*.[37]

Some of these schools, as Swift points out, had "good foundations and rents to support them," that is, they were endowed and could be expected to survive indefinitely, whereas many of them had only "the casual goodwill of charitable persons,"[38] that is, they were supported by subscriptions solicited from individuals, by church-door collections, and by donations from cathedral chapters or city corporations. By 1725 the movement had lost its momentum and criticism of the schools was rife, until new enthusiasm was generated in 1733 with the formation of the Incorporated Society in Dublin for Promoting English Protestant Schools in Ireland. Of this organization, whose announced purpose was to advance the "true religion" and increase the Protestant interest in Ireland, Swift was a charter member.[39]

Swift's general attitude toward the charity school movement is evident from his sermon, "Causes of the Wretched Condition of Ireland," preached when the movement was waning and critics, friendly and otherwise, were assessing the achievements. Here he set forth his conception of the purposes of the schools in Ireland and suggested needed reforms. These purposes, as they were conceived by his contemporaries, were both economic and religious. The combination of the two was aptly stated by Peter Brown, Bishop of Cork and Rosse, in an appeal for funds in 1716 to support a charity school in St. Andrews parish, Dublin. The money, Bishop Brown told his auditors, would be laid out in providing the pupils with

Cloaths, and *Books*, and *Schooling;* in giving them Instruction in the first Rudiments of the Christian Religion, and acquainting them with the Doctrines and Principles of our holy Church; in teaching them such Things as may qualify them for Trades and Callings; in binding them out Apprentices, and so putting them into a Condition of earning Bread for themselves, and being some way useful to the Publick.[40]

Similarly, the Incorporated Society in an official statement appealed to the landed gentry of Ireland for support because it converted Popish children into Protestants and added wealth to the nation by increasing the number of laborers. "So that," the document added, "if the Charter-Schools could be sufficiently extended and diffused, they would be the Means of increasing Industry and Trades, and Useful Manufactures, which must of course improve every Gentleman's Estate."[41]

[37] *Methods of Erecting, Supporting, & Governing Charity Schools: with an Account of Charity Schools in Ireland* (3rd ed.; Dublin, 1721), p. 4. See also M. G. Jones, *The Charity School Movement: a Study of Eighteenth Century Puritanism in Action* (Cambridge, 1938), pp. 222 ff. and Appendix III.

[38] *Works*, IV, p. 214.

[39] See *An Abstract of the Proceedings of the Incorporated Society in Dublin, for Promoting English Protestant Schools in Ireland from . . . 1733 to . . . 1737* (Dublin, 1737), p. 36. In the "Alphabetical Table of Members" Swift is listed as a charter member.

[40] *A Sermon, Preach'd at the Parish Church of St. Andrew's Dublin, on Sunday the 15th of April, 1716. For the Benefit of the Charity-School for Boys in that Parish* (Dublin, 1716), p. 36.

[41] *A Brief Review of the Rise and Progress of the Incorporated Society in Dublin, for Promoting English Protestant Schools in Ireland. From the Opening of His Majesty's Royal Charter, February 6th, 1733, to November 6th, 1743* (Dublin, 1744), p. 11. See also Henry Downs, *A Sermon Preach'd in the Parish Church of St. Warbrough, Dublin, May the 7th, 1721, at the Annual Meeting of the Children Educated in the Charity-Schools in Dublin* (Dublin, 1721), pp. 17–18.

With the religious and economic purposes of the schools as stated Swift had no quarrel; but he realized that the economic intention was not being fulfilled in a manner consistent with the best interest of the country. He therefore recommended in his sermon that the few schools in Ireland possessed of permanent endowments limit themselves to the children of "decayed citizens and freemen" who are to "be bred up to good trades," and that the small parish charity schools, concerned with larger numbers of the Popish natives, train their pupils only for "the very meanest trades."[42] By this last phrase Swift meant the menial services to be performed in homes, agriculture, and commerce. He made the distinction between the two types of training because he agreed with the current criticism—that the schools were flooding the labor market in the better trades with charity-trained apprentices who competed with the sons of respectable and self-supporting citizens.[43] There was no little fear that the charity schools were creating an educated class out of the ignorant poor, who were useful to society as long as they remained ignorant and poor but who could not be effectively absorbed in their improved status into the economic life of the nation. The enemies of the movement seized upon this point and violently denounced the charity schools as inimical to the welfare of the nation because they withdrew the poor from the menial occupations to which they would otherwise naturally gravitate. In England this indictment was effectively voiced by Bernard Mandeville, recognized as a leading opponent of the charity school movement, who based his attack upon an assumption that his mercantilist contemporaries could appreciate—"in a free Nation where Slaves are not allow'd of, the surest Wealth consists in a Multitude of laborious Poor."[44]

The friends of the charity schools moved warily in the face of this criticism. They were not disposed to interfere with the natural functioning of the labor supply—or elevate the poor unduly. Swift's good friend, Sir William Fownes, pointed out that there is a "want of Trade sufficient" for the many apprentices.[45] Swift, too, recognized the danger. He complains that Ireland is "overstocked with 'prentices and journeymen" from the charity schools, more than can possibly find employment; and he maintains that the small parish charity schools must revise their educational aims downward.[46] If these schools are to serve the economic welfare of the nation, they ought not to have an exalted idea of the training to be given: the pupils should "be taught to read and write, to know somewhat in casting accounts, to understand the principles of religion, to practise cleanliness, to get a spirit of honesty, industry, and thrift."[47] Swift's program is the same modest program of education that James Talbott had set forth in *The Christian School-master* (1707), a work dedicated to the Society for Promoting Christian Knowledge and widely accepted as a statement of the educational aims of the charity schools.[48] The danger of over-educating the poor

[42] *Works*, IV, 214–215.   [43] *Works*, IV, 215
[44] *Essay on Charity, and Charity Schools* (1723), in *Fable of the Bees*, ed. F. B. Kaye (Oxford, 1924), I, 287–288; cf. also pp. 316–317. See also John Trenchard's criticism in the *British Journal*, June 15, 1723, printed as *Cato's Letter*, No. 133.
[45] *Op. cit.*, p. 10.   [46] *Works*, IV, 215.   [47] *Works*, IV, 216.
[48] See *The Christian School-master*, pp. 79, 83, and *passim*. Each of the items named by Swift receives separate discussion in Talbott's work. For an Irish document stating the simple educational aims of the schools see *Methods of Erecting, Supporting & Governing Charity-Schools* .... (3rd ed.; Dublin, 1721), p. 10.

was apparent even to the most enthusiastic supporters of the schools, who themselves issued warnings that the pupils should not be taught anything which would make them "less fit for that low and laborious Station of Life, in which Divine Providence hath plac'd them."[49] When Edmund Gibson, Bishop of London, addressed the masters and mistresses of the charity schools in 1724, he made some pointed remarks on this subject:

... if Charity-Schools should grow by degrees into a more polite sort of Education; if the Boys should be taught fine Writing, and the Girls fine Working, and both of them fine Singing; in which Cases also the Masters and Mistresses would hardly refrain from teaching the Children to *value* themselves upon these Attainments; all this, I own, would have a natural Tendency to set them above the meaner and more laborious Stations and Offices of Life. And therefore all these Things should be carefully kept out of our Charity-Schools ....[50]

It is quite clear from Swift's discussion that he had no desire to educate the poor children above their station. He thought the small parish charity schools could be most effective if they confined their efforts to training a large body of well-behaved servants—an understandable view in the light of his personal difficulties with servants.[51] But this was no mere personal matter; his fulminations against servants were loudly echoed by other Irishmen, who agreed that servants had "become one of the many public grievances of the Kingdom."[52] Indeed, in Ireland the proponents of the charity schools had officially recognized the grievance and affirmed that they would solve the problem:

The Practice of some *Charity-Schools* in putting out several of the Children to good *Services*, stands in need of no recommendation, but will be universally approved and followed. Nothing has been more generally, and indeed justly complained of, than the Ignorance, Negligence and Dishonesty of Servants; but that Misfortune, 'tis hoped, may now in a great Measure cease in Families. For by Means of these Schools, Gentlemen and Others will have it in their Power to furnish themselves with such Persons for their Services, who having *born the Yoke in their Youth*, been held to Discipline and Order, practiced Humility and Obedience, used bodily Labour, and acquired all necessary Learning; will be equally *capable* and *willing*, to *serve them well in all Things.*[53]

Both in England and Ireland supporters of the movement asked for contributions on the ground that the schools constitute a "Means to furnish your Country with a Set of People of both Sexes, better qualified to make good Servants, than could otherwise be expected."[54] Nevertheless, continued complaints indicate that the schools, despite their intentions, had not been able to supply the demand for good servants.[55] Thus in his suggestions for

[49] Thomas Mangey, "The Gospel Preach'd to the Poor. A Sermon Preached in the Parish-Church of St. Sepulchre, June, 2, 1726," in *Twenty Five Sermons* (London, 1729), p. 512.

[50] Abel Boyer, *The Political State of Great Britain*, Nov., 1724, Vol. XXVIII, 485–486.

[51] Swift was highly vocal on the subject of his servant troubles. Readers of the *Journal to Stella* will not need to be reminded that his man-servant, Patrick, was a constant source of vexation. See also *Works*, VII, 76, 133; XI, 307–364.

[52] See, for example, Samuel Madden, *Reflections and Resolutions proper for the Gentlemen of Ireland* (Dublin, 1738), 1816 ed., pp. 61–63.

[53] *Methods of Erecting, Supporting & Governing Charity-Schools* .... (Dublin, 1721), p. 39. See the section headed "Some Observations and Proposals grounded on the Foregoing Account."

[54] John Watson, "Preventive Charity the best Method of Doing Good. A Sermon preached in the Parish-Church of St. Sepulchre, May 25, 1727," in *Twenty Five Sermons* (London, 1729), p. 538. See also Hugh Boulter, soon to become the Lord Primate of Ireland, in his *Sermon preach'd ... May the 17th, 1722, at the Anniversary Meeting of the Children Educated in the Charity-Schools in and about the Cities of London and Westminster* (London, 1722), pp. 21–22.

[55] In England the schools were severely criticized for their failure to produce good servants. As a matter of fact they were accused of inculcating bad qualities in those who otherwise might

reforming the small parish schools, we find Swift emphasizing the means by which the children of the Irish natives can be turned into acceptable domestics.[56]

Although Swift recorded comparatively little concerning the charity school movement, his brief discussion reveals his interest and his decisive reactions to what was being accomplished. He probably did not share the highly enthusiastic expectations of the more sanguine proponents of the movement in Ireland, that the schools could be the means by which "the whole nation might become Protestant and English."[57] Unquestionably the purposes of the movement strongly appealed to him. The attempt to teach English to the children of the poor natives was consistent with his desire, expressed on several occasions, "to abolish the Irish language in this kingdom." This, he declared, "would, in a great measure, civilize the most barbarous among them, reconcile them to our customs and manner of living, and reduce great numbers to the national religion. . . ."[58] So far he could agree with his enemy, Archbishop Boulter, who pleaded for more charity schools to teach the children of the papists the English tongue.[59] Nor is it to be doubted that he had anything but the highest approval of the Incorporated Society in Dublin for Promoting English Protestant Schools in Ireland—he was a charter member—whose purpose was to strengthen the Protestant interest: "Every *Popish* Child turned out a *Protestant* from these Schools, will bring an Accession of Strength to the *Protestant* Interest."[60] But the evidence suggests that he had more faith in the economic functions of the schools. Whatever his enthusiasm for converting the Popish natives, he tended, I believe, to view the charity school movement primarily as a means for achieving economic ends and secondarily for achieving religious ends.

Swift was, first of all, a practical humanitarian interested in the economic betterment of Ireland and in preparing the poor for agriculture, trade, and domestic service. Thus he views their problems chiefly from the realistic vantage of economic cause and effect. But he was also a Christian divine in an age which had inherited an elaborate body of traditional theory concerning charity and the poor in the Christian scheme of things. It is not surprising therefore to find that aspects of this theory, mainly some of the

---

make good servants. See Mandeville, *Fable of the Bees*, ed. F. B. Kaye, I, 306–307; John Trenchard, *Cato's Letters*, No. 133.

[56] *Works*, IV, 215–217.

[57] See *Methods of Erecting, Supporting & Governing Charity-Schools* . . . . (3rd ed.; Dublin, 1721), p. [3].

[58] *Works*, VII, 133; see also *Works*, IV, 214; VI, 199; VII, 345–346.

[59] *Letters written by His Excellency, Hugh Boulter, D.D.* (Dublin, 1770), II, 9. Feeling as he did, Swift would not take part in the movement in Ireland, of which Archbishop King was a proponent, to utilize the Irish tongue to convert the natives. He had some contact, as early as 1710, in London with the most indefatigable person in this cause, the Reverend John Richardson, Rector of Armagh and later Dean of Kilmacduagh, whose *Proposal for the Conversion of the Popish Natives of Ireland to the Established Religion* appeared in 1711. Shortly before its appearance Swift attempted to gain access for Richardson to certain people of influence, as is indicated by entries in the *Journal to Stella* for March 6, 23, 1710/11, and March 14, 1711/12.

[60] *A Brief Review of the Rise and Progress of the Incorporated Society of Dublin* (Dublin, 1744), p. 11. See also *An Abstract of the Proceedings of the Incorporated Society in Dublin, for Promoting English Protestant Schools in Ireland from . . . 1733 to . . . 1737* (Dublin, 1737), pp. 4–5: "The Society proposes to strengthen His Majesty's Government, and the Protestant Interest of *Ireland*, by encreasing the Numbers of *Protestants* in the only Christian and Reasonable Way . . . by providing fresh Recruits of *Protestants* out of their Schools."

more obvious and conventional aspects, are reflected in his utterances. As a Christian divine who preached that all men are equal in the sight of God,[61] Swift was ready enough to give some explanation of the social and material inequalities that seemed to work to the advantage of the rich and powerful —and that made charity necessary. He warned the poor against the great sin of "murmuring and repining, that God hath dealt his blessings unequally to the sons of men."[62] They must not impugn the justice of God. The problem of satisfying the poor, of showing them that their lot was not the effect of wanton or blind providence, was of course a persistent one in theology; and eighteenth-century clergymen had nothing to add to the traditional explanations. It is not surprising that the charity sermons of the period were frequently used to rationalize the existing order in society. They were a natural medium for the purpose. If Swift preached any charity sermons in the usual sense, they have not survived;[63] but two of his extant sermons, being concerned with a frequent theme of such sermons, the division of the world into rich and poor, offer excellent substitutes.

For these two sermons, "On Mutual Subjection" and "On the Poor Man's Contentment," no date can be assigned; but I think they may be said to represent an abiding rather than a transient element in Swift's social and religious views. The first of the two to be published, "On Mutual Subjection" (1744), is concerned with showing that a Christian commonwealth, despite its diversity—its hierarchal and stratified structure—can be brought to Christian unity and brotherhood if the duty of mutual subjection recommended by the Apostles Peter and Paul is practiced. Swift argues that no member of a Christian society, regardless of what the inequalities in station and wealth seem to imply, is more important than another member. Particularly no member is self-sufficient: the relation between king and subject, master and servant, merchant and laborer, rich and poor, is reciprocal. To enforce the point he expounds the Pauline conception of society as a living organism in which all the parts are vitally interrelated. Those in inferior stations are warned to accept their subjection; but Swift is less concerned with these than with the powerful and wealthy, who are exhorted to recognize that they are in certain respects subject to those below them. Theirs is the Christian duty—and this is the most significant point for our purposes—of using their talents and fortunes unselfishly for the less fortunate and for the good of the whole community because, so far as their possessions are concerned, they are merely stewards or trustees of God and not outright owners.

The theory of the stewardship of the wealthy which Swift sets forth was an essential aspect of the Christian theory of charity as it had developed from the Middle Ages. By the eighteenth century it was indeed a hoary conventionality. Throughout the ages homiletic literature had abounded in demonstrations that a Christian may with good conscience possess riches only on the assumption that he is a steward of God ready to dispense alms for the relief of the needy.[64] In Swift's day this sentiment was an ever recurring theme in the charity sermons. In 1708, for example, Robert Moss,

---

[61] *Works*, IV, 112, 202.   [62] *Works*, IV, 207; cf. also IV, 217–218.
[63] See above, footnote no. 32.
[64] See R. H. Tawney, *Religion and the Rise of Capitalism* (London, 1929), pp. 261–262; Helen G. White, *Social Criticism in Popular Religious Literature of the Sixteenth Century* (New York, 1944), pp. 263 ff.; Richard B. Schlatter, *The Social Ideas of the Religious Leaders, 1660–1688* (Oxford, 1940), pp. 125 ff.

Preacher at Gray's Inn, selected to deliver the annual sermon before the children of the London and Westminster charity schools, told his auditors that

the Man, that in the Vogue of the World passes for the Master of many Thousands, is not the proper Owner of what he hath; He is only God's Steward, and the larger Estate he hath to manage, so much the greater is his Trust and Care in the Family; and he ought accordingly to give to every one their *Portion* in due Season, and in full Measure: Which if he neglects to do, he is guilty of foul Ingratitude as well as Disobedience to his Lord, and manifest Wrong to his Fellow-Creatures, over whom he is made a kind of *Ruler*. In Discharge of which honourable Trust, he ought to be both faithful and wise . . . .[65]

In the following year under the same circumstances Samuel Bradford, later Bishop of Rochester, declared that "Those who abound in the Good Things of this Life are always to consider themselves as the Stewards of Almighty God, to dispense his Gifts to the indigent, and to remember that they must give an Account of the Management of this their Stewardship."[66] And in 1725 before the same group—to quote one more typical utterance, William Berriman, Rector of Undershaft, elaborated the theory carefully to show that it is a compound of justice and mercy.

The Duty now of Almsgiving . . . is founded in the Rules of Justice, and the express Command of the Supream Lord and Proprietor of all Things, who has not made over his Right to us, but only entrusted us with our respective Stewardships, which we are bound to discharge conformably to his Directions. From hence it is easie to perceive, that they who give not in some just Proportion to that Ability which God has given them, detain what really is not their own, and in this Respect stand on the same Foot with them who spoil their Neighbour by Treachery or Violence. . . . The Portion of the Poor, which lies mix'd and undistinguish'd from their own, will be likely to draw down such a Curse upon their Wealth, that it shall moulder and consume away. . . . The Extravagance of some, or the Negligence of others . . . shall frequently spoil them of those Riches, which heap'd up without Regard to that Mercy, which is indeed a necessary Part of Justice, and without which we can never be reckon'd faithful in our Stewardship.[67]

This then is the attitude toward wealth expounded by Swift in "On Mutual Subjection" to enforce the duty of charity, a theory which he expresses briefly but in the precise terminology of his predecessors and contemporaries: ". . . no man ought to look upon the advantages of life, such as riches, honour, power, and the like, as his property, but merely as a trust, which God hath deposited with him, to be employed for the use of his brethren."[68] Under such a theory charity is obviously not a mere voluntary act of the rich man—a mere gesture of kindliness or mercy. It becomes an act of justice, an obligation not to be scanted. As Swift says, if the rich man does not employ his wealth for the benefit of others, he is committing a breach of the trust conferred by God and will certainly be punished for his

[65] "The Providential Division of Men into Rich and Poor. A Sermon preached in the Parish-Church of St. Sepulchre, May 27, 1708," in *Twenty Five Sermons* (London, 1729), p. 113.

[66] "Unanimity and Charity, the Characters of Christians. A Sermon preach'd in the Parish-Church of St. Sepulchre, June 16, 1709," in *Twenty Five Sermons* (London, 1729), pp. 129–130.

[67] "The Excellency and Reward of Charity. A Sermon preached in the Parish-Church of St. Sepulchre, May 20, 1725," in *Twenty Five Sermons* (London, 1729), pp. 488–489. See also p. 481 where Berriman says that to give charity is an act of justice, yet since God has left the amount to the giver's discretion he who gives cheerfully and liberally is also doing an act of mercy: " . . . as the Practice of our Duty in this Instance, cannot but argue an inward Affection and Sympathy with our Brethren, from hence it comes to pass that this, which is really an Act of *Justice*, has yet the Credit to be deemed an Act of *Mercy* and *Compassion*." For additional statements of the theory of stewardship see *Twenty Five Sermons* (London, 1729), pp. 31, 199, 249.

[68] *Works*, IV, 116.

violation.[69] Undoubtedly Swift agreed with his contemporary who maintained that "though the *Poor* have no Legal Demand upon the *Rich* . . . yet they have a Right that is Superiour and Antecedent to all Human Constitutions: For they claim under God. . . ."[70]

The theory of the stewardship of wealth was in certain respects a comforting one by virtue of acting as a solvent for the severe strictures on the rich that were commonplaces in Christian thought. It permitted wealth to be viewed as in itself morally neutral—Swift wrote that "wealth and power are in their own nature, at best, but things indifferent"[71]—but gave to it a social purpose which justified its existence. For a person of Swift's conservative habit of mind the theory was an acceptable rationalization. It was congenial to his thinking in that it made room for the amelioration he ardently desired without in any respect suggesting that fundamental social changes were necessary in the rigid structure of society.

If Swift's view of the rich man is in accord with long established Christian tradition, his view of the poor man is not less so. His sermon "On the Poor Man's Contentment"—a tissue of commonplaces—is not distinguishable from innumerable sermons devoted to the camel and needle's eye text or to the beatitude which promised the poor the kingdom of God. He recognizes the difficulty of making the poor understand that theirs is a satisfactory state. "It is certain," he declares, "that no rich man ever desired to be poor, and that most, if not all, poor men, desire to be rich."[72] Nevertheless, he asserts, the rich do not have an advantage. It need hardly be said that Swift had no intention of glorifying the monastic ideal of poverty—an ideal that could find little response in the wqrldly-minded Anglican clergymen of the eighteenth century. The problem as he conceived it was to convince the deserving and industrious poor—it was generally agreed that the undeserving poor, by their idleness and debauchery, suffered a just fate[73]—that the unequal distribution of worldly goods was not a bar to their happiness. We need not follow Swift's logic in detail. His point of departure is "a certain truth, that God Almighty hath placed all men upon an equal foot, with respect to their happiness in this world, and the capacity of attaining their salvation in the next. . . ."[74] Then, as if to deny this assertion, he contrasts in detail the worldly condition and immortal expectations of rich and poor to show that in actuality the poor have a definite advantage—that the presumed temporal advantages of the rich are illusory and that the poor have both more temporal blessings and a better prospect of entering the kingdom of heaven. The sermon as a whole rests on an asumption that, once again, brings Swift close to the spirit of contemporary charity sermons, in which divines felt a certain compulsion to explain, in the words of one of them, that "it is agreeable to the Will of God, that there should be a great Variety and Disparity in Men's Conditions; that some should be high and others low; that some should be richer, and others poorer."[75] It would be an easy matter to multiply instances in which the poor were told that they must be content with a lot which was theirs by the ordinance of God. A typical one must suffice, from a sermon whose revealing title is "The Providential Division of Men into Rich and Poor."

---

[69] *Ibid.*   [70] Robert Moss, *op. cit.*, p. 113.
[71] *Works*, IV, 207.   [72] *Works*, IV, 202.
[73] For Swift's views on this point see *Works*, IV, 203, 217–218; VII, 330.
[74] *Works*, IV, 202.
[75] Ofspring Blackall, *The Rules and Measures of Alms-giving* (London, 1709), p. 7.

For since it is God's own Appointment, that some should be Rich and some Poor, some High and some Low, that so, by a due Subordination, Government might be better maintain'd, and the Ends of Society answer'd, no doubt This infers an Obligation upon those of inferior Degree, to keep their Rank, and observe *Decorum* in it; and not look up with an evil and envious Eye upon those who are plac'd above them; much less to behave themselves Rudely and Disrespectfully towards them, or to turn Refractory and Contumacious, because such disorderly Behaviour would be an Act of Disobedience against God, and a Resistance of his Ordinance.[76]

The frequency and vigor with which the clergy of Swift's day felt the need of defending the thesis—again I quote from a charity sermon—that "the different Orders and Degrees of Men are from the Hand of God"[77] suggests an uneasy conviction on their part. Nevertheless, they never faltered; and we have in Swift's two sermons, "On Mutual Subjection" and "On the Poor Man's Contentment," evidence that he accepted the justice of a society so constructed. In the first of these he observes and condones the hierarchal nature of society, delaring that "our particular stations are appointed to each of us by God Almighty."[78] "On the Poor Man's Contentment" supports the sentiment. Like his contemporaries—and his predecessors—Swift thought it incumbent on his order to explain to those in lower stations the purposes of the deity in creating what seemed, viewed superficially, to be injustices from the hand of God. ". . . let me," he wrote, "humbly presume to vindicate the justice and mercy of God and His dealings with mankind."[79] The sin of those who do not have wealth is "murmuring and repining, that God hath dealt his blessings unequally to the sons of men."[80] This "false and wicked" opinion he endeavors to expose by revealing to the poor wherein their contentment lies. Thus it is that Swift justifies the ways of God to the poor.

[76] Robert Moss, *op. cit.*, p. 110.
[77] Thomas Sherlock, "A Sermon preached in the Parish-Church of St. Sepulchre, May 21, 1719," in *Twenty-five Sermons* (London, 1729), p. 360 [misnumbered 260].
[78] *Works*, IV, 112.   [79] *Works*, IV, 217.   [80] *Works*, IV, 207.

JONATHAN SWIFT:
"NOT THE GRAVEST OF DIVINES"

On this occasion it is fitting to make at least a modest inquiry into a major aspect of Swift's life which, curiously, has received less attention then it merits. Swift as a writer, Swift engaged in political activity, Swift in love, even Swift not in love — these have been the constant subjects of scrutiny. The drama inherent in these phases of his career has understandably attracted attention not to be expected of that aspect of his life preoccupied with the presumably sober duties of a clergyman. But Swift as a churchman is a more interesting and dramatic figure than is customarily realized; and something of the desperation, the conflicts, irritations, and ironies which constituted the ambience of his life generally were present in its clerical phase. The most obvious preliminary point is a quantitative one: more of his time and energy were devoted to the Church than to any other preoccupation. Ordained in 1694, he rose from an obscure cleric in a remote corner of Northern Ireland to a dignitary of renown by 1713, and continued an active churchman until the last few years of his life, when illness and the decay of his mind left him helpless. Thus he was an active churchman for over forty years, though we must allow for an intermission of a few years when he engaged in political journalism for the Harley ministry in the last four years of Queen Anne's reign.

But even in those years of intense involvement in the political scene, the Anglican Establishment being what it was in the eighteenth century, a clergyman in the good graces of powerful statesmen, as Swift was, could perform certain services for the Church more valuable than remaining in his diocese. At the risk of seeming facetious, I submit that Swift did indeed do the Irish Establishment a considerable service by virtue of his political alignment with the Harley ministry, not the least being that he obtained for himself the deanery of St. Patrick's — and became one of the most effective and brilliant deans in its history. In that capacity he has a secure place as a defender of the Irish Establishment, surpassed by few or none. Observe that I say 'defender of the Establishment'—not defender of the faith. That is another matter, in which he qualifies less well.

It is ironic that he did not wish to be a dean of St. Patrick's —nor, apparently, did anyone else wish him to be. He himself aspired to be a canon of Canterbury or Westminster, to occupy one of the royal prebends much sought after because emoluments were high and duties light.[1] Even in 1713, when he was an eligible (if not a wholly logical) candidate for a bishopric, his own expectations were somewhat restrained, and he would have acquiesced in a lesser preferment to remain in England. He had little faith in the rumours which elevated him to the episcopal bench; and in those days of intense manoeuvring in April, 1713, when the Queen was being pressed by the Harley ministry to give him preferment, Swift looked on with weariness and irritation, insisting merely that something honourable be done for him immediately. At that juncture he might well have been given one of the vacancies at Ely, Windsor, Lichfield, or Wells, and thus might have passed his life in England. But the Queen, it appears, did not relish the prospect of having him that near, despite pleas from her favourite and confidante, Lady Masham, who shed tears at the very thought of Swift's being sent, to use his words of a later date, to 'miserable Dublin in wretched Ireland.'[2] When the decision was finally made, he was both relieved and resigned, and puzzled that his powerful friends in the government would let him go. To Stella he wrote: '... perhaps they can't help it'.[3] In the light of history it is not easy to feel sorry for Swift. If he was leaving an exciting existence in a brilliant circle, he was going to one of the best deaneries in the Establishment, to a position of power and influence, and in material terms more rewarding than a number of bishoprics in England and Ireland.

At the time of his installation as dean, June 13, 1713, he was 45 years of age and had been in orders 18 years. It would be gratifying to be able to say that he had some special distinction as a divine which impelled his appointment.

Like innumerable deans and bishops of the English and Irish Establishments of the eighteenth century, he gained his eminence by talents of another kind. Nevertheless, the criticisms of him, both contemporary and later, as excessively ambitious, scheming, and undeserving are more severe than the facts warrant, and they ignore the basic historical reality: that the Anglican Establishment was a political institution as well as a religious one and that deaneries were political plums to be disposed of. Swift was a man of his times, one who accepted the inevitability of patronage in a state church even as he observed the inevitability of abuses in the system. We must remember too that he was a political animal, as much so as his friends the Earl of Oxford, the Lord Treasurer, and Viscount Bolingbroke, the Secretary of State. In 1719, after six years as dean, Swift wrote to his friend Charles Ford, 'No Cloyster is retired enough to keep Politicks out, and I will own they raise my Passions whenever they come in my way'.[4] It could be argued that Swift was in the wrong profession, that by talent and temperament his forte was politics; and it is true that he wavered in his decision to take Orders, that he was amenable to a different career had the opportunity offered. Yet once he had taken Orders he accepted the responsibilities as these responsibilities were conceived (all too flexibly) in his day: 'I look upon myself,' he remarked, 'in the capacity of a clergyman, to be one appointed by providence for defending a post assigned me, and for gaining over as many enemies as I can.'[5]

I would hesitate to interpret this remark as reflecting an unusual sense of mission. It does reflect convictions and a sense of purpose. However disillusioned he may have become as the years passed, he never lost his respect for the clerical function. He had indeed a great contempt for many individual clergymen, but not for the clerical order. He was frequently distressed that so few who wore the cloth wore it becomingly. He had a sense of the dignity of the priesthood, coupled with a commitment to work for its improvement, both well exemplified in his actions, his letters, and his writings. Two

of his pieces, little known but characteristic, reveal his painful reflections on the nature and status of the clerical
profession; one written in 1728, entitled *Essay on the Fates
of Clergymen*, the other, *Concerning that Universal Hatred
which prevails against the Clergy*. Both are laments over the
state of the clergy; but the second is the more interesting,
showing Swift taking the long view and relating the contempt
of the clergy to historical causes, economic in nature. In a
sense this brief fragment is Swift's most pessimistic utterance
about the Church. When we view it in conjunction with
similar remarks he made over the years, we can understand
why he has been given the appelation which has clung to
him, *the* gloomy dean. But the implications of this descriptive
phrase and of the dark misanthropic strains in *Gulliver's
Travels* have often led to a misreading of his character and
have even obscured the very facts of his life. In 1853 a
great Victorian novelist remarked on 'the caverns of his
gloomy heart' and pictured him as 'always alone — alone and
gnashing in the darkness, except when Stella's sweet smile
came and shone upon him.'[6] Recently an echo of this view
appeared in a magazine read by millions on several continents:
'Night after night the old churl sat by a snug fire in his
splendid mansions and wrote hate letters to a world he
chose to think had cheated him.'[7] This is the gloomy dean
with a vengeance; and sensational as it is, a scholar who
wishes to portray Swift in a clerical or in any capacity must
take note of it in passing.

If we are to explain and understand the not inconsiderable
pessimism which characterized him as a churchman and to
arrive at a more accurate and balanced conception, we must
reject these imaginary, melodramatic flights and rely austerely
on certain known facts, some trivial and some important,
some peculiarly personal and some significant only in the
context of the historical conditions Swift faced in common
with scores of other clergymen — and to which he reacted
very much as they did. The essential questions are: what
were the causes and the nature of his clerical jeremiads?

Do his occasional gloomy pronouncements deserve the emphasis they have received? Is he in fact *the* gloomy dean?

I wish to put forward as a reasonable hypothesis the view that there is nothing about Swift's pessimism as a churchman that is strange or pathological or wilful or self indulgent or even uniquely personal and temperamental — or even anything that one of his contemporaries aware of conditions in the Church of Ireland would have found surprising. But let me emphasize that I wish to explain his pessimism, not explain it away.

At the very outset of his career one can see an emerging pattern of disappointment, frustration, and disillusionment. He faced disconcerting delays in being ordained, and these were followed by defeated expectations. Neither his patron, Sir William Temple, nor family friends secured for him what he had hoped. Instead he was assigned a prebendal stall in the Cathedral of Down and Connor, in County Antrim; and here began his disenchantment. What did he find? He entered into a diocese which even for the Church of Ireland in the period was in a dire state — churches in ruins, non-residence of the clergy widely prevalent, incumbents, where there were incumbents, illegally abused by patrons and parishioners, church lands alienated, in short, desolation everywhere apparent at a glance; and the dry rot in the temporalities matched by spiritual dry rot.[8] Shortly before Swift began residence in the northern parish of Kilroot, in the spring of 1695, the diocese had been wracked by scandals which involved the Bishop of Down and Connor, the Dean of the Cathedral, the Treasurer, the Precentor of Connor, as well as others. An ecclesiastical commission, appointed in response to rumours and complaints which had been reaching authorities in both England and Ireland over a period of years, discovered conditions so sordid and corrupt that the bishop and other dignitaries, and some of the inferior clergy, were deprived, suspended, or excommunicated for such varied offences as adultery, fornication, drunkenness, neglect of cures, diversion of funds, illegal use of the bishop's seal, and simony. The very prebend to which Swift was assigned was involved: his predecessor was deprived for non-residence, intemperance, and incontinence, thus paving the way for Swift to become Prebendary of Kilroot. When Swift arrived to take over his duties, the noise and the scandal had not subsided. It takes very little imagination to gauge the disillusioning impact on this proud and spirited young man, already conscious of his gifts and used to the cultivated and genteel atmosphere of Moor Park.

To these sordid conditions must be added another aspect of the desolate circumstances into which he was plunged. Although he had, as the core of his prebend, three parishes to serve, he had no parish church in two of the three. The third parish did have a church, without a roof. Furthermore, in his three parishes he had almost no parishioners. Nevertheless he preached some sermons which he later described as 'the idlest trifling stuff that ever was writ, calculated for a Church without a company or a roof.'[9] Even more galling, though the Irish Establishment was moribund, the Presbyterian meeting-houses flourished. Anglican parishes often could not boast more than ten, sometimes not more than six, whereas 'the Presbyterian meetings [were] crowded with thousands'; so reported an Anglican dignitary three years before Swift arrived, adding that 'the county of Antrim especially . . . is the most populous of Scots of any in Ulster.'[10] As Swift looked at his own Church, surely in despair, and at the flourishing condition of the Kirk, he must have reflected in grim irony over the presumed exclusive status of the Anglican Church. We have little information about Swift in this first phase of his career, but it seems not too venturesome to suggest that here developed or intensified that fear and dislike of nonconformity which persisted throughout his life, and also the lasting concern for the temporalities of the Church which made him later such a fierce opponent of any encroachments by laymen on the material welfare of the Establishment. To the Anglican clergy of the eighteenth century it was axiomatic that the spiritual health of the Church depended on flourishing temporalities. Tithes, the divine tenth, were indeed divine. It was Archdeacon Grantly in Anthony Trollope's novel, *The Warden*, who 'did not believe in the Gospel with more assurance than he did in the sacred justice of all ecclesiastical revenues.' So with Swift and his contemporaries.

Swift was prebendary of Kilroot for three years, January, 1695, to January, 1698, though his actual residence in his parishes was a bare year or less. By the middle of 1696 he had returned to the household of Sir William Temple, once again seeking and expecting through Temple's influence a satisfactory appointment in England — not necessarily a place in the Church. It is instructive to observe how fortune played waggishly with his hopes. He could turn to two men, the Earl of Sunderland, then in the government, and Sir William Temple. Now political accident and death played their parts. 'My Ld Sunderland fell and I with Him,' Swift wrote lugubriously in the spring of 1698,[11] and, as he tarried expectantly, Temple most inopportunely died at the beginning of the new year, leaving his protégé unprovided for and with no other dependable, influential person to whom he might turn for assistance. Swift, at the age of 32, was still seeking his place in the Church. Once again he was to experience delays and defeated hopes. The coveted royal prebend, in his dreams from the very beginning, eluded him once more. It is clear that he hoped for more than he might reasonably expect, now that he had no influential person to advance his claims. As for deserts, not even the most sympathetic observer can discover at this point in his career any special merit as a clergyman which would have justified the preferment he desired. To those who had the power to appoint he would have seemed little more than a place-seeker; and it was his misfortune that he sought preferment at a moment when the King had appointed a clerical commission, consisting of two archbishops and four bishops, with instructions to approve preferment for only the worthiest clergymen.

Once again he returned to Ireland to try his fortunes, in the fall of 1699, as domestic chaplain to the Earl of Berkeley, who was assuming his duties as a Lord Justice. Although the office of domestic chaplain was paltry, it had, as a temporary place, certain advantages. The Chaplains of Lord Justices expected as a matter of course to be preferred when a suitable vacancy occurred; and Swift could hope, through intercourse at Dublin Castle with people of power, to increase the possibilities of preferment. In the meantime he would have limited duties, little more than family prayers or an occasional sermon at the Castle, and these without parochial duties or vexatious dependence on tithes. There was time for reading, for social intercourse, and for writing those amusing occasional poems which survive from this period. And time, of course, to scan the clerical scene for preferment.

The opportunity came quickly: in a matter of months the lucrative deanery of Derry fell vacant, with its disposal presumably in the hands of the Earl of Berkeley. Years later, in his Autobiographical Fragment, a disgruntled Swift asserts that through bribery Derry was conferred on another and that he himself was 'put off with some other Church-livings not worth above a third part of that rich deanery.'[12] That Swift was wrong about the facts (he seems not to have received serious consideration) does not concern us here. What is significant (and fortunate) is that his failure to be preferred to Derry left him free to become predendary of Dunlavin in St. Patrick's Cathedral (in September, 1700) and to begin his association of forty-five years with that Cathedral. The 'other Church-livings' which Swift refers to with some scorn contained the parish of Laracor in the diocese of Meath, the only parish of the six he had in his life to bring him any satisfaction. Not that Laracor and Meath at the moment were a vast improvement over Kilroot and Antrim. A few years before Swift's incumbency the Bishop of Meath reported that of 197 parish churches in the diocese only 43 were in repair and that a mere forty clergymen resided in their parishes.[13] The resemblance to Down and

Connor was striking in other respects as well: lay impropria-
tion of tithes, lack of manses for the clergy, and neglect
of cures because of pluralities. Though Swift was himself
a pluralist (he held a union of three parishes), this time he
had a church in reasonably good repair. Swift as a dedicated
parish priest: it is not a role that one can easily conceive;
yet Laracor does show us an aspect of the man which in
some respects softens the asperities of his character so often
emphasized. Laracor became for him a haven, offering
interludes of tranquillity, even an outlet for domestic instincts
and the country gentleman's urge to cultivate and improve
his estate. When he was fiercely engaged in the political
machinations of the Harley ministry, his thoughts often
turned to this serene country parish — Laracor with its
canal, its apples and willows and thorns, its river with
the cherry trees on the bank. This is a recurring strain in
his letters to Stella. As the political scene palled and disgusted,
he writes feelingly: 'I wish my self more and more among
my willows.' He pictures himself pleasantly 'in his morning-
gown in the garden' at Laracor; and often he reveals great
satisfaction in the improvements he made in this country
parish.[14] Nevertheless we cannot turn Swift into an active
parish priest. He did not serve the cure. He did choose
conscientiously the curates and kept them under close
supervision. On occasional visits he preached, as he said,
to a gathering 'of at least 15 people, most of them Gentle, and
all Simple.'[15] Fifteen parishioners! In any event this was
an improvement over Kilroot, where his even fewer members
of the Establishment were engulfed by nonconformists. In
Laracor the preponderant population was Catholic. Perhaps
enough has been said to indicate that the Church of Ireland
in Swift's day, particularly in the country parishes, could
generate only the deepest distress in those devoted to it.
We hardly need seek beyond Swift's experiences with his
parishes in both the north and the south to explain his
pessimism about the Establishment, a pessimism which was
to intensify as the years passed and to culminate in the

gloomy pronouncement of 1736: 'I have long given up all hopes of Church or Christianity.'[16]

In the perspective of history we can see that the years 1700 to 1713, when Swift was a canon of St. Patrick's, constituted a sound apprenticeship for the deanery. Though the chapter minutes are all too sparse, they give evidence of his increasing importance in cathedral affairs; and other events reveal that he steadily gained valuable experience, not only in the internal affairs of the chapter but also in knowledge of ecclesiastical precedents and prerogatives, all of which served him well as a dean. Two matters, both of which took him beyond the confines of the cathedral, deserve mention. In 1707 he was elected proctor to represent St. Patrick's in the Lower House of Convocation; and later in the same year he interested himself seriously in the most momentous endeavour of the years before the deanship: the attempt to gain for the Irish Establishment remission by the Crown of the imposts known as the First Fruits. These Crown levies on clerical holdings were not great (Swift estimated them at £1000 annually) but they were vexatious, particularly to the lower clergy. Since Queen Anne had remitted them to the Church of England, the Church of Ireland had legitimate expectations that it too would be so favoured.

For a period of three years Swift's chief preoccupation was to win this bounty for the Church, in the course of which he acted as a representative of the Irish bishops, who apparently recognized his competence to negotiate this delicate matter, at the same time that they were aware he had access to powerful statesmen in England. In England Swift pleaded his cause with the Earl Godolphin, then First Lord of the Treasury, and with such other powerful Whigs as Somers, Pembroke, Wharton and Sunderland, all to no avail; and finally, when the Godolphin ministry fell, with Robert Harley and others among the Tories. So much has been said of Swift's inordinate ambition, of Swift the place-seeker, that we must look at this project from that vantage. He was not so naïve that he did not realize what might accrue to him from success, yet he could be selfless when his deepest convictions were affronted. Godolphin made clear that his government would consider favourably the pleas for remission of the First Fruits if the Irish churchmen supported the ministerial policy in Ireland, i.e., easing the plight of the nonconformists by removing the Test Act.[17] Although we cannot in this day admire Swift's inflexible antagonism to dissent, we can understand it. Godolphin's bribe, as Swift conceived it, aroused his instincts for the safety of the Establishment. It should be remembered that Swift is much more a man of the seventeenth century than of the eighteenth, at least he is so in his uncompromising resistance to nonconformity. His views were formed in the wake of the Cromwellian revolution; and he was unable to erase from his memory what the Anglican Establishment had undergone in that turbulent period. His vivid imagination never freed him from the thoughts that it might happen again. When he was confronted by Godolphin with the harsh political realities, at a moment when inevitably he had in mind his own advancement, all that was required of him was a letter to the Irish bishops urging a sympathetic gesture of assent to ministerial policy.

He did not hesitate: a shining personal moment, one must say, in an illiberal cause. He urged his correspondents in Ireland not to barter the privileged position of the Establishment for the First Fruits; and he suggested that the Irish clergy should prepare addresses to the throne, making clear its opposition to the removal of the Test.[18] In so doing, he was well aware that he had not served his own interest or, indeed, that of the Church; and in the following months, as he continued his efforts, he added to his fund of pessimism and cynicism as he watched the delays, excuses, and tortuous evasions of the statesmen upon whom he depended to further the cause of the Irish Church. Fortunately, in the light of later events, he did not succeed with the Whig ministry. After an interlude in Dublin, he returned to

England in September, 1710, once again an emissary to seek Queen Anne's bounty, to look on with satisfaction as the Godolphin ministry was succeeded by the moderate Tories led by Robert Harley, later Earl of Oxford. In less than two months Swift had succeeded with Harley; and he was soon to begin his brilliant association with Queen Anne's last ministry, as its chief political journalist.

The eventual reward was the deanery of St. Patrick's. All things considered, Swift made an easy transition from political journalist to dean. He had become adept in controversy (very useful for an Anglican dean of the period) and had become accustomed to vicious attacks from the journalistic enemies of the Harley ministry. They did not let him forget the profane wit of *A Tale of A Tub*; and even on the day of his installation (so legend has it) verses were affixed to the door of the Cathedral, one of which read:

> Look down, *St. Patrick*, look we pray,
>   On thine own *Church* and *Steeple;*
> Convert thy *Dean*, on this *Great Day;*
>   Or else God help the People![19]

His great neighbour, William King, Archbishop of Dublin, disturbed by rumours that Swift would get a bishopric, expressed relief that it was only a deanery because 'a Dean could do less mischief than a bishop.'[20] Swift was aware of the antagonisms that enveloped him then and throughout his career. Nevertheless, though his temper was often ruffled, his witty perception of himself and his circumstances did not desert him. This is well illustrated in a poem he composed soon after his installation, which took place on June 13, 1713. The poem, an imitation of Horace, is a mock account of Harley's determination to make Swift a dean despite his modest desire to be a canon of Windsor.

> [Harley] down to Windsor takes his Guest.
> S - - - t much admires the Place and Air,
>   And longs to be a *Canon* there;

In Summer round the Park to ride,
In Winter — never to reside.
A *Canon*! that's a Place too mean:
No, Doctor, you shall be a *Dean;*
Two Dozen *Canons* round your Stall,
And you the Tyrant o'er them all:
You need but cross the *Irish* Seas,
To live in Plenty, Power and Ease.[21]

This is the Swift who humorously described to Alexander
Pope his jurisdiction over the Liberty of St. Patrick's:

I am Lord Mayor of 120 houses, I am absolute Lord of
the greatest Cathedral in the Kingdom: am at peace with
the neighbouring Princes, the Lord Mayor of the City,
and the A. Bp. of Dublin, only the latter, like the K. of
France sometimes attempts encroachments on my Dominions . . . .[22]

This, too, is the Swift who took time from the duties and
vexations of the decanal office to write an epigram upon the
'fall' of a bishop, Rundle of Derry, who had taken a spill:
'Friend Rundle fell with grievous bump/Upon his reverential
rump'.[23] The strain of ribaldry and frivolity, so essential a
part of Swift's nature, was not concealed behind the clerical
habit. As it is an aspect of the man, so is it an aspect of the
churchman. I am, therefore, a little restive when confronted
by lines which seem to brush aside this fundamental view of
humour and playfulness, such lines as came from Ireland's
great poet, depicting Swift as

... beating on his breast in sibylline frenzy blind
Because the heart in his blood-sodden breast had dragged
him down into mankind.[24]

It is a little disconcerting to find Yeats reflecting the traditional legendary view which scholars struggle to counteract.
As Professor George Sherburn brilliantly demonstrated, we
shall not see Swift plain until the emphasis is removed from

this horrendous collection of psychological traits which stress gigantic and demonic passions — fierceness, malignity, misery, intensity, violence, and brooding misanthropy.[25] So far as I am aware, Swift did not appear to his contemporaries or his associates in the church to be a gloomy dean in any sense that might not be applied to many other contemporary churchmen in Ireland. Admittedly his pessimism about both the Establishment and Ireland was strong and vocal, but it is difficult to find any of his contemporaries who were not similarly distressed and gloomy over almost every aspect of Irish life.

Swift's indictments are darker and fiercer because he had a talent for violent rhetoric. To speak of an *optimistic* Irish churchman or an *optimistic* public-spirited Irishman in the eighteenth century may well be a contradiction in terms. We get a better measure of the man and cleric if we refuse to catch him up in such a phrase as the gloomy dean, if we view him (except for those last few years of infirmity) as active, staunch, zealous, alert, often irritating and tough and uncompromising, in affairs relating to church and state. I suggest that we shall see him even plainer if we observe his day-by-day clerical routine, the preponderance of hours he spent in the important or trivial concerns of a great cathedral. The chapter minutes of St. Patrick's, along with Swift's letters and the letters of other churchmen, tell us much in this respect. Swift presiding over his chapter, Swift looking carefully at the selection of a vicar choral, Swift attending to leases on Cathedral lands, seeing to such matters as the repair of the fabric, guarding the quality of the services, attentive to Cathedral charities, improving the Cathedral school. These and numberless other preoccupations engaged him week after week, month after month, year after year. In a sense these are the matters which constituted the basic texture of his life and defined its quality.

To maintain balance and proper perspective in assessing the churchman we cannot minimize this aspect of his existence, just as we may not ignore the Swift who, however much he was immersed in church affairs, was also a genial, witty guest at great houses, a persistent punster, a delightful correspondent of both sexes, young and old, and a writer of lively squibs and poems. As he himself said, he was 'not the gravest of Divines';[26] and despite the numerous and striking pessimistic utterances, we find evidence in his daily life of many satisfactions, of zest, vitality, and wholesome interests. In his poem, *The Author upon Himself*, he wrote:

S[wift] had the Sin of Wit no venial Crime,
Nay, 'twas affirm'd, he sometimes dealt in Rhime:
Humour, and Mirth, had Place in all he writ:
He reconcil'd Divinity and Wit.[27]

This is an image of himself that he took seriously. He reconciled divinity and wit, he asserts. Perhaps he did not wholly reconcile them; he did sometimes bring them into a curious juxtaposition, as in his sermon, *Upon Sleeping in Church*, the text of which is *Acts*, xx.ix, concerned with the young man who sank into a deep sleep 'as Paul *was long preaching.*' The hapless young man fell from his precarious perch in a window of the third loft and was 'taken up dead,' but miraculously restored by St. Paul. Swift tells his auditors that he has chosen the text 'with Design, if possible, to disturb some Part in this Audience of half an Hour's Sleep, for the Convenience and Exercise whereof this Place, at this Season of the Day, is very much celebrated:

The Accident which happened to this young Man in the Text, hath not been sufficient to discourage his Successors: But, because the Preachers now in the World, however they may exceed St. *Paul* in the Art of setting Men to Sleep, do extremely fall short of him in the Working of Miracles; therefore Men are become so cautious as to chuse more safe and convenient Stations and Postures for taking their Repose, without Hazard to their Persons...[28]

This (it is supererogation to say it) is no mere interlude of comic statement and witty apprehension. It is a persistent strain reflecting facets of the man which balance the darker side; and in this delightful opening to his sermon, in which his comic vision becomes the instrument of homiletic purposes, we can see an undeniable affinity between the divine and the wit. Then, too, for Swift and his contemporaries, as we well know, the witty satirist was a serious moralist, one who engaged himself on the side of the virtues and chastised men for their vices and follies and institutions for their abuses. It is not accidental that he defended John Gay's *The Beggar's Opera* as a 'moral Play' and thought it might do more good 'than a thousand Sermons' by a certain court chaplain who had attacked it.[29] One of the reasons for satire, Swift asserted, is that men of public spirit may 'mend the World as far as they are able.'[30] He agreed with Sir Richard Steele's remark, that 'the greatest evils in human society are such as no law can come at, but satire can, and ought to be praised for doing so.'[31]

Swift's defence of satiric wit was, of course, a defence of himself. Twenty-five years after the publication of *A Tale of a Tub* (1704), which may be called his original sin of wit (and for which he believed he had been amply punished), we still find him commenting on the fate of the witty clergyman. He reflected on the inevitable success in the Church of the dull, discreet man, cold in temper, grave in deportment, and by contrast, the man of parts 'to whose Preferment nothing is so fatal as the Character of Wit, Politeness in Reading, or Manners, or that Kind of Behaviour, which we contract by having too much conversed with Persons of high Station and Eminency; these Qualifications being reckoned by the *Vulgar* of *all Ranks*, to be Marks of *Levity*, which is the last Crime the World will pardon in a *Clergy-Man*....'[32] One can hardly doubt that this was Swift thinking of himself. It is reminiscent of the picture he drew in his poem mentioned earlier, *The Author upon Himself*, written soon after his installation as dean:

Humour, and Mirth, had Place in all he writ:
He reconcil'd Divinity and Wit.
He mov'd, and bow'd, and talk'd with too much Grace;
Nor shew'd the Parson in his Gait or Face;
Despis'd luxurious Wines, and costly Meat;
Yet, still was at the Tables of the Great.
Frequented Lords; *saw those that saw the Queen;*

. . . . .

But, after sage Monitions from his Friends,
His Talents to employ for nobler Ends;
To better Judgments willing to submit,
He turns to Pol[it]icks his dang'rous Wit.[33]

But if Swift had a 'dang'rous Wit,' he was deadly serious
in his decanal capacity. He wished to be a good dean, not
necessarily a loved one; and from the outset he seemed to
take it as axiomatic that a good dean is a strong dean. This
meant to him, among other things, a refusal to compromise
in defence of the prerogatives of the decanal office. Attacks
on his prerogatives came as a matter of course, perhaps
the most dangerous from Archbishop King, who had vigorous
adherents in the Cathedral chapter. King's endeavour to
nullify Tory influence in St. Patrick's brought him into
conflict with Swift on various occasions; and for a number
of years we have the spectacle of two firm-minded dignitaries
in a constant state of irritation with each other. Yet after
a decade they had arrived at a *modus vivendi*, with the
Archbishop eventually granting that Swift had 'behaved
him Self very well in his Station, very agreeable to me,
and been usefull to the Publick both by his Charity and
his Labours....'[34] But this genial attitude of 1726 had been
of slow growth. In the intervening years Swift had to
accustom himself to intractable canons within the chapter.
His first biographer depicts him sitting in the chapter house
'like Jupiter in the Synod of the Gods,'[35] an image of power
and serenity not supported by the evidence. He was vexed
by the frequent political manoeuvring of the Whiggish

canons, who also challenged his decanal prerogatives on occasions. His remark to Pope, 'I am absolute Lord of the greatest Cathedral in the Kingdom,' was by no means true. He had great power, the power of negative or veto, but otherwise he was merely *primus inter pares*. In 1716, several of the canons challenged the dean's right of veto, though it was based, Swift maintained, on 'constant immemorial custom.' To Swift, the opposition to him seemed often to rise out of political differences often inspired by Archbishop King. 'I am here,' he complained to his old friend, Francis Atterbury, then Bishop of Rochester, 'at the head of three and twenty dignitaries and prebendaries, whereof the major part, differing from me in principles, have taken a fancy to oppose me upon all occasions in the chapter house; and a ringleader among them has presumed to debate my power of proposing, or my negative, though it is what . . . has never been once disputed.'[36] A year later he complained again that opposition 'in everything relating to my station, is made a merit in my Chapter.'[37]

This atmosphere of dissension and wrangling in which he carried on his duties as dean clearly had an effect on his spirits and probably contributed to his pessimism. But Swift's complaints, I am inclined to believe, do not tell us anything uniquely about Swift himself. The cathedrals of the eighteenth century (as earlier) were battlegrounds: bishops and deans and canons were in constant conflict. The respective rights of deans and chapters were more frequently than not ill defined and open to varied interpretations. Though political antagonisms played a part, the conflicts were inherent in vague charters and confused precedents. One can only stand amazed before the spectacle of those who preached amity on the Lord's day and indulged an unceasing vein of litigiousness on the other six days. Of Swift we may say that he was restive in the face of opposition; but perhaps not more so than other deans. He did indeed interpret opposition to his wishes as politically motivated. Like Dr. Johnson, he was determined not to let the Whig dogs have the better of it; and in some instances his Whiggish canons were determined not to let him have the better of it. There is, for example, the occasion in 1716 when he proposed a certain canon as representative of the chapter in Convocation. His proposal was voted down, whereupon he proposed himself, only to be rejected by the same majority.[38] With the passing of the years the tensions faded, partly because Archbishop King's influence waned (he died in 1729), partly because the new men who moved into the prebends became Swift's staunch friends. He still complained as late as 1728 of 'the tricks used by my Chapter to teize me,'[39] though it is revealing that in 1731, when he again proposed himself as proctor to represent St. Patrick's in Convocation, he was this time unanimously approved.[40]

Swift's relations with the Irish bishops, sharp and bitter at the beginning, also eased with time, particularly with those bishops of Irish birth and education. One of his great causes was the Irish 'interest' in the Church, that is, he was highly critical of the English policy of filling Irish bishoprics and deaneries with clergymen sent over from England, an attitude which he shared with Archbishop King and which brought them into an amicable relationship.[41] Although Swift was severely critical of the Anglo-Irish gentry, he thought they were justifiably bitter over the failure of their sons and relatives to obtain a fair share of good appointments in the Church. In part he felt that merit was being neglected, that an inferior clergyman from England was often preferred at the expense of a superior Irishman; but he was also keenly aware of the importance of an alliance between the Church of Ireland and the lay gentry. The welfare of the Establishment was threatened if this powerful group, exacerbated by tithes and resentful of English policies, did not receive fair treatment. Thus, when Carteret was Lord Lieutenant, Swift, relying on an old friendship, appealed to him to end the discrimination. Bestowing the best ecclesiastical preferment on strangers, he wrote to Carteret, has discouraged learning and the study of divinity in Ireland:

... the young Men sent into the Church from the University here, have no better prospects than to be Curates, or small Country-Vicars, for Life. It will become so excellent a Governor as you, a little to moderate this great Partiality wherein you [will] take away one great Cause of universal Discontent.[42]

The dichotomy in the Irish Establishment between the English and the Irish 'interests' was most bitterly felt at the episcopal level; and in espousing the Irish 'interest' Swift was opposing himself to the English government's attempt to establish a Whiggish episcopal bench to counter Tory influence among the lower clergy and the gentry. If Swift in this instance aligned himself with the gentry, he was their fierce antagonist when they made periodical attempts to escape tithes or alienate church lands. He was keenly aware of the constant struggle between powerful laymen and churchmen for a larger share of the national wealth; and, interestingly, he saw the struggle in the context of history, ranging from the Reformation to his own day. The history of the Church, as he viewed it, was a history of plundering, despoliations, persistent alienations of church possessions, beginning with Henry VIII, who had robbed the English and Irish Establishments of two-thirds of their legal possessions. In Swift's words, Henry was variously described as a sacrilegious tyrant, an infernal beast, a wicked prince, a monster. 'I wish,' he adds, 'that he had been Flead, his skin stuffed and hanged on a Gibbet, his bulky guts and flesh left to be devoured by Birds and Beasts, for a warning to his Successors forever. Amen.'[43]

It is passion of this intensity which Swift brought to the controversy over tithes in 1734, and again in 1736, when the Irish House of Commons attempted to reduce tithes on hemp, flax, and grazing lands. In poetry and prose he assumed the role of ecclesiastical polemist, a defender of the patrimony of the Church. His well known poem, *The Legion Club* (1736), is mainly Juvenalian invective. To discover the rationale of his position, one must turn to the prose pamphlets. On an occasion when he was vexed (as he often was) by the difficulty of collecting his tithes, he remarked wryly that though 'tithes be of Divine institution' they are of 'diabolical execution.'[44] But in fact Swift, who entered into the contemporary controversy over the exact status of tithes, was not inclined to insist that they were due the clergy by divine right. He contented himself with maintaining that tithes are of great antiquity and are vested in the Church as a property right, an argument that he shrewdly recognized would have greater appeal to the landed gentry, who in self-interest hesitated to tamper with property rights.[45] But even such an argument did not prevail with many of the powerful laity; and we can attribute no small part of Swift's pessimism to his awareness that a State Church has little defence against a civil power with designs on ecclesiastical property. As I have already indicated, Swift was a typical churchman of the period in his conviction that the spiritual welfare of the Church depended on its material welfare. He would assent to the remark by the historian, F. W. Maitland, that 'the attempt to draw an unwavering line between "spiritual" and "temporal" affairs is hopeless.'[46] Thus it is that Swift spent an incalculable amount of time on church economics, in the despairing hope that the Irish Establishment as the embodiment of Christianity might be more vital and effective. Clerical leases and rents, tithes, glebes, parsonages, the poverty of the lower clergy, the whole economy of the Church, these are pervasive matters in his writings from 1723 to 1736. He insisted that he was not thinking merely of Church and churchmen, that a temporally strong Church nourished the economic life of the nation because the clergy as landlords and makers of leases played a vital part in the economic health of the whole people.

At the very root of his pessimism was a subtle, larger historical view which he barely enunciates, the view that in the course of British constitutional history a persistent process could be detected, great shifts in social and political power resulting from the transference of property from one group to another. As we have seen, Swift thought Henry VIII the one who began shifting property and thus power from the Church into the hands of laymen, a prevailing view in the period among church historians. The process, Swift conceived to be still running a violent course in the Irish Establishment; and to a large extent he thought this was the ultimate reason for the ineffectiveness of the Establishment, its lost vigour, a clergy held in contempt. It would be pretentious to call Swift an economic determinist, yet economic causes played a significant part in his assessment of the position of the contemporary Church.

Clearly then we are not to brush aside wholly the traditional view of Swift as the gloomy dean. We need to modify and understand the phrase in the context of a large body of facts, personal and historical, which give it meaning and fix its limits. I suggest that we may go so far as to refer to him as *a* gloomy dean, not *the* gloomy dean, viewing him in the light of numerous other gloomy deans in the Irish Establishment of the period and of ecclesiastical conditions generally in contemporary Ireland. Let us perhaps content ourselves with admitting that among the gloomy deans of his day he was *primus inter pares*. Unquestionably his gloomy comments increase after 1730, intensified by his ill health, his impotence in getting preferment for deserving clergymen, his inability to collect his tithes, the encroachments by laymen on church property, and his realization that he could accomplish little for Ireland. It may be true, as he admitted, that he had 'composed more Libels than Sermons,'[47]; but not his most bitter enemies could accuse him of neglecting his stewardship of St. Patrick's even as he took his place on the stage of national affairs. As Herbert Davis has said, Swift's conception of pastoral care widened out to embrace the nation. He accepted the obligations expected of a distinguished churchman of his status, to act in a larger sphere than the merely clerical, to be a force in the cultural, political, social, and economic life of the nation. In these varied spheres he utilized frequently his great talent, the witty perception of men and affairs, the astringent realism, which make appropriate his characterization of himself as 'not the gravest of Divines.'

NOTES

1 In the autobiographical fragment on his family Swift asserts that King William promised Sir William Temple that 'he would give Mr. Swift a Prebend of Canterbury or Westminster.' See *The Prose Works of Jonathan Swift*, ed. Herbert Davis, (Oxford, 1939—), V, p.195. Hereafter referred to as *Prose Works*.

2 See *Jonathan Swift: Journal to Stella*, ed. Harold Williams, (Oxford, 1948), II, 66off.

3 *Ibid.*, 662.

4 *The Letters of Jonathan Swift to Charles Ford*, ed. David Nichol Smith, Oxford, 1935, p.82.

5 *Prose Works*, IX, 262.

6 William Makepeace Thackeray, *The English Humourists of the Eighteenth Century* (1853), Furniss Centenary Edition, London, 1911, pp.31 - 2.

7 *Time*, Jan. 15, 1965, p.90.

8 Here and elsewhere in this essay I have drawn freely on the facts in my book, *Swift and the Church of Ireland*, Oxford, 1954. I am grateful to the Clarendon Press for giving me full latitude. For a more extensive treatment of the events in this paragraph, see my book, pp.11 ff.

9 *The Correspondence of Jonathan Swift*, ed Harold Williams, Oxford, 1963, I, 31.

10 In a letter of Bishop Leslie to William King, quoted by James Seaton Reid, *History of the Presbyterian Church in Ireland*, Belfast, 1867, II, 391.

11 *Corres.*, I, 26, to the Rev. John Winder, 1 April, 1698.

12 *Prose Works*, V, 195.

13 Marsh's Library, MS. Z 3.1.4 (5), f. 142: *The State of the Diocese of Meath . . .* 1693. For Laracor, see Landa, *op. cit.*, pp.37 ff.

14 *Journal to Stella*, I, 197; II, 573, and *passim.*

15 *Corres.*, I, 163; II, 193.

16 *Ibid.*, IV, 505.

17 *Ibid.*, I, 85 - 6.

18 *Ibid.*, I, 77 - 8, 79. Swift's letters from London to his correspondents in Ireland in the months of April, May, and June tell the story of his attempts to gain remission of the First Fruits from the Godolphin ministry. By November he was weary of the project and would gladly have accepted a government post abroad. See his letter to King, Nov. 9, 1708, in *Corres.* I, 105.

19 [Jonathan Smedley], *Gulliveriana: or, A Fourth Volume of Miscellanies*, London, 1728, p.78.

20 Gilbert Collection, Dublin, MS. 28, King to Wake, 8 May, 1713(?).

21 'Part of the Seventh Epistle of the First Book of Horace Imitated,' in *The Poems of Jonathan Swift*, ed. Harold Williams, 2nd ed., Oxford, 1958, I, 173. Hereafter referred to as *Poems*.

22 *Corres.*, IV, 171.

23 'On Dr. Rundle, Bishop of Derry,' in *Poems*, III, 822.

24 William Butler Yeats, 'Blood and the Moon.'

25 'Methods in Books about Swift,' *SP*, XXXV (1938), 635 - 56.

26 'Stella's Birthday, March 13, 1726/7,' in *Poems*, II, 764.

27 *Ibid.*, I, 193 - 4.

28 *Prose Works*, IX, 210.

29 *Ibid.*, XII, 36: 'The Intelligencer,' No. III.

30 *Ibid.*, p.34.

31 *The Tatler*, No. 61.

32 *Prose Works*, XII, 40.

33 *Poems*, I, 193 - 4.

34 *King Correspondence*, vol. 1725 - 7, Trinity College, Dublin, Letter to Francis Annesley, May 30, 1726.

35 John, Earl of Orrery, *Remarks on the Life and Writings of Dr. Jonathan Swift*, London, 1752, p.51.

36 *Corres.*, II, 194.

37 *Ibid.*, 279.

38 St. Patrick's Cathedral, Chapter Minutes, March, 17, 1716.

39 *Corres.*, III, 289.

40 St. Patrick's Cathedral, Chapter Minutes, March 17, 1731.

41 For a fuller treatment of this matter, see my book, *Swift and the Church of Ireland*, pp.169 - 77.

42 *Corres.* III, 70 - 1.

43 Lord Rothschild, *Some Unpublished Marginalia of Jonathan Swift*, Cambridge, 1945, pp.7 - 8; *Prose Works*, XIII, 121 - 6.

44 *Corres.*, III, 374 - 5.

45 See Landa, *op. cit.*, pp.123 ff.

46 *Roman Canon Law in the Church of England*, London, 1898, p.56.

47 *Corres.*, I, 414. Swift's characterization of himself as 'not the gravest of Divines' and his assertion that he 'reconcil'd Divinity and Wit' may be related in a vague and subtle way to contemporary rejections of a gloomy Calvinism, a view reflected in the *Spectator*, no. 494, where Addison remarks that 'the Saint was of a sorrowful Countenance, and generally eaten up with Spleen and Melancholy' (see also *The Spectator*, nos. 381, 387). Anglican writers thought it a mistaken notion of piety which associated gloom, melancholy, and undue gravity with a true religious spirit. The grave, formal, starched man had long been under attack (see Swift's *Intelligencer*, nos. V and VII); and Swift unquestionably would have agreed with Shaftesbury's remark that '*Gravity* is of the very Essence of *Imposture* (*Letter concerning Enthusiasm*, sec. ii). Likewise he would find comfort in Shaftesbury's insistence 'That Wit and Humour are corroborative of *Religion* and promotive of *true Faith*,' a comment made 'to defend an Author . . . charg'd as too presumptuous for introducing the way of Wit and Humour into *Religious Searches*' (*Miscellaneous Reflections*, Miscellany II, ch. iii: Shaftesbury asserted: 'we may justly be said to have in the main, *A witty* and *good-humour'd Religon*'). It is this strain of thought which seems to have culminated in Sterne's conviction that 'Joy is another name for Religion,' a view embodied in 'The Grace' in *A Sentimental Journey*, where Yorick beholds '*Religion* mixing in the dance.'

SWIFT, THE MYSTERIES, AND DEISM

In 1705 William Wotton, well known for his controversy
with Swift's patron, Sir William Temple, over the respective
merits of the Ancients and the Moderns, indicted *A Tale
of a Tub* as "one of the Prophanest Banters upon the
Religion of *Jesus Christ* . . . that ever yet appeared."[1]
There is no way of determining accurately how widely this
indictment was accepted as just, but certainly a segment
of the reading public—vocal if not numerous—agreed that
the author stood properly accused of irreverence and
impiety. This charge has clung to Swift. It is reflected in
certain commentators of the later eighteenth and the nineteenth centuries, and indeed still has a faint persistence.[2]
Among other accusations, Wotton specifically accused the
author of *A Tale* of copying from the deist Toland, "who
always raises a Laugh at the Word *Mystery*"[3]— a suspicion
of Swift's soundness on the Christian mysteries that has had
enough vigor to persist and to be revived in recent years by
so penetrating a scholar as Emil Pons.[4] Certainly it cannot
be denied that *A Tale* lends some support to the charges of
irreligion, particularly if it is isolated from Swift's other
utterances and if his "Apology"—in which he insists that
the work is a satire on the corruptions of religion—is
ignored. Even sympathetic critics have not always been

---

[1]See *Reflections upon Ancient and Modern Learning*, 3rd ed. corrected (London, 1705), p. 534. Wotton did not know at the time that
Swift was the author.

[2]See Donald M. Berwick, *The Reputation of Jonathan Swift, 1781–
1882* (Philadelphia, 1941), *passim*, and C. Looten, *La Pensée Reli-
gieuse de Swift et ses Antinomies* (Lille and Paris, 1935), *passim*.

[3]*Op. cit.*, p. 525.

[4]See *Swift: les Années de Jeunesse et le "Conte du Tonneau"*
(Strasbourg, 1925), pp. 332–3. Cf. also Looten, *op. cit.*, pp. 69 ff. and
p. 117n., where Looten says that Swift's real view of the Trinity is
"à certains égards, plus voisine de celle de [the deist] Collins qu'il ne
le pense et qu'il ne le voudrait."

able to forgive Swift for writing the *Tale;* yet one looks in vain beneath the violent language, the caustic and degrading symbols, and the energy of the satire, for any views regarding Catholics and dissenters that were not being voiced by hundreds of Anglican clergymen from their pulpits or that had not been published widely in works devoted to the triangular controversy among Catholics, Anglicans, and dissenters.[5]

Among Swift's other works *Gulliver's Travels*, particularly Part IV, has been singled out by commentators as further evidence of irreligion. The indictment has usually been directed against the dangerous misanthropy which, in the words of an eighteenth-century commentator, "goes so far in sapping the very foundations of Morality and Religion, that . . . the last part of *Swift's Gulliver* [is] a worse Book to peruse, than those which we forbid, as the most flagitious and obscene."[6] Swift had, of course, ardent defenders from the beginning, and continued to find them in each succeeding generation. Today the violent and extreme accusations of the past are generally discounted as ill considered and as failing to present a well-rounded conception, being based on only two works. Still it is a striking fact that Swift as a Christian divine has received comparatively little attention. His mystifying personal relationships, his political activities, his defense of Ireland— in these and other aspects he has been examined minutely, but no satisfactory detailed analysis of his religious views has yet appeared to provide a basis for a complete judgment.[7] The sermons, which might be expected to offer evi-

---

[5]For many earlier attacks on the Puritans, which reveal the conventionality of Swift's satiric themes in the *Tale*, see the articles by C. M. Webster in *PMLA*, XLVII (1932), 171–8; XLVIII (1933), 1141–53; L (1935), 210–23.

[6]James Harris, *Philological Enquiries* (1781), in *Works* (London, 1803), V, 543–4.

[7]The only extended study of Swift's religious views other than that by Looten, already mentioned, is that by Hans Reimers, *Jonathan Swift: Gedanken und Schriften über Religion und Kirche* (Hamburg,

SWIFT, THE MYSTERIES, AND DEISM

dence of his sincere and considered opinions in religion, have been strangely neglected.[8] It is true that Swift appeared not to value his sermons and made no effort, so far as is known, to publish them (only eleven undoubtedly authentic ones have been printed) ; but his attitude may indicate nothing more than his personal feeling that they deserved no wide audience. It certainly does not vitiate their significance as a dependable, if not the best, source of his religious views. In the hope of exposing a segment of his religious thought, I propose in this article to examine one of these sermons, "On the Trinity," and to view it in its relations to contemporary religious ideas and controversies. In certain respects this is the most important of the surviving sermons. It is the only point at which Swift has expressed himself more than casually on a fundamental Christian doctrine. It is, furthermore, the only point at which we find anything resembling an articulated defense of the Christian mysteries. Here we can observe Swift engaged in meeting a challenge to orthodoxy; and in particular we see that he had a reasoned opposition to the deists, not a mere reliance upon irony and ridicule. Here also, briefly, he sets the boundaries as he conceived them of reason and faith.

"On the Trinity"—a Trinity-Sunday sermon—was first published in 1744. Unfortunately there is no way of determining when it was preached. In a eulogistic comment the Earl of Orrery called it "one of the best in its kind"[9]— a eulogy that does more than justice to Swift's effort, especially if Orrery meant that Swift had produced some-

---

1935). Although it leaves much to be desired, Max Armin Korn's brief treatment, in ch. II of his *Die Weltanschauung Jonathan Swifts* (Jena, 1935), deserves mention.

[8]But see the Introduction to Volume IX, now in the press, of Herbert Davis's edition of *The Prose Works of Jonathan Swift*. Cf. also the brief article by F. M. Darnall, "Swift's Religion," *JEGP*, XXX (1931), 379–82. Looten's discussion of the sermons is cursory.

[9]*Remarks on the Life and Writings of Dr. Jonathan Swift* (London, 1752), p. 293.

thing unusual or original. Actually his is a fairly conventional Trinity-Sunday sermon. He was content to repeat the ideas, even the phraseology, that contemporary clergymen had often used in their defenses of the Trinity and the other mysteries of Christianity. The tone and the point of view Swift adopts are explicable in terms of the controversy at the end of the seventeenth century when Anglican clergymen fought vigorously against exponents of a Socinian or an anti-Trinitarian viewpoint and at the same time quarrelled violently among themselves as to what constitutes an orthodox view of Christianity's fundamental doctrine. Among those who published elaborate explanations and debated the Trinity on a highly abstruse plane were such famous figures as William Sherlock, Dean of St. Paul's; Dr. John Wallis, divine, mathematician, and an original member of the Royal Society; Robert South, Canon of Christ Church, Oxford, as well as many of lesser note. The bitterness of the controversy grew to such proportions that in desperation the Archbishop of Canterbury remarked of the Athanasian Creed: "I wish we were well rid of it."[10] Legislation in 1698 "for the suppressing all pernicious books and pamphlets, which contain in them impious doctrines against the Holy Trinity"[11] had little effect; and the controversy moved vigorously into the eighteenth century, to receive fresh impetus in 1712 with the appearance of Samuel Clarke's *The Scripture Doctrine of the Trinity*. This work, eventually condemned by the Lower House of Convocation, was widely denounced as Arian; and to refute this revival of an old heresy a number of divines published their minute inquiries into the nature of the Trinity, each claiming for himself the true interpretation.

---

[10]See Thomas Birch, *The Life of the Most Reverend Dr. John Tillotson*, 2nd ed. (London, 1753), p. 315.

[11]See Robert Wallace, *Antitrinitarian Biography* (London, 1850), I, 385–6. For accounts of the controversy see, in addition to Wallace, John Hunt, *Religious Thought in England* (London, 1871), II, 201 ff.; C. J. Abbey and J. H. Overton, *The English Church in the Eighteenth Century* (London, 1878), I, 480 ff.

To these attempts to explain the Trinity by "studied niceties" and "metaphysical subtilties," there was in many quarters a violent reaction. The learned divines who thought they were ably defending the faith found themselves being charged with needlessly creating scruples and perplexities by their "minute inquiries into the *modus* of what they cannot comprehend."[12] Swift assumes this attitude in one of his random utterances on religion, where he criticizes clergymen who are "too curious, or too narrow, in reducing orthodoxy within the compass of subtleties, niceties, and distinctions";[13] and he repeated the criticism in *A Letter to a Young Clergyman* (1720), pointing out that nothing in the canons or articles of Christianity warrants the attempts of divines to explain the mysteries and that such attempts serve no useful purpose. A safer procedure, he insisted, is "upon solemn days to deliver the doctrine as the Church holds it, and confirm it by Scripture."[14] Such is the attitude that informs Swift's sermon. The majority of mankind, Swift maintains, is obliged to accept the doctrine of the Trinity only in the brief form in which it appears in Holy Scripture, without reference to the meaning of the word "Person," the exact nature of the union and distinction in the Godhead, or the "nice and philosophical points" of the Athanasian Creed. Divines who have attempted "farther explanations of this doctrine of the Trinity, by rules of philosophy . . . have multiplied controversies to such a degree, as to beget scruples that have perplexed the minds of many sober Christians, who otherwise could never have entertained them."[15] Characteristically Swift condemns abstruse terms and accepts the prevalent contem-

---

[12]This is a typical accusation, made by Samuel Clarke's able opponent, the Rev. Daniel Waterland; see his *Works* (Oxford, 1823), I, pt. ii, 213.

[13]*The Prose Works of Jonathan Swift, D.D.*, ed. Temple Scott (London, 1897–1908), III, 308. This edition is hereafter referred to as *Works*.

[14]*Works*, III, 213.

[15]*Works*, IV, 129–30.

porary notion that subtle speculations and philosophical intricacies are a violation of common sense. Thus it is that he is critical of those culpable, though well-meaning, clergymen who engage in heated controversies—among themselves or with the enemies of Christianity—involving learned discussions of modes, consubstantiality, and degrees of subordination. His indictment of the prying intellect will be readily recognized as an expression of that anti-intellectualism discernible at other points in his works and widely current in his day, particularly in theology, where divines exhorted their hearers to avoid an "over-anxious scrutiny" into the mysteries. Such exhortations were frequent in the sermons delivered on Trinity Sunday; and we may take as typical the attitude of one of Swift's fellow clergymen, who declared: "We shall better celebrate the Holy Trinity by a profound Silence and Adoration, than by disputing about it, or prying too curiously into the Manner of it."[16]

But Swift was not content with mere condemnation of "idle Speculation and a needless Curiosity." He wished also to expose the false reasoning of those who attacked the doctrine of the Trinity, the Socinians for example, who "would shew how impossible it is that three can be one, and one can be three."[17] The Trinitarian view of the nature of God—"there are three Persons who are *severally and each of them true God,* and yet there is but one true God"— involves, so the Socinians insisted, an inescapable contradiction; this faith in a trinity in unity is "absurd, and contrary both to Reason and *to itself,* and therefore not only false, but *impossible.*" It is, the argument ran, *"an Error in counting* or numbring" and imposes "false Gods on us; by advancing two to be Gods, who are not so."[18]

---

[16]Matthew Hole, *Practical Discourses . . . to be Us'd Thro-out the Year* (London, 1716), IV, pt. ii, 83.

[17]*Works,* IV, 136.

[18]See the Socinian position as represented by Stephen Nye, *A Brief History of the Unitarians, called also Socinians* (London, 1687), pp. 24–5.

The Socinian attack on the triune nature of God depended, Swift's contemporaries frequently pointed out, on bad logic —on an invalid analogy between known and unknown natures: the Socinians reasoned falsely that since three cannot be one in known natures (in man, for example), three cannot be one in unknown natures (God, for example). The Trinitarians—and Swift—granted that to speak of three as one with respect to man is a self-evident contradiction. If, Swift writes, "I were directly told in Scripture that three are one, and one is three, I could not conceive or believe it in the natural common sense of that expression . . ."; and he adds that "if any one told me that three men are one, and one man is three," he would reject the idea as "absurd and impossible."[19] But the analogy does not apply to the divine nature. It has a way of subsistence different from created nature. Thus the Socinian cannot argue tenably that what is true of finite nature is necessarily true of infinite nature. As Charles Leslie, able opponent of the Socinians, stated the case for the Trinitarians in 1708: "We cannot charge that as a contradiction in one nature because we find it so in another, unless we understand both natures perfectly well. And the divine nature being allowed on all hands to be incomprehensible, consequently we cannot charge anything as a contradiction in it because we find it so in our frail nature."[20] This in effect is the position Swift adopts—with the insistence that since the union and distinction in the divine nature is affirmed in Scripture, it must be accepted however "dark and mystical." His attitude is predicated on the fundamental tenet of the sermon, the incomprehensibility of the divine nature.

But "On the Trinity" transcends the treatment of a single doctrine, to become a defense of the Christian mysteries in general. In its wider scope the sermon constitutes Swift's answer to "those who are enemies to all revealed religion."

[19] *Works*, IV, 130, 131.

[20] *The Socinian Controversy* (1708), in *Theological Works* (Oxford, 1832), II, 56.

It is his defense of the faith against the challenge of those
extreme rationalists, the deists, who denied that the mysteries are credible when subjected to the test of human
reason. As is well known, Swift joined in the general
clamor against the deists. He gave them special attention
in the unfinished notations he made in 1708 for an attack
upon Matthew Tindal's *The Rights of the Christian Church*
(1706), in the *Argument against Abolishing Christianity*
(1709), and in his abstract of Anthony Collins's *Discourse of
Free-Thinking* (1713); but one looks in vain in these works
for a straightforward or a really substantial discussion of
the religious issues raised by the deists. Swift is characteristically lavish of irony and ridicule. He disdains a controversy in which the fundamental issues are seriously and
objectively considered; yet "On the Trinity" testifies to his
realization that the deists were not merely to be laughed
out of countenance. Here at least is evidence that he had
thought seriously about deism and that he had reasoned
grounds for his opposition.

Swift centers his attack on one of the fundamental con-
tentions of the deists, that what a man assents to, those
doctrines or mysteries which are the object of his faith—
particularly those vital to his salvation—must be clear and
intelligible to his reason, whose function is to judge of their
truth or falsity. An effective and disturbing statement of
this view—and one we may take as typical of early eighteenth-century deism—came from a person Swift enjoyed
attacking, John Toland, whose *Christianity not Mysterious*
(1696) was ordered burned, the same Toland whose attitude
toward the mysteries, according to Wotton, had influenced
the author of *A Tale of a Tub.*[21] Toland contended that the
word "mystery" in the New Testament is never applied to a
doctrine which is inconceivable or which cannot be understood by the ordinary faculties of man. On the contrary,
he asserted, when once revealed by the deity a mystery,
by the very fact of its revelation, becomes the object of

---

[21]See above, p. [240], note 3.

human reason as inevitably as is any fact in nature. Thus Toland insists that if the doctrine of the Trinity or any other mystery is to receive assent it must be clearly comprehended and be subjected to the test of reason.[22] As we shall see, the crux of the difference between Swift and the deists is in a sense epistemological: the issue is the manner in which the mysteries may be "known" or received by the mind; or perhaps more accurately the issue is not merely a matter of *how* the mysteries become knowledge but also a question of *whether* they do.

What Swift does in effect is to deny that the deistic epistemology and criterion of truth have relevance in the sphere of religion. It seemed to him unwarranted to attempt an explanation of a mystery, by its very nature something incomprehensible and above reason. He falls back on the traditional distinction used in defending the mysteries: ". . . things may be above our reason, without being contrary to it." Granting that certain things may be above reason, the deist maintained that by virtue of being so these things cannot receive assent or be the objects of faith. How is it possible, the deist Anthony Collins asked, to assent to that which is above reason and not therefore presented to reason so that the agreement or disagreement of ideas may be perceived? The truth or falsity of a proposition cannot be determined when no ideas are presented to reason. He applied this logic to the doctrine of the Trinity, with the following prefatory remarks:

By things above Reason is sometimes understood things of which we have no Idea, and which yet may be the Objects of our Assent. Now tho, beyond dispute, a great many things exist of which we have no Idea; yet Ideas and Acts of the Mind being relative, there can be no Act of the Mind where there is no Idea, or no Object: and therefore tho there is a just ground from the narrowness of our Understanding to say things exist of which we have no Idea; yet there is no ground, in this sense, to apply the Distinction to Objects of the Understanding: for then a thing might be an Object of the Understanding, and not an Object at the same time.[23]

---

[22]*Christianity not Mysterious* (London, 1696), pp. 41–2, 111.

[23]*An Essay concerning the Use of Reason in Propositions* (London, 1707), p. 30.

Similarly John Toland insisted that "the conceiv'd Idea's of things are the only Subjects of Believing, Denying, Approving, and every other Act of the Understanding: Therefore all Matters reveal'd by God or Man, must be *equally intelligible and possible.*"[24] Thus the deist contended, in the words of Thomas Morgan, that "Revelation it self, [should] be brought down to our Understandings, and Capacities, so as to enable us to form some clear consistent Notions and Conceptions."[25] The deist was firm in maintaining that knowledge is prior to assent or faith—indeed, to enforce the point Toland declared that *"Faith* is *Knowledg"*[26]—and that the instrument for discovering the truth is the reason of man operating on clear ideas.

To Swift and his contemporaries who combated the deists, this excessive reliance on human reason was altogether unwarranted; and in their answers they frequently set out to define its limitations. Swift's antirationalism is well known from his other works, but perhaps we may glance at it briefly in "On the Trinity" as an example of how he applied it in defense of religion and the mysteries. Here it has a dual aspect. One aspect is the familiar indictment on psychological grounds: "the reason of every particular man is weak and wavering, perpetually swayed and turned by his interests, his passions, and his vices."[27] With reason under the sway of sub-rational impulses and inclinations, it cannot be accepted, Swift argues, as a trustworthy instrument of interpretation. But he obviously wished to avoid a wholly skeptical position: the "right rule of reason" and the "general reason of mankind" are dependable. Nor does he want to reject human reason completely: "It must be allowed," he declares, "that every man is bound to follow

---

[24]*Op. cit.,* p. 42.

[25]See *The Nature and Consequences of Enthusiasm Consider'd* (London, 1719), p. 19.

[26]*Op. cit.,* p. 145; but see p. 133, where Toland writes that "all Faith or Perswasion must necessarily consist of two Parts, *Knowledg* and *Assent."*

[27]*Works,* IV, 135.

the rules and directions of that measure of reason which God hath given him. . . ."[28] Yet the emphasis throughout the sermon is on the fact that man has only a "measure of reason," a narrow and circumscribed capacity; and herein is the second aspect of the antirationalism Swift sets up as a corrective to the extreme rationalism of the deists—a limited or partial skepticism which views man's reason as operating effectively only in a restricted sphere. The wisest man, Swift points out, is baffled by the "commonest actions of nature." His vaunted reason is at a loss to explain such mysteries in nature as growth in animals and plants or the operation of the loadstone. If human reason cannot fathom the mystery of "the smallest seed," who will say that it is adequate to comprehend divine mysteries?

Contemporary divines, eager to defend the mysteries of Christianity and to deny the possibility of that clear perception which deists held necessary, relied again and again in their arguments on this important analogy between natural and supernatural mysteries. The analogy was particularly favored in discourses on the Trinity. Take, for example, the sermon on the Trinity by Archbishop Tillotson in which he explains to his auditors, in typical phraseology, that they can hardly expect this great and mysterious doctrine to be comprehensible to their reason since their understanding cannot reach to lesser mysteries:

There are a great many things in nature which we cannot comprehend how they either are, or can be: as the continuity of matter, that is, how the parts of it do hang so fast together, that are many times very hard to be parted: and yet we are sure that it is so, because we see it every day. So likewise how the small seeds of things contain the whole form and nature of the things from which they proceed and into which by degrees they grow; and yet we plainly see this every year.[29]

In the same vein William Sherlock, Dean of St. Paul's, declared to his congregation that "Nature is as great a Mystery as Revelation, and it is no greater affront to our

---

[28]*Works*, IV, 130.

[29]*Works*, ed. Thomas Birch (London, 1820), III, 425–6.

Understandings, no more against Reason for God to reveal such things to us as our Reason cannot comprehend, than it is to make a whole World, which Reason cannot comprehend."[30] If, it was earnestly maintained, "there is not the meanest part of the Creation, not a Worm, not a Flie, not a very Mite, nor ev'n a spire of Grass, but what is an Overmatch for the Understanding of the greatest Philosopher in the World," who can justly cavil at the lack of comprehension of religious mysteries?[31] This insistence that "Our philosophy dwells in the surface of nature"—the phraseology is William Wollaston's[32]—will be recognized as a kind of skepticism, of a long and respectable lineage, widely current in Swift's day. John Locke gave it forceful philosophic expression in the *Essay concerning Human Understanding* (1690), where he contended that man can know only the nominal, not the real essences of things. Man is involved in darkness, Locke insisted, and he emphasized the narrow limits of the understanding, often in the terminology and with the illustrations repeatedly used in theological literature. Indeed, Swift's sermon echoes some of the passages in the *Essay*. "The clearest and most enlarged understandings of thinking men," Locke wrote, "find themselves puzzled and at a loss in every particle of matter."[33] And at another point:

Concerning the manner of operation in most parts of the works of nature; wherein, though we see the sensible effects, yet their causes are unknown, and we perceive not the ways and manner how they are produced. We see animals are generated, nourished and move; the loadstone draws iron; and the parts of a candle successively melting, turn into flame, and give us both light and heat. These and the like

---

[30]*Sermons Preach'd upon Several Occasions* (London, 1700), pp. 298–9.

[31]See *The Doctrine of the Blessed Trinity Stated and Defended. By Some London Ministers* (London, 1719), p. 17. For the deistic attack on this analogy see Toland, *op. cit.*, pp. 80–9, and Thomas Morgan, *op. cit.*, pp. 20–1.

[32]See *The Religion of Nature Delineated*, 7th ed. (London, 1750), p. 146.

[33]Bk. IV, ch. iii, sec. 22.

effects we see and know; but the causes that operate, and the manner they are produced in, we can only guess and probably conjecture.[34]

Here then is the conventional skepticism that Swift utilizes as one means of defending the credibility of the mysteries and as the basis of his protest against the rationalists. Thus it is that he asserts: "How little do those who quarrel with mysteries, know of the commonest actions of nature!"[35]

But, as we have observed, Swift was wary of falling into a thoroughgoing skepticism by rejecting human reason altogether. He saw the need of rescuing faith from the malign charge that it is opposed to reason. Faith, he insists, is "highly reasonable." It may be acquired "without giving up our senses or contradicting our reason." Two questions of importance are suggested by Swift's utterances. What part, however insignificant, does human reason play in the sphere of religion? What precisely is the nature of faith? The second of these questions receives a clear and positive answer. The first is answered only negatively and by implication. The whole tenor of the sermon emphasizes the part human reason does not play, in opposition to the extreme rationalists who "lay so much weight on their own reason in matters of religion, as to think everything impossible and absurd which they cannot conceive."[36] Though he does not explicitly make the point, Swift apparently would accept the current view—it is implicit in and a condition of his argument—that human reason has a significant function: to examine the credentials of revelation. Reason determines whether or not a particular doctrine or mystery is God's pronouncement. In the phraseology of Locke, "the proper object of faith" is a revelation from God, "but whether it be a divine revelation or no, reason must judge."[37] Or as another of Swift's contemporaries expressed it more elaborately:

[34]Bk. IV, ch. xvi, sec. 12.
[35]*Works*, IV, 133.
[36]*Works*, IV, 135.
[37]Bk. IV, ch. xviii, sec. 10.

. . . when a thing is proposed to me as from God, all that my Reason has to do in this Case is Seriously, Soberly, Diligently, Impartially, and (I add) *Humbly* to Examine whether it comes with the true *Credentials* of his Authority, and has him for its real Author or no. This is all that Reason has to do in this Matter, and when she has done this, she is to rise from the Seat of Judgement, and resign it to Faith, which either gives or refuses her Assent.[38]

In the final analysis then, Swift's defense of the mysteries rests upon the reasonableness of faith—the view, as it was sometimes expressed, that faith is itself a higher form of reason; and this sermon belongs to the extensive literature of the period in which attempts are made to distinguish carefully the respective provinces and validity of faith and reason. The crux of Swift's position is evident in his definition of faith: "a virtue by which anything commanded us by God to believe appears evident and certain to us, although we do not see, nor can conceive it."[39] Applying this definition to the Trinity, Swift declares that we must accept the doctrine as "in itself incapable of any controversy: since God himself hath pronounced the fact, but wholly concealed the manner."[40] This conception of faith is what Swift's contemporaries—he himself does not use the term in "On the Trinity"—called implicit faith, that is, assent to a doctrine on authority, even though the doctrine is not fully comprehended. In the instance of revealed religion a doctrine or mystery deserves acceptance, no matter how incomprehensible, if it has divine authority. Explicit faith, the opposite of implicit, involved assent only when reason clearly perceived the nature of the doctrine or mystery.[41]

---

[38]John Norris, *An Account of Reason and Faith* (London, 1697), pp. 292–3.

[39]*Works*, IV, 133.

[40]*Works*, IV, 136.

[41]The distinction between implicit and explicit belief as given by Edward Synge, Archbishop of Tuam, may be taken as typical: "To *know*, is to give Assent to a Proposition, when it evidently appears to be built upon Reason. But when the Truth of a Proposition is assented to, not upon Arguments drawn from the Reason, or the Nature of the thing, but upon Account of the Veracity and Authority

This important distinction measures the difference between the deists and the divines who combated them. It was at the very basis of the orthodox answer to the rationalists, and was expounded frequently in sermons and tracts to explain how man, though endowed with reason, must nevertheless accept the unintelligible. The argument in its typical form, and as it underlies Swift's defense of the mysteries, began with the assumption that a revelation from God must be believed (even the deists did not deny that it is the highest reason to believe an infallible God). Assent to a particular revealed doctrine is not grounded necessarily upon any internal reason or evidence—that is, upon clear perception as the criterion of truth, as the deists insisted—but rather upon authority. Assent upon reason or knowledge, admittedly one ground of assent, is subject to error and uncertainty because of the nature and limitations of man's reason; but assent upon the authority of God —implicit faith—is firm and certain. The argument involved a distinction between the object of faith, that is, the doctrine or mystery believed, and the reason or motive for believing it, referred to as the formal reason of faith. Faith, it was contended, is not necessarily concerned with the meaning of a proposition or doctrine, that is, with its intelligibility (the object of faith may or may not be clearly perceived), but with the truth of that proposition or doctrine, that is, with the ground for believing it. As George Stanhope, chaplain to William and Mary and later Dean of Canterbury, declared in the Boyle Lectures of 1701–2: ". . . the particular Thing Reason is to regard in Matters of Faith, is the Evidence upon which we are

---

of the Person or Persons who affirm it; such a Proposition as that is said to be *believed*. Farthermore, if a Man understands not the Meaning of a Proposition, and yet believes that it contains a Truth in it, because of the deference he pays to the Person who speaks it; this I call an *Implicit Belief:* And, properly speaking, the Object of such a Belief is not the Truth of the Proposition it self, but only the Veracity of the Speaker. But where a Man understands the Meaning of the Proposition, which he believes, this I call an *Explicit Belief"* (*A Gentleman's Religion* [1698], in *Works*, London, 1744, II, 283–4).

moved to receive them, which is the Evidence of Testimony.
And consequently it is not the Condition of the Thing
revealed, but the Certainty of the Revelation, that makes the
proper Subject of our Enquiry."[42] Discussing the same
problem in a later series of the Boyle Lectures, Brampton
Gurdon answers the question: " . . . why may not Authority, affirming the Truth of a Proposition, be a sufficient
Evidence to warrant our Assent?"

'Tis true, Authority, as *such*, does not help us to understand the
Proposition better than we did before; and yet the Opinion we have
of the Skill and Veracity of the Person who tells us the Proposition
is true, may be to us, a probable Evidence of its Truth, and a rational
Ground of Persuasion. And therefore a clear Understanding of a
Truth, cannot be previously necessary to every Assent of the Mind of
Man.[43]

Thus these divines could argue that one assented to the
mysteries, not because he perceived them clearly but because
he had the authority of God for them: the proper object of
faith is not "the Truth of the Proposition it self, but only
the Veracity of the Speaker." In Swift's own words in this
sermon: "God commandeth us, by our dependence upon His
truth, and His Holy Word, to believe a fact that we do not
understand. And, this is no more than what we do every
day in the works of nature, upon the credit of men of
learning."[44] Swift finds it wholly reasonable that "God
should require us to believe mysteries, while the reason or
manner of what we are to believe is above our comprehension, and wholly concealed from us."[45] He obviously
agrees with his contemporaries in holding that faith may
be "inevident and obscure" so far as the doctrine is concerned if the ground for believing is clear and acceptable.
There was no tendency to minimize the rationality of this

---

[42]See the abbreviated version as printed in *A Defence of Natural
and Revealed Religion*, ed. Gilbert Burnet (London, 1737), II, 10.

[43]*Ibid.*, III, 393.

[44]*Works*, IV, 137.

[45]*Works*, IV, 132.

"dark" faith. As John Norris expressed it in his elaborate
analysis of reason and faith: this implicit faith "resolves
at last into a Ground highly Rational, and so may be said
in that respect to be the highest Reason. For certainly
nothing can be more Reasonable than to believe whatever
God (who is infallible) reveals."[46] It is this implicit faith
which Swift says "we may acquire without giving up our
senses, or contradicting our reason."[47] The deists, as we
have seen, demanded "the same perspicuity from God as
from Man."[48] In other words, they believed explicit faith
valid and implicit faith invalid. "To be confident of any
thing without conceiving it," wrote John Toland, "is no real
Faith or Perswasion, but a rash Presumption and an ob-
stinate Prejudice."[49] He held firmly to his main position,
that *"REASON* is the only Foundation of all Certitude; and
that nothing reveal'd, whether as to its *Manner* or *Existence,* is more exempted from its Disquisitions, than the
ordinary Phenomena of Nature."[50]

One of Swift's contemporaries pictured himself as exposing the fashionable heresies of the times—as being engaged
"in Vindication of the Christian religion against the *Deist;*
and of the Divinity of Christ against the *Arian* and the
Socinian."[51] I suggest that Swift's "On the Trinity" is most
profitably read and understood in the light of contemporary
reactions to these fashionable heresies. It presents a clue
to the possible lines of his arguments had he attempted
something formidable in the field of Christian apologetics.
They are arguments which would have sounded familiar to
any literate person of the day. Swift characteristically has
been content to take the familiar and give it vigorous and

---

[46]*Op. cit.,* p. 94.

[47]*Works,* IV, 137.

[48]Anthony Collins, *op. cit.,* p. 12 ff.

[49]*Op. cit.,* p. 132.

[50]*Ibid.,* p. 6.

[51]Richard Blackmore, *Just Prejudices against the Arian Hypothesis*
(London, 1721), p. 11.

effective statement. He has himself supplied us with a single principle which serves as an excellent comment on the nature of his orthodoxy in this sermon, in his statement to Dr. Delany that "the grand points of Christianity ought to be taken as infallible revelations."[52] Indeed, that statement may well serve as a key to much of his religious thinking.

---

[52]*The Correspondence of Jonathan Swift, D.D.*, ed. F. Elrington Ball (London, 1910–14), IV, 289.

SWIFT'S DEANERY INCOME

SWIFT's tendency to present a situation in its darker aspects, however well it served as a literary manner, is likely to be misleading if taken seriously with respect to his personal affairs. His correspondence offers certain instances in point, none more striking than the persistent gloom with which he represents, in the last decade of his active career, the state of his finances. When writing to various friends, or even to acquaintances where reserve on such a topic is normally expected, he bemoaned his lowered income and—bad prophet that he was— his impending poverty. Typical is the lament in May 1729, to one of his correspondents, that like all men in Ireland dependent on tithes and rents he is on 'the high road to ruin'. 'I do expect,' he adds, 'and am determined in a short time to pawn my little plate, or sell it for subsistence.'[1] Three years later he wrote to Gay in a similar doleful strain, again announcing that he is on the verge of ruin: '. . . all my revenues which depend on tithes are sunk almost to nothing, and my whole personal fortune is in the utmost confusion. . . .'[2] Charles Ford, Arbuthnot, Barber, Pulteney, Lord Oxford, and Pope heard the same tale.[3] It was Pope particularly who after Gay's death received the burden of these woes: 'I know not any man,' Swift wrote to him in 1733, 'in a greater likelihood than myself to die poor and friendless.'[4] When Pope showed this plaint to the Duchess of Queensberry, that pleasant, forthright lady wrote to Swift: 'I differ with you extremely that you are in any likelihood of dying poor or friendless.'[5]

As we well know, Swift did not die poor; and he undoubtedly realized after his appointment to the deanery that he was to

---

[1] To Knightley Chetwode. See *The Correspondence of Jonathan Swift, D.D.*, edited by F. Elrington Ball (London, 1910–14), iv. 81. Cited subsequently as *Corres.*

[2] Ibid. iv. 351.

[3] *The Letters of Jonathan Swift to Charles Ford*, edited David Nichol Smith (Oxford, 1935), pp. 142, 163; *Corres.* iv. 150, 219, 316, 351; v. 107, 223.

[4] Ibid., p. 380.

[5] Ibid., p. 399.

possess a life-long comfortable income.[1] It is true that he had financial difficulties of a certain kind, but there was only one serious threat to his fortune. This occurred in 1725 when John Pratt, Deputy Vice-Treasurer of Ireland, who had £1,200 belonging to Swift in his possession, was imprisoned for defalcations amounting to over £70,000. Fortunately Pratt proved a man of honour, and Swift 'miraculously escaped being perfectly worth nothing'.[2] What touched Swift more were the vexatious delays in rents and interests, and particularly the reduced return from tithes. Doubtless these occasioned momentary pinches and account for his troubled words—for example, the reiterated statement between 1733 and 1735 that his income had been reduced by £300.[3] Yet his prophecies of ruin are belied by the steady accumulation of that sizeable fortune remaining at his death to endow his hospital. The fact is, that with respect to his income, as elsewhere, Swift writes more darkly than the situation warrants, indulging himself—surely half seriously—in remarkably obvious distortion of the realities. It is probable that he did not expect to be taken literally. Nor is it likely that his friends were perturbed: report had it that the deanery made a good return. Nevertheless it is not possible to speak with any finality concerning Swift's financial affairs: they have never received careful investigation, not even the easily available documents, such as the account books. Though doubtless many revealing documents are lost beyond recovery, I have recently found a manuscript which sheds light on the exact return from the deanery. This document, which has escaped the notice of modern scholars, offers further testimony that Swift's income was ample. It is an undated and unsigned manuscript among the records in St. Patrick's Cathedral, Dublin, inscribed 'Of Dr Swift's Effects'; and it sets forth item by item the sources—rents, tithes, and fees—from which Swift's

---

[1] Shortly after his appointment he writes to Stella of the heavy initial expenses for the deanery house, the First Fruits, and the Patent, amounting to £1,000 (cf. *Journal to Stella*, 23 April 1713), but a year later, in a letter written to Archdeacon Walls, filled with calculations, he is obviously feeling secure financially. See *Corres.* ii. 147.

[2] Swift wrote to Ford that Pratt 'owed me all and something more than all I had in the World'. He was proud of the resignation he displayed in the face of this great loss: 'I despaired of every Penny, and yet I have legall Witness that I was a great Philosopher in that Matter.' See *Letters of Swift to Ford*, ed. David Nichol Smith, pp. 121, 125; *Corres.* iii. 241, 251, 252.

[3] Ibid. v. 107, 163, 223.

annual deanery income was derived, with the amount each returned.[1] After careful comparison of the hand with that of the Reverend John Lyon, the Prebendary of St. Patrick's to whose care Swift was committed in 1742, I am convinced that the document was compiled by Lyon; and I surmise from the evidence immediately following that it was prepared in 1742 for the Commission of Lunacy which found Swift to be 'a person of unsound mind and memory'.

The writ under which the Commission acted, dated 12 August, directed an inquiry not only into Swift's sanity but also. if he were found insane, into his income and possessions: '... what lands and tenements, goods and chattels, the said Doctor Jonathan Swift was possessed of at the time he became of unsound mind and memory, or at any time since, and what is the yearly value thereof. ...'[2] The report of the Commission a few days later showed that Swift possessed as of 20 May 1742, and did still possess, 'lands, tithes, and tenements of the clear yearly value of eight hundred pounds sterling' as well as goods and chattels estimated at ten thousand pounds sterling.[3] The manuscript under discussion has the heading, 'The Yearly Value of Lands, Tithes, Ground Rents & Fees belonging to the Dean of St Patrick's Dublin', and the figures totalled at the end amount to £807, which corresponds to the 'clear yearly value of eight hundred pounds sterling' mentioned in the report of the Commission of Lunacy. That the Reverend John Lyon should be asked to compile the document for the Commission was fitting in view of his position at this time as Swift's almoner and of the important additional fact that he had perhaps a better knowledge of the chapter records than any other member of the Cathedral. It was natural therefore that he should be chosen to draw up an account of deanery income, just as he was the obvious person to be entrusted with the care of Swift once the affirmation of lunacy had been made, and later to act as secretary to Swift's trustees. There is further evidence that Lyon was given the task of compiling a list of Swift's effects at this juncture: there exists a catalogue of Swift's books in his hand drawn up apparently as a result of the proceedings of the

[1] For permission to use this manuscript I am greatly indebted to the present Dean of St. Patrick's, the Right Reverend David F. R. Wilson, a staunch admirer of his predecessor. I am also greatly obliged to the Dean's Vicar, the Reverend J. W. Armstrong, who patiently dug through masses of manuscripts for my benefit.

[2] *Corres.* vi. 183.   [3] Ibid. 184–5.

Commission—so Mr. Harold Williams, who discovered the document, thinks.[1]

In attempting to discover the circumstances which gave rise to a document concerning income and possessions, one must at least examine the hypothesis that this newly discovered manuscript dates from Swift's death—that it was prepared for his executors who would, of course, need the information it sets forth. The tone of the document at certain points, with the reference to Swift in the past tense and to his executors, at first glance faintly suggests that it was prepared at the time of his death. This tone, however, is just as appropriate for one who was already known to have lost his faculties and who, though physically alive, was dead in the eyes of the law, as Swift was according to the report of the Commission. The allusion to Swift's executors will not be puzzling when it is recollected that his will was made and witnessed long before 1742 and was easily available to Lyon and the Commission. But the evidence is final at least on this one point, that Swift was alive when the document was drawn up: the reference (see the eleventh item below) to the 'present Bishop of Clogher', to 'the present Dean', and their financial settlement concerning the deanery house which both occupied permits no other interpretation. The Bishop of Clogher can be no other than John Stearne, Swift's predecessor at St. Patrick's and afterwards Bishop of Clogher from 1717 to 1745. Since he predeceased Swift by a few months in 1745, the mention of him gives us one terminal date and proof that Swift was still alive. The latest date mentioned in the manuscript is 25 March 1741, which thus establishes that it was written between 1741 and 1745.

If, then, we take into account the circumstances, the nature of the document, and the various pieces of evidence—that the Commission of Lunacy was directed to make a valuation of Swift's income, that its report of the annual return of his 'lands, tithes, and tenements' tallies with the sum given in the manuscript under discussion, that the hand is that of John Lyon, an obvious choice to serve the Commission, that Swift was alive

---

[1] *Dean Swift's Library* (Cambridge, 1932), pp. 10, 13. From this same period is extant an inventory of Swift's personal property. From a photostat of the original in Swift's Hospital I find that though most of the items listed are in an unknown hand some are in the hand of Dr. Lyon, a further indication that he was making an accounting of Swift's possessions at this time. This inventory has been reprinted by T. P. Le Fanu in *Proceedings of the Royal Irish Academy*, xxxvii, sec. c (1927), 263–75.

when the document was compiled—we may reasonably assume that the manuscript was prepared by John Lyon in 1742 for the Commission of Lunacy. It appears to be, however, not an official return so much as a rough or preliminary draft, as is indicated by words crossed through and interlinear corrections. In what follows I propose to quote each item in the document in its order, and to make notations where these may be relevant. As already stated, the document is headed 'The Yearly Value of Lands, Tithes, Ground Rents & Fees belonging to the Dean of St Patrick's Dublin'.

The first item is concerned with deanery possessions in County Kildare:

> The Lands & Tithes of ye Manor of Kilberry & Cloney near Athy in ye Co: of Kildare yield now p[er] Ann: £200—N: The Lease was renewed from March 25: 1741 to J: Stopford Esq And 400£ paid as a Fine. Mr Stopford owns these Lands to be worth to him 500£ p[er] Ann: The Vicarage is Non-Cure of 60£ p[er] Ann: is in ye Dean's Gift. The Dean appoints his Seneschal in this Manor.

Swift paid a visit to County Kildare in January 1714–15 to make a personal appraisal of the worth of these deanery lands. In a letter written soon after he lists his holdings in this region, including, to use his phrase, such 'cursed Irish names' as Tullygorey, Shanraheen, and Clonwannir; and he calculates that the entire holdings at full rent are worth £475 per annum.[1] Since he was receiving only £120 yearly, he proposed to revise his leases upward; indeed, he had written from London six months earlier to his agent that no land rents from deanery holdings should be accepted pending a review of leases.[2] The Cathedral records show four leases of these lands in the period of Swift's deanship, with increasing rentals from an annual return of £150 in a lease of 1716 to the £200 mentioned in this manuscript.[3] His well-known insistence upon an increased rental at each renewal is exemplified in his dealings with Stopford; and Stopford's significant admission that the lease was worth £500 annually to him, whereas Swift was returned only £200, is evidence in support of what Swift and other Irish

---

[1] *Corres.* ii. 266.   [2] Ibid., p. 148.

[3] See the register of leases in St. Patrick's Cathedral, Dublin. My information is taken from the section headed 'The Dean's Property'. For the lease to J. Stopford listed in the first entry, see the 'Chapter Minute Book of St. Patrick's Cathedral, Dublin, 1720–1763', f. 116 v. The lease was confirmed by the Chapter at a meeting on 15 May 1741.

clergymen constantly maintained, that a churchman is fortunate to receive half the value of his lands.

The second item concerns deanery lands in County Dublin:

The Lands of Dean Rath, Priest Town, Ballibane & Angerstown
containing 357 Acres near Clondolkan yield p[er] Ann. £90. This
Lease was renewed from 25: Dec[r] 1740 And £   was paid by way
of Fine. N:B: M[r] Pearson the Tenant pays 20[s] p[er] Acre for these
Lands.

Swift's predecessor, Stearne, had leased these County Dublin
holdings in 1709 for an annual rental of £54. Swift appears to
have induced the lessee to surrender this lease in 1720 for one
returning a rental of £70 annually. In addition he reserved to
himself during the last eleven years of the term of the lease
thirty acres of Priest Town and 'all the Tythes for some time'.
The lease on these lands was re-negotiated or renewed at least
twice before Swift's death, and by 1740 he had almost doubled
the yearly sum returned when he first became dean.[1]

The third item is concerned with tithes:

The Rectorial Tythes of Tallaght, Esker, Clondolkan, Tassagard
& Rathcool, which y[e] Dean in his own Accompts rates at 420£
p[er] An: com[m]unibus Annis deducting all charges We reckon
only at £400. Mem: A Piece of Land near Tallagh Ch: belonging
to y[e] Dean called y[e] Dean's Croft is now inclosed with y[e] Gardens as
I am informed of his Grace of Dublin.

The places mentioned are in County Dublin, and the tithes
due from them account for approximately one-half of the total
deanery income. It was here that Swift's revenues were most
vulnerable: as he wrote to Pope, '. . . although tithes be of
divine institution, they are of diabolical execution', and he
regularly registers complaints about the difficulties of collection.[2] The whole matter of tithes was extremely complicated
by, among other things, conflicting claims and divided owner-
ship. For example, in three of the above-mentioned parishes
Swift had claims to only portions of the tithes. In Tallaght all
tithes were in the hands of lay impropriators except the great
tithes, which were appropriate to the deanery of St. Patrick's;
from Rathcool also Swift received only the great tithes, from

---

[1] See 'The Dean's Property' in the register of leases in St. Patrick's Cathedral;
see also the 'Chapter Minute Book, 1720–1763', f. 100 v.

[2] *Corres.* iv. 127; cf. also iv. 81, 150, 219, 316, 351; v. 107.

Tassagard two-thirds of all tithes.[1] Tassagard and Rathcool are of some interest for the early relationship between Swift as dean, and his Archbishop, William King. A month after his installation, these two parishes being vacant, Swift appealed to King 'as a personal favour' to give the benefices to his curate at Laracor, Thomas Warburton—an appeal as little successful with the Archbishop as the one Swift had made a few weeks earlier in behalf of Thomas Parnell.[2]

The fourth item:

The Tenements East & West of ye Deanery are in Lease viz: Worrall from 25 Mar: 1732 for 40 Years at 5£ p[er] Ann. Mr J^n Connly for his Holding East of ye Deanry pays £9 p[er] Ann. Whose Lease was renewed from 25 Mar: 1732 for 39 Years.

The first-named lessee, John Worrall, held a portion of deanery property located in St. Kevin Street and Deanery Lane.[3] He was a member of the Cathedral chapter; in fact he had a longer connexion with St. Patrick's than Swift, having begun as a minor canon in 1690 and then serving as Dean's Vicar from 1695 to well beyond Swift's death.[4] His relations with Swift were the subject of some controversy among the early biographers, but there can be no doubt that for a long period Swift's feeling toward him was friendly and companionable and that he was trusted with Swift's personal affairs as well as with Cathedral business.[5] That portion of the item concerning Connly is crossed through; nevertheless the annual return of £9 is figured in the total at the end of the manuscript, and rightly so as indicated by a clause in Swift's will leaving the profits from Connly's lease to Anne Ridgeway, deanery house-keeper in Swift's last years. The holding consisted, we learn from the will, of two houses.

The fifth item:

Mr Goodman for his Holding West of ye Deanry pays £10 p[er] Ann: Whose Lease was renewed from— .

[1] See a parochial return—an uncatalogued manuscript—in the Register of the Diocese of Dublin, dating from 1725. Tassagard (or Saggart) meant more than tithes to Swift: Vanessa had a bower there.   [2] *Corres.* ii. 56; 23–4.

[3] See the 'Chapter Minute Book, 1720–1763', f. 68 r., for 28 Nov. 1732, and 'The Dean's Property' in the manuscript book of leases.

[4] Hugh Jackson Lawlor, *The Fasti of St. Patrick's Cathedral, Dublin* (Dundalk, 1930), pp. 203, 216.

[5] See *Corres.* iii. 263 *et passim.* It was to Worrall that Swift gave credit for saving the money in Pratt's hands in 1725. See *Corres.* ii. 251–2.

This property is described in Swift's will as 'two houses or more lately built'. The lease, which was for a term of forty years, he bequeathed to his cousin Mrs. Whiteway. I have not been able to supply from existing documents the date of the renewal left blank in the manuscript.

The sixth item:

The Residentiary House yields £5 which is paid by ye Proctor of ye Oeconomy—who also pays ye Dean's Duties reserved in all chapter Leases worth £10 p[er] Ann:

This item is of more than ordinary interest. It involves the two-way transaction which brought Swift the land for his famous garden, Naboth's Vineyard. The Residentiary House, deanery property located in Deanery Lane, was so named because it served as a place of residence for visiting canons when they came to serve their turns in the Cathedral. It was leased with clauses calling for a certain number of rooms to be kept free for this purpose.[1] In 1721 Swift agreed to renew a lease of the Residentiary House to the chapter of St. Patrick's for the sum of £5 annually; in return the chapter granted to Swift and his successors a lease on two acres of land belonging to the economy of the Cathedral, to run for a term of forty years provided that the lease of the Residentiary House should continue in force.[2] The two acres thus secured Swift turned into Naboth's Vineyard, the garden which he prized so highly and which served as a place to stable his horses and entertain his friends.

The seventh item:

The Dean's fees by renewing Leases, Burials & other Contingencies worth £10 p[er] Ann.

The eighth item:

There is also a small Tenement somewhat ruinous now in Deanery Lane or Mitre Ally worth £3 p[er] Ann.

The ninth item:

The Dean's House Garden & Excellent offices all in very good Condition we value but low at £70.

---

[1] See the lease in the records at St. Patrick's Cathedral, Dublin, between John Rous, Verger, and John Stearne, Dean, 1711.

[2] See the 'Chapter Minute Book, 1720–1763', f. 18 r.; cf. also f. 57 r., 17 April 1730, when the chapter sublet the Residentiary House to its sexton for £12 per annum.

This item refers to the annual rental—the estimated valuation of the deanery house as a place of residence—and is considered part of the revenue of the dignity, though no actual monetary return as such is involved.

The tenth item:

There was £20 p[er] Ann: paid to yᵉ Dean out of yᵉ Oeconomy by way of Repairs, because he laid out above £200 in improving yᵉ Deanry-House, no part [of] wᶜʰ if I mistake not, he has charged to his Successors.

I have found no record of any single undertaking by Swift involving repairs to the Deanery for the amount mentioned. It is possible that the chapter granted him this annual sum to compensate for cumulative repairs, such as those entered in his accounts for 1718.[1] This annual grant of the chapter to Swift is not totalled with the other figures at the end of the manuscript.

The eleventh item:

'However there is yᵉ Sum of £300 to be paid to yᵉ Dean's Executors being yᵉ Third of what the present Bp of Clogher Expended in building yᵉ Deanry—The present Dean having paid his L[ordshi]p £600.'

This is a reference to the deanery house built by Swift's predecessor John Stearne when Swift was only a prebendary of St. Patrick's. The construction, which Swift watched with great interest, was begun in 1707 and ranged over four years. It was in December 1711 that Swift, then in London, wrote to Stearne: 'I reckon your hands are now out of mortar, and that your garden is finished.'[2] Within two years Stearne was translated to the bishopric of Dromore (later to Clogher) to make way for Swift as Dean of St. Patrick's. When Swift took possession of the deanery house he became Stearne's debtor. According to this item in the manuscript he paid Stearne £600 and Swift's executors were to receive £300, stated to be a third of Stearne's expenditure.[3] This arrangement was not the result

[1] See 'Personal Expenses and Income of Jonathan Swift, 1717–1718', Forster Collection, MS. 510. 48. D. 34/6, Victoria and Albert Museum.

[2] *Corres.* i. 311; for other references see pp. 82, 85, 91, 124, 181, 311.

[3] In the *Journal to Stella*, under entry of 23 April 1713, Swift writes to Stella that he had expected to pay £600 for the deanery house but had been informed by St. George Ashe that the sum would be £800. This manuscript confirms that Swift's original expectation was right. See also *Corres.* ii. 124, 147.

of free bargaining between Stearne and Swift but was necessitated by an Irish statute passed in the reign of William III
(10 Wm. III, c. 6) to encourage the building of houses and
other improvements upon church lands. It provided that any
clergyman who built a residence should receive two-thirds of
the expenditure from his immediate successor and that this
successor (or his heirs) in turn should receive one-third of the
original expenditure from the next successor.[1] Thus of the £900
spent by Stearne to construct the deanery house Swift paid him
£600, the two-thirds demanded by statute, and Swift (in this
case his executors) could expect £300, the one-third of the
original disbursement as demanded by the statute. This sum
of £300 is not figured in the final total in this manuscript,
properly so because it was to accrue at some future date whereas
this compilation is concerned with the *annual* return from
deanery possessions.

The twelfth item concerns Naboth's Vineyard:

> The Dean took about 2 Acres of Land adjoyning yᵉ South side of
> yᵉ Cabbage Garden which he called Naboth's Vineyard from yᵉ
> Chapter subject to £3 p[er] An: besides 5ˢ Dean's Duties & 3ˢ
> Proctors fees. Which Ground (except a Garden being part thereof
> leased to one White at 5£ p[er] Ann:) was enclosed by a good
> Stone Wall yᵉ South side of which is lined with Brick & plantd with
> yᵉ best Fruit trees, & is separated from yᵉ remainder laid out for
> pasture by a quick Set Hedge—To which yᵉ Servants have access
> by a Gate at yᵉ West end. This Naboth's Vineyard with White's
> Garden, the Dean has bequeathed to his Successor[s], provided they
> pay £300 to his Executors towards building his Hospital—otherwise
> yᵉ Interest of it is to be sold to yᵉ Highest Bidder.

Naboth's Vineyard, we learn from this item, was leased to
Swift for a rental of £3 per annum, probably a fair rental in
its unimproved state. After Swift had built the 'cursed wall'
which cost him over £600, planted the fruit-trees, the quickset
hedge, and made other improvements, its value was so en-
hanced that his trustees could lease it in 1743 for four times that
sum.[2] Naboth's Vineyard is the subject of a clause in Swift's
will in which he expresses the earnest hope that his successors

---

[1] *The Statutes at Large passed in the Parliaments held in Ireland from . . . 1310 to . . . 1786*
(Dublin, 1786), iii. 473 ff.

[2] See the lease between Arthur Lamprey and Swift's trustees, dated 25 Dec.
1743, in the records of St. Patrick's Cathedral, Dublin.

will preserve it—'to be always in the hands of succeeding Deans during their office'. Thus, though he empowers his executors to sell the remainder of the lease to the highest bidder, he directs them to give his successor in the deanery the first refusal. This item in the manuscript concerning Naboth's Vineyard, like the preceding item, has strictly speaking no place in a list touching on annual income; and it presents no figure to be totalled with those from rents, tithes, and fees. Its inclusion is puzzling, unless the intention was to supply information concerning Swift's 'goods and chattels' which the Commission of Lunacy was also directed to evaluate.

The manuscript concludes with a column of figures, the total of which constitutes Swift's deanery income from the various sources—lands, tithes, ground rents, and fees. The total set down is £807; but one annual return, of £5, was apparently omitted inadvertently, and with this added we find that Swift's annual revenue from the deanery was £812. Thus St. Patrick's was not the most valuable deanery in Ireland in point of income (those of Derry, Raphoe, and possibly Down returned more); nevertheless it was a satisfactory one—and in point of prestige a surpassing one. Swift could have held no other with the same satisfaction. A qualification must be made concerning Swift's income from the deanery: it was reduced, as he complained, by arrears and defaults. To what extent, it is difficult to determine. That there were such we know from the scattered accounts available, but I am inclined to believe that Swift suffered less in this respect than most clergymen in similar positions; in any case, less than his constant complaints would indicate. He was too much a master of the art of persuasion and of applying pressure to forgo his rights. It would have brought some satisfaction to Swift's enemies to learn that his deanery income was not so high as they believed. They reported it to be £1,000—far too much for a divine hardly suspected of being a Christian, who nevertheless barely missed being a bishop:

> A Place he got, yclyp'd a *Stall*,
> And eke a Thousand Pounds withal,
> And, were he a less *witty Writer*,
> He might, as well, have got *a Mitre*.[1]

[1] [Jonathan Smedley,] *Gulliveriana; or, a Fourth Volume of Miscellanies* (London, 1728), p. 109.

'What Pretence', asked the anonymous author of an attack on *Gulliver's Travels*, 'has he more than any other Man, to a Thousand a Year for doing nothing, or little more than strutting behind a Verger, and Lording it over men honester, and more deserving than himself...?'[1] Although the deanery income was substantial in itself, it was of course not the whole of Swift's annual income. Since the manuscript under discussion is concerned with deanery possessions, it does not include Swift's income from the three parishes he held along with the deanery —Laracor, Rathbeggan, and Agher. Swift, one must remember, was a pluralist. Doubtless the tithes from these additional benefices decreased from the pleasing figure of £200 for which they were set in 1708 and 1714;[2] still the decrease came at a time when it could not seriously affect Swift's standard of living. Finally it should be observed that when Swift was most vocal and uneasy about his financial affairs he was accumulating that substantial sum which by 1736 amounted to £7,500. This money drew interest at rates ranging from 5 to 6 per cent.[3] As a matter of fact, ready money he found rather troublesome—so he indicated in an Advertisement in 1738 announcing that he 'is now able to lend two thousand pounds at five per cent upon good security'. His complaint is that since he cannot purchase a good estate for endowing his hospital, he is forced to keep his fortune in mortgages on lands and the like securities.[4]

On the whole, then, Swift deserves no great sympathy when he cries out his financial woes. The clue to his attitude is not so much in the actual state of his finances as in his temperament. It may be the truth, as he wrote to the Earl of Oxford in 1735, that his revenue had decreased by £300; but he adds a more significant truth with characteristic understatement: '. . . with good management I still make a shift to keep up, and am not poor, nor even moneyless'.[5]

[1] *A Letter from a Clergyman to his Friend, with an Account of Capt. Lemuel Gulliver* (London, 1726), p. 20. For another report that the deanery was worth £1,000 annually see E. Curll's *Dean Swift's Literary Correspondence, for twenty-four years; from 1714 to 1738* (London, 1741), p. 16.

[2] See Forster Collection, MS. 505. 48. D. 34/1, 'Private Expenses of Jonathan Swift, 1708–1709'. See also *Corres.* ii. 147. Swift's accounts for 1717 and 1736 show decreases, but apparently they do not give full information.

[3] *Corres.* vi. 87 n. But entries in his accounts for 11 April 1737 show arrears in interest. See Forster Collection, MS. 512. 48. D. 34/8.

[4] *Corres.* vi. 86–7.

[5] Ibid. v. 223.

JONATHAN SWIFT

IT IS RARE INDEED that a commentator appraises any work of Jonathan Swift without reference to biographical fact. If one of Swift's minor efforts is under discussion, as the poem "The Lady's Dressing Room," we may expect the critical judgment to rest upon some such basis as that presented by Sir Walter Scott, who wished the poem to be interpreted in the light of the author's peculiar habits and state of mind. If Part III of *Gulliver's Travels,* where Swift attacks the corruptions of learning, is the object of consideration, the commentator is certain to make an excursion back to Swift's student days at Trinity College, Dublin, to explain that here began his life-long hatred of science and philosophy. And so with the other works, to the point that the criticism of Swift is a sustained endeavor to interpret the writings in the light of the man, although anyone who reads the critics of Swift will be aware too of a simultaneous and converse process—attempts to interpret the man in the light of the works.

With respect to Swift we are often confronted not

only with the critical significance of biographical evidence but as well with the biographical significance of critical evidence. It is easy to find commentators who will have it both ways, commentators, for example, who assume a morbid state of mind in Swift as an explanation of his scatalogical verse, then use the scatalogical verse to prove that the author undoubtedly was morbid. Traditionally the criticism of Swift's works is so inextricably mingled with biography that one looks almost in vain for critical judgments based upon merely aesthetic assumptions.

The persistent tendency of the commentators has been to assume a direct and fairly simple reflection in the works of the nature and personality of Swift; and such a work as *Gulliver's Travels* has as often as not been viewed as both a strange and puzzling psychological case history and a representation of its author's objective experiences. No one can doubt for a moment the validity and the fruitfulness of the biographical approach to *Gulliver's Travels* in particular or to Swift's works in general. Considering the character of his writings—their personal, intimate, and topical nature—this approach is the natural one. Yet I think that the interpretation of Swift has at times suffered somewhat from this tendency, this unwillingness of the commentator to detach the work from the man. But the overemphasis upon this approach is rather less disturbing than its misapplication or its loose and incautious use. Commentators who would doubtless feel some hesitation in equating Fielding with Tom Jones or Sterne with Tristram Shandy can accept with ap-

parent ease as a premise of their criticism that Swift is
Gulliver. In what follows I wish, first of all, to comment on certain recurring biographical considerations
which have played a part—a not very happy part—in
the criticism of Swift's works for a period of two centuries, and, secondly, to present some instances in
which other biographical considerations of value for
criticism have not been explored sufficiently.

The problem which has most preoccupied Swift's
critics has been the pessimism and misanthropy of
Gulliver's Travels and the endeavor to explain these
qualities in the work by searching for exactly corresponding qualities in Swift himself. Part IV of *Gulliver's Travels,* with its contrasting picture of Yahoo
and Houyhnhnm, has been the focal point of the discussions, and ordinarily the commentators have acted
on the assumption, though not always consciously,
that here in Part IV is the real key to Swift. It is maintained or implied that in Part IV are the possibilities of
a final comprehension and the basis of a final judgment. The image of Swift—the rather horrendous
image—which has been transmitted from generation
to generation is chiefly the image deduced from Part
IV, enforced by a careful selection of biographical
fact or myth appropriately chosen to stress the severe
lineaments of his character. Only occasionally is the
image, a monochrome, softened by reference to the
playful Swift, to Swift the author of delightful light
verse, the punster, the genial companion of Queen
Anne's Lord Treasurer and her Secretary of State, or to
the Swift who was a charming guest at great houses and

who had a genius for friendship among both sexes.

Perhaps for purposes of discussion we may ignore the volume and range of Swift's works and grant the unwarranted assumption that the masterpiece is somehow the man, and that a particular portion of the masterpiece—Part IV of *Gulliver*—is of such fundamental significance as to outweigh various other considerations. If we trace the progress of the criticism of *Gulliver's Travels* from Swift's earliest biographer, the Earl of Orrery, to the twentieth century, we find preponderantly and repetitiously a set of severe judgments passed on Part IV, judgments referable back to Swift the man. In his *Remarks on the Life and Writings of Dr. Jonathan Swift* (1752), Orrery climaxes his comment with the statement that "no man [was] better acquainted [than Swift] with human nature, both in the highest, and in the lowest scenes of life" (p. 338). Yet, contradictorily, in discussing Part IV of *Gulliver* he observes that Swift's misanthropy is "intolerable," adding that "the representation which he has given us of human nature, must terrify, and even debase the mind of the reader who views it" (p. 184). Orrery then proceeds to a lengthy vindication of mankind mingled with violent charges against Swift, among them that in painting the Yahoos Swift became one himself and that the "voyage to the Houyhnhnms is a real insult upon mankind" (p. 190). Orrery is significant because with few exceptions his is the tone and pretty much the method of criticism of the Fourth Voyage for a century and a half. The fundamental points raised are concerned with the motives or the personality of the author who would present this particular conception of human nature; and Orrery's explanation of Part IV in terms of injured pride, personal disappointments, and a soured temper becomes as time goes on the traditional one.

Even an occasional defender of Swift, as his good friend Patrick Delany, who answers Orrery point by point, is unwilling to undertake the defense of the last book of *Gulliver;* and he too lets fall such phrases as "moral deformity" and "defiled imagination." The eighteenth-century commentators, taking a high moral line, maintained that Swift's misanthropy had led him to write, as James Beattie phrased it, "a monstrous fiction." It was variously and characteristically stated: the gloomy and perverse Dean had talents that tended toward the wicked rather than the sublime; he was motivated by a malignant wish to degrade and brutalize the human race; he had written a libel on human nature. Though generally these commentators prefer to denounce the moral aspects of the Voyage to Houyhnhnmland and the degraded nature of the author, they leave no doubt that they think Part IV an artistic failure as well. In their eyes moral culpability and artistic failure have a necessary connection. The premise seems to be that a person of unsound views concerning human nature or of false moral views cannot write an artistically sound work. It is as though a Buddhist should deny literary value to Dante's *Divine Comedy* or Milton's *Paradise Lost* because these works are ethically and religiously unsound.

Yet it ought to be said to the honor of the eighteenth-

century commentators that they generally paid the
author of *Gulliver* the compliment of believing him a
sane man. It remained for certain nineteenth-century
critics to take a new tack and to elaborate a less defensible charge. Though they accepted the view that the
Fourth Voyage could be explained in terms of a depraved author, they *added* that it might well be explained in terms of a mad author. The charge of madness was usually presented with a certain caution. Two
commentators in the middle of the century may be
taken as examples of the willingness to accuse Swift
of insanity and the unwillingness, at the same time, to
come out unreservedly. In the *North British Review* of
1849 a reviewer writes of Swift's work that it is *"more
or less* symptomatic of mental disease" (italics mine);
and in the following year, in the London *Times*, a
writer says that Swift was "more or less mad." It is
possible that Sir Walter Scott is responsible for this
wavering between outright and qualified assertion. In
his edition of Swift's *Works* (1814) he writes that we
cannot justify, by saying that it has a moral purpose,
"the nakedness with which Swift has sketched this horrible outline of mankind degraded to a bestial state"
(1883 ed., I, 315). He prefers to explain the misanthropy of *Gulliver* as the result of "the *first* impressions
of . . . *incipient* mental disease" (italics mine). There
are nineteenth-century commentators who felt that the
Fourth Voyage should not be read. Thackeray gave
such advice to the audience who listened to his lectures
on the English humorists of the eighteenth century in
1851; and, later, Edmund Gosse—using such phrases as

"the horrible satisfaction of disease" and a brain "not wholly under control"—declared that the "horrible foulness of this satire on the Yahoo . . . banishes from decent households a fourth part of one of the most brilliant and delightful of English books." It is somewhat more surprising to find W. E. H. Lecky, who usually showed a well-balanced and sympathetic understanding of Swift, falling into the jargon. He can see Swift's misanthropy as a constitutional melancholy "mainly due to a physical malady which had long acted upon his brain." [1] It is not surprising, however, that in the twentieth century the psychoanalysts have seized on so attractive a subject as Swift; and now we find *Gulliver* explained in terms of neuroses and complexes. The following quotation is taken from the *Psychoanalytic Review* of 1942: *Gulliver's Travels* "may be viewed as a neurotic phantasy with coprophilia as its main content." It furnishes

abundant evidence of the neurotic makeup of the author and discloses in him a number of perverse trends indicative of fixation at the anal sadistic stage of libidinal development. Most conspicuous among those perverse trends is that of coprophilia, although the work furnishes evidence of numerous other related neurotic characteristics accompanying the general picture of psychosexual infantilism and emotional immaturity.

By a diligent search this psychoanalyst was able to discover in *Gulliver's Travels* strains of misogyny, misanthropy, mysophilia, mysophobia, voyeurism, exhibitionism, and compensatory potency reactions. If

[1] Introduction to the *Prose Works of Jonathan Swift,* ed. T. Scott, 1897, I, lxxxviii.

this psychoanalytic approach seems to have in it an element of absurdity, we should recognize that it is only a logical development of the disordered-intellect theory of the nineteenth-century critics, the chief difference being that the terminology has changed and that the psychoanalyst frankly sees *Gulliver's Travels* as case history, whereas the critics were presumably making a literary appraisal. Perhaps these crude and amateur attempts deserve little attention, yet they are a phenomenon that the serious student of Swift can hardly ignore in the light of their recurrence and their effectiveness in perpetuating myths. And they sometimes come with great persuasiveness and literary flavor, as witness Mr. Aldous Huxley's essay in which, by virtue of ignoring nine tenths of Swift's works, he can arrive at an amazingly oversimplified explanation of Swift's greatness: "Swift's greatness," Mr. Huxley writes, "lies in the intensity, the almost insane violence, of that 'hatred of bowels' which is the essence of his misanthropy and which underlies the whole of his work" (*Do What You Will*, 1930, p. 105).

I suggest that the commentators who have relied on a theory of insanity or disordered intellect to explain Swift's works have weakened their case, if they have not vitiated it entirely, by resorting to ex post facto reasoning. The failure of Swift's mental faculties toward the end of his life—some fifteen or sixteen years after the publication of *Gulliver's Travels*—was seized upon to explain something the critics did not like and frequently did not understand. It seemed to them valid to push his insanity back in time, to look retrospectively at the intolerable fourth book of *Gulliver's Travels,* and to infer that Swift's insanity must have been at least incipient when he wrote it. One recent commentator, rather more zealous than others, hints that the madness can be traced as far back as *A Tale of a Tub.* Commentators who observe manifestations of a disordered intellect in the Fourth Voyage have not thought to question the intellect behind the Third Voyage, yet we know now that the third was composed in point of time after the fourth. And these commentators have nothing but praise for the vigor, the keenness, the sanity, and the humanity of the mind that produced the *Drapier's Letters,* yet we have reasonable assurance that Swift completed the draft of Part IV of *Gulliver* in January of 1724 and was at work on the first of the *Drapier's Letters* in February.

Another procedure of which the critics of Swift are fond deserves to be scanned: the habit of taking an isolated statement or an isolated incident and giving it undue significance to support their prepossessions. In a recent study of Swift, in many respects of more than ordinary perceptiveness, the author considers Part IV of *Gulliver* as an embodiment of the tragic view of life. In so doing he passes from the work to the facts or presumed facts of Swift's life to enforce his interpretation, adducing as evidence the report of Swift's manner, in his later years, of bidding friends good-by: "Good night, I hope I shall never see you again." If Swift really used this remark, if he used it seriously, some weight may be attached to it; but I should want to know to whom he used it and in what tone or spirit.

It sounds very much like his usual banter, his manner
of friendly insult and quite genial vituperation which
so often distinguishes his letters to friends who understood his ironic turn and his liking for the inverted
compliment. How can we rely on such casual remarks
or possibly know what weight to give them? But such a
remark is related to Swift's habit of reading certain
parts of the Book of Job to prove that he hated life,
and is made to seem of a piece with the Fourth Voyage
of *Gulliver's Travels*. This is typical of the commentators who have culled from Swift's letters, from the
biographies, and from other documents all the presumed evidence of gloom and misanthropy in order to
uncover what they have a strong prepossession to uncover, the essential misery of his existence. This is the
way to prove, in support of the interpretation of the
Fourth Voyage, that "Swift's life was a long disease,
with its disappointments, its self-torture, its morbid
recriminations."

But a matter of statistical balance is involved here:
the facts listed and weighted heavily have been too
much of one complexion. Too much has been made of
the last years of Swift's life, when he bothered less to
conceal his moods and his irritations—and when he
seemed to get a certain satisfaction in talking about his
ailments. I should like to see some biographer counter
the gloomy approach by emphasizing Swift's zest for
life, his vitality, and the playfulness of his mind. There
is ample evidence in his letters—and in what we know
of his activities—of high spirits, good humor, and
daily satisfactions. Such a study might very well, with-

out distortion, evidence an unexpected mathematical balance between happiness and unhappiness.

I should not want to be put into the position of denying Swift a considerable pessimism and a fair share of misanthropy. These qualities, however, were not so raw or so unassimilated or so crudely operative in his daily existence as has been often represented. The manner in which these personal qualities have been used to explain *Gulliver* deserves to be questioned. It has been an overly simple process of equating biographical fact and artistic statement, of viewing the work as a transcription of the author's experiences or as a precise and complete representation of his personal philosophy—or as a final explanation of his personality. There is an obvious danger in seeing an artistic or imaginative construction as mere duplication. *Gulliver's Travels* is a work of mingled fantasy and satire; it is Utopian literature, highly allusive and symbolic, charged with hidden meanings and projected to a level several removes from the real world of its author.

To leaven the biographical approach other questions deserve attention. What are the artistic necessities of a work of this type? What are the aesthetic principles, quite apart from other considerations, that shape the work? To what extent is there a compromise between these principles and the conscious or the undeliberate tendency of the author to reflect his experiences and his personality?

If the biographical approach to Swift has been crudely used or overemphasized in certain respects,

there are other respects in which biographical considerations of critical value have been left almost
wholly unexplored. The most significant of these
seems to me to be Swift's profession as a Christian
divine. Is there in this some clue to an explanation of
Part IV of *Gulliver?* If a reading of the sermons can
be trusted, the eighteenth-century divine relished his
duty to expatiate on the evils and corruptions of this
world and the inadequacies of this life. He seemed to
enjoy measuring the imperfections before him against
a higher set of values. Swift, I think, would have held
an optimistic divine to be a contradiction in terms;
and his own pessimism is quite consonant with the pessimism at the heart of Christianity. One of Swift's sermons begins as follows:

The holy Scripture is full of expressions to set forth the
miserable condition of man during the whole progress of
his life; his weakness, pride, and vanity, his unmeasurable
desires, and perpetual disappointments; the prevalency of
his passions, and the corruptions of his reason, his delud-
ing hopes, and his real, as well as imaginary, fears . . .
his cares and anxieties, the diseases of his body, and the
diseases of his mind. . . . And the wise men of all ages
have made the same reflections.[2]

If Swift had written his own comment on *Gulliver's
Travels,* he might very well have used the words of
this sermon. *Gulliver's Travels* certainly is full of expressions to set forth the miserable condition of man—
his weakness, pride, and vanity, his unmeasurable desires, the prevalency of his passions and the corrup-

[2] *On The Poor Man's Contentment.*

tions of his reason—and so on through the catalogue.
Indeed, Swift's few sermons and those of other eighteenth-century divines could easily be used to annotate
Gulliver's Travels. It is difficult for me to believe that
a contemporary could fail to see the affinity between
the Fourth Voyage—or the whole of *Gulliver*—and
many of the conventional sermons on human nature
and the evils of this life. Swift's emphasis on depraved
human nature and his evaluation of man's behavior
are certainly *not* at odds with Christian tradition.
There is no need to ascribe such views solely to personal bitterness or frustrations or melancholia. His
thinking and status as a divine had an effect much
more profound than is generally recognized. A good
case can be made for Part IV of *Gulliver* as being in
its implications Christian apologetics, though of
course in nontheological terms; in a sense it is an al-
legory which veils human nature and society as a
Christian divine views them. It is by indirection a defense of the doctrine of redemption and man's need of
grace.

Only an occasional commentator has recognized and
stressed the essentially Christian philosophy of the
Fourth Voyage. The first was Swift's relative, Deane
Swift, who declared that the Christian conception of
the evil nature of man is the "groundwork of the whole
satyre contained in the voyage to the Houyhnhnms."
Then this cousin of Jonathan Swift, this lesser Swift,
delivers himself of a catalogue of vices worthy of his
great cousin:

Ought a preacher of righteousness [he asks], ought a watch-
man of the Christian faith . . . to hold his peace . . .
when avarice, fraud, cheating, violence, rapine, extortion,
cruelty, oppression, tyranny, rancour, envy, malice, detrac-
tion, hatred, revenge, murder, whoredom, adultery, lasciv-
iousness, bribery, corruption, pimping, lying, perjury,
subornation, treachery, ingratitude, gaming, flattery,
drunkenness, gluttony, luxury, vanity, effeminacy, cow-
ardice, pride, impudence, hypocrisy, infidelity, blasphemy,
idolatry, sodomy, and innumerable other vices are as
epidemical as the pox, and many of them the notorious
characteristicks of the bulk of mankind? [3]

"Dr. Swift," he adds, "was not the first preacher,
whose writings import this kind of philosophy." Surely
those clergymen who week after week exposed the
deceitfulness of the human heart would have agreed
with Deane Swift.

It seems to be true, as T. O. Wedel has pointed out,[4]
that Swift's view of human nature was opposed to certain contemporary attitudes in which the passions of
men were looked on kindly and in which the dignity
of human nature was defended in such a way that the
doctrine of original sin lost its efficacy. In his *Reasonableness of Christianity* (1695) John Locke could deny,
without raising much serious protest, that the fall of
Adam implies the corruption of human nature in
Adam's posterity. It is this same current of thought

---

[3] *Essay upon the Life, Writings, and Character of Dr. Swift* (1755),
pp. 219–20.
[4] For the relationship between Swift and Wesley stated in this paragraph see an article to which I am much indebted, T. O. Wedel, "On
the Philosophical Background of *Gulliver's Travels,*" *Studies in Philology,* XXIII (1926), 434–50.

that later in the century disturbed John Wesley, who complains in one of his sermons (No. XXXVIII, "Original Sin") that "not a few persons of strong understanding, as well as extensive learning, have employed their utmost abilities to show, what they termed, 'the fair side of human nature in Adam's posterity.'" "So that," Wesley continues, "it is now quite unfashionable to say anything to the disparagement of human nature; which is generally allowed, notwithstanding a few infirmities, to be very innocent, and wise, and virtuous." Is it not significant, when Wesley comes to write his treatise on *The Doctrine of Original Sin* (1756), that he should turn to Swift, to Part IV of *Gulliver* for quotations? In this treatise Wesley refers scornfully to those "who gravely talk of the dignity of our nature," and then quotes several times from what he calls "a late eminent hand." The "late eminent hand" is Swift's, whose words from Part IV of *Gulliver* describing man as "a lump of deformity and disease, both in body and mind, smitten with pride" Wesley has seized on. Wesley refers again and again to the "many laboured panegyrics . . . we now read and hear on the dignity of human nature"; and he raises a question which is, I think, a clue to Swift. If men are generally virtuous, what is the need of the doctrine of Redemption? This is pretty much the point of two sermons by Swift, where he is obviously in reaction to the panegyrics on human nature which came from Shaftesbury and the benevolists, from the defenders of the Stoic wise man, and from proponents of the concept of a man of honor. Swift sensed the

danger to orthodox Christianity from an ethical system or any view of human nature stressing man's
goodness or strongly asserting man's capacity for virtue. He had no faith in the existence of the benevolent
man of Shaftesbury and the anti-Hobbists, the proud,
magnanimous man of the Stoics, or the rational man of
the deists; his man is a creature of the passions, of pride
and self-love, a frail and sinful being in need of redemption. The very simple and wholly unoriginal
strain of apologetics in Swift's sermons is based upon
an attitude common in traditional Christian thought;
and to my way of thinking Swift the clergyman repeats
himself in *Gulliver's Travels.*

It might be of value to carry the consideration of
Swift the clergyman beyond application to *Gulliver,* to
discover whether his activities in his profession may
not throw some light on his other works—the Irish
tracts, for example. Those who make a case for Swift's
misanthropy, his pessimism and gloom, his tragic view
of life, can point to these tracts to enforce their views.
Can we accept the Irish tracts as "monuments to
despair, pessimism, bitterness, hopelessness and hate;
and like his other works . . . distillations of the
man"? It is certainly true that the tracts reflect disillusionment, and are filled with statements that reflect hopelessness. Undoubtedly they are charged with
bitterness; yet it is not necessarily the bitterness of a
man who hates his fellow men or thinks them not
worth saving. The real note is perhaps despair, despair
at corruption and weakness; but it is obvious that
Swift's *words* of despair were tempered by hope that

something might be achieved to relieve the Irish people. Until the end of his active life he persisted in writing and working to achieve reforms. His continued zest for reform is significant, even though he assures us frequently that he is without hope. He did not withdraw to nurse his bitterness or his misanthropy. Is it not conceivable that the tone, the emotional coloring, the violent rhetoric of the Irish tracts are susceptible to an explanation in terms other than personal bitterness or pessimism? Are not the rhetorical qualities, the strong expressions, appropriate to the purpose in hand and proper from a clergyman and reformer bent on seeing maladjustments corrected? Swift's occupation, his position as dean and dignitary, gave him the opportunity and imposed on him the obligation to take cognizance of private and public distresses. He dispensed the Cathedral funds for private and public benefactions; he sat on numerous charity commissions; he was requested and expected to make his views known on public ills. As a dignitary in a hapless country, it was—to say the least—mathematically probable that he should encounter conditions to call forth gloomy expressions. If a sensitive, public-spirited, socially conscious Irishman of Swift's day were anything but gloomy, then indeed we would need an explanation. Irish conditions being what they were, Swift's lamentations, the fierce and desperate rhetoric, are a natural product of a man doing his duty in an appropriately chosen diction. It was Swift's job to spy out the worst and to call attention to it in the strongest language he could command. By his calling he was a specialist in disorders; and here we have possibly a sufficient explanation of the tone of the Irish tracts without recourse to any theory of personality or misanthropy.

The Irish tracts, including the *Drapier's Letters,* offer another instance of the way in which interpretation and biographical considerations enforce each other—and at the same time a further instance of how easily divergent views may be arrived at. If a person without any knowledge of Swift came to the tracts without prepossessions, he would carry away with him, despite certain qualifications, the general impression of an Irish patriot moved by a genuine desire for the national welfare. Swift would obviously appear to be concerned to protect Ireland from exploitation at the hands of a powerful England. There is, certainly, a note of scorn for the slothful and dirty native Irish; but there is also a note of strong compassion and a tendency to absolve them from blame in the light of intolerable conditions which they could hardly be expected to transcend. In a letter of 1732 he writes that the English ought to be "ashamed of the reproaches they cast on the ignorance, the dulness, and the want of courage, in the Irish natives; those defects . . . arising only from the poverty and slavery they suffer from their inhuman neighbors . . . the millions of oppressions they lie under . . . have been enough to damp the best spirits under the sun." [5] It is not accidental that the English authorities viewed Swift as dangerous, and certain of his tracts as openly inciting

[5] *Correspondence,* ed. E. Ball (1910–14), IV, 328.

the Irish to make themselves independent of England. Indeed his sense of Ireland's rights as a nation to develop its own economy and to control its own destiny is at times so vigorously expressed—his words probably go beyond his intention—that he can easily be taken as a confirmed nationalist.

And thus the Irish claim Swift as the Hibernian Patriot. In 1782, when Grattan secured the adoption of the declaration of Irish independence in the Irish House of Commons, he took the floor to apostrophize Swift (and Molyneux) in these words: "Spirit of Swift! Your genius has prevailed. Ireland is now a nation!" This view of Swift as the "first and greatest of Irish nationalists" found stronger and stronger proponents as time went on. In the last part of the nineteenth century we find this not uncharacteristic utterance: "No one can now talk of Irish liberty, the Irish nation, Irish manufactures, Irish grievances, and Irish rights without speaking the language and echoing the thoughts of Swift. When [he] denounced Wood's Halfpence he was not thinking at all of finance and currency. He was after quite other game. He meant to build up an Irish nation." In the twentieth century such enthusiasm eventuates in the view, recently propounded, that Swift's sympathies were with the silent and hidden Ireland rather than with the Protestant Ascendancy and that the native Irish "made him a God of their Gaelic Olympus, and even imagined that he was secretly of their faith." A year does not pass without discussion in some Irish journal of the exact nature of Swift's Irishism.

Yet there is the other side, equally well supported by biographical materials. Certain fierce defenders of Irish nationalism will have none of Swift. Admitting that some of his efforts had good results, they still insist that the facts of Swift's biography leave no interpretation possible but that Swift was an Englishman of the hated Protestant Ascendancy. The Irish nation was for him the English Pale. Catholic and Celtic Ireland hardly existed for him. It has been pointed out that in Swift's day the Gaels had hundreds of poets to express their feelings and that these poets were often politically self-conscious; yet in their works are no references to the Dean or the Drapier.

The case is strengthened by a careful selection of biographical fact: Swift's insistence that his birth in Ireland was mere accident; his pride in his Yorkshire ancestry; his desire for residence and a career in England; and his reference to his being exiled in Ireland; his resistance to any attempt to spread the use of the Irish language. But what weighs most heavily with the proponents of this view is that Swift had, they insist, no real concern for Catholic Ireland, that he favored the harsh penal laws against the Catholics, and that his concern was only for the Anglo-Irish Anglicans. As usual, Swift's words and actions are interpreted with considerable asperity, and he is seen as defending Ireland less out of humanity than out of a desire to revenge himself on his enemy, Robert Walpole and the Whig administration in England. This is the familiar Swift—and the familiar application of his biography to interpretation—Swift, the man of violent personal prejudices, moved by envy and disappointed ambition, whose every act, known or surmised, whose every utterance, public or private, and whose personality in every facet, real or imagined, are brought to bear in the interpretation of his works.

THE SHANDEAN HOMUNCULUS:
THE BACKGROUND OF
STERNE'S "LITTLE GENTLEMAN"

I WISH there was not a clock in the kingdom."[1] This heartfelt lament from the lips of Mr. Shandy comes parenthetically as he is paraphrasing some of Locke's remarks on the succession of ideas. For Mr. Shandy, the word "clock" had associations, as it must have for even the least alert reader of *Tristram Shandy*, with Mrs. Shandy's untimely "silly question" (*"Pray, my dear . . . have you not forgot to wind up the clock?"*), uttered at the precise and fateful moment of Tristram's begetting, fateful because, as Mr. Shandy says, Tristram's misfortunes resulted from it: they *"began nine months before ever he came into the world."*[2] Tristram was indeed a "child of interruption."[3] But Mrs. Shandy, so culpable in the eyes of her husband, should be viewed with compassion. She was merely an innocent "victim" of the logical processes of the mind (as Locke viewed it), and her question

---

[1] Laurence Sterne, *The Life and Opinions of Tristram Shandy, Gentleman*, ed. James Aiken Work (New York, 1940), III, xviii, 190. All references are to this edition. For designating chapters, I substitute roman numbers for the arabic in Work.

[2] I, iii, 7. As a gloss on the remarks of Tristram and his father concerning *tempore coitionis* (I, i, 4; II, xiv, 149), a subject that had received attention from the time of the ancients, one may turn to a controversy some three decades before Sterne published his novel. The chief antagonists were Dr. James Augustus Blondel and Dr. Daniel Turner, both members of the Royal College of Physicians. See Blondel's *The Power of the Mother's Imagination Examin'd, in Answer to Dr. Daniel Turner's Book* (London, 1729), pp. 9–10, 114, and Turner's *De Morbis Cutaneis* (3d ed.; London, 1726), pp. 161–62; *A Discourse concerning Gleets . . . to which is added A Defence of . . . the 12th Chapter of . . . De Morbis Cutaneis, in respect of the Spots and Marks impress'd upon the Skin of the Foetus* (London, 1729), pp. 69 ff. If certain current embryological views, defended in medical circles, had been valid, Tristram might well have been born with the image of a clock clearly defined on his body. See also Turner's *The Force of the Mother's Imagination upon her Foetus in Utero . . . in the Way of A Reply to Dr. Blondel's Last Book* (London, 1730), pp. 168, 170.

[3] IV, xix, 296.

was inevitable in terms of the theory of the association of ideas—and quite appropriate to the moment. It came on the first Sunday night of the month when Mr. Shandy, "one of the most regular men in every thing he did," followed his undeviating custom of winding the large house-clock and got out of the way at the same time "some other little family concernments [so as to] be no more plagued and pester'd with them the rest of the month."[4] Unlike Sterne, who once described himself as "totally spiritualized out of all form for connubial purposes,"[5] Tristram's father, aged between fifty and sixty at the time of his son's conception, was clearly not in that condition, even though he was rather abstemious; and the "sagacious *Locke*" would have been the first to understand the peculiar linkage of ideas in Mrs. Shandy's mind of two activities so ordinarily unrelated. As Tristram himself explained, "from an unhappy association of ideas which have no connection in nature . . . my poor mother could never hear the said clock wound up,—but the thoughts of some other things unavoidably popp'd into her head,—*& vice versa.*"[6]

It may be thought that this witty, if somewhat indelicate, opening of *Tristram Shandy*, with its description of the homunculus, has received its full measure of attention; but it has, in fact, implications and complexities hitherto unexplored. Sterne's knowledgeable contemporaries would have read the opening chapters with special understanding in the context of eighteenth-century medical and biological science, and particularly in the light of a long continued controversy in the field of embryology. We have here one more example, actually one of the best examples, of what has frequently been remarked, Sterne's use of learning for purposes of wit. A clue to what an eighteenth-century reader found in Tristram's account of his begetting comes from a pamphlet published soon after the appearance of the first volume of *Tristram Shandy*—a brief, anonymous scribble titled *The Clockmaker's Outcry against the Author of the Life and Opinions of Tristram Shandy* (1760).[7] This is a pretense that Sterne, who is described as a "forerunner of Antichrist,"[8] has come close to destroying the clockmaker's trade because "no modest lady now dares to mention a word about *winding-up a clock*, without exposing herself to the sly leers and jokes of the family." The anonymous pam-

---

[4] I, iv, 8.

[5] *Letters of Laurence Sterne*, ed. Lewis Perry Curtis (Oxford, 1935), pp. 240–41. In this amusing and suggestive letter to Mrs. F., Sterne tells her: "I have not an ounce of carnality about me."

[6] I, iv, 9.

[7] I use the Second Edition, Corrected, London, 1760.

[8] *Ibid.*, p. 10.

phleteer complains that "hitherto harmless watches are degraded into agents of debauchery" and reputable hoary clocks excite to "acts of carnality."[9] Sterne is accused of beginning his novel "like one of Priapus's lecherous priests in Pagan times."[10] In the midst of the tirades are two significant relevant remarks, the insistence that most of what is said in *Tristram Shandy* about the homunculus is false and absurd[11] and that Sterne has contradicted himself by espousing two opposed hypotheses in embryology—a reference to the diametrical views of the ovists and the animalculists, whose controversy dominated that science.[12]

For our purposes the key passage in *Tristram Shandy* is the whole of Book I, chapter ii, in which Tristram complains that his mother's "unseasonable question" so ruffled the animal spirits that they failed to perform their function of conducting Homunculus safely "to the place destined for his reception." Then we are given an account of the homunculus:

The HOMUNCULUS, Sir, [is] to the eye of reason in scientific research . . . a Being guarded and circumscribed with rights:—the minutest philosophers . . . shew us incontestably That the HOMUNCULUS is created by the same hand,—engender'd in the same course of nature,—endowed with the same loco-motive powers and faculties with us:—That he consists, as we do, of skin, hair, fat, flesh, veins, arteries, ligaments, nerves, cartilages, bones, marrow, brains, glands, genitals, humours, and articulations:—is a Being of as much activity,—and, in all senses of the word, as much and as truly our fellow-creature as my Lord Chancellor of England.[13]

The witty context of this description and the humorous tone, as well as its remoteness from modern embryological theory, should not mislead us into believing that Sterne has greatly distorted certain scientific views of his time. Actually Tristram's account of the "little gentleman" is based on the microscopic investigations and the speculations of such respected biologists of the late seventeenth century as Harvey, Swammerdown, Malpighi, Leeuwenhoek, de Graaf, and others whose embryological views were accepted and disseminated in the eighteenth century. These views were reflected in a theory called "preformation" and in two schools of thought concerning human conception, the ovists and the animalculists, whose clashing ideas throw light on the opening chapters of *Tristram Shandy*.[14]

[9] *Ibid.*, pp. 42, 43.

[10] *Ibid.*, p. 11.

[11] *Ibid.*, p. 10.

[12] *Ibid.*, pp. 34–35.

[13] I, ii, 5.

[14] For the historical development of embryological theories, see R. C. Punnett, "Ovists and Animalculists," *American Naturalist*, LXII (1928), 481–507; F. J. Cole, *Early The-*

The school of ovists derived from the famous dictum enunciated by Harvey in 1651, *ex ovo omnium,* a principle further demonstrated by the work of Swammerdown and de Graaf, especially the latter's discovery of the mammalian egg. Scientists and others inclined to this school maintained the primacy of the female in generation and believed, with varying degrees of assurance, that "the first Bud of the future larger Animal [is] pre-existent . . . in the Egg of the Mother."[15] This "Ovarian Doctrine" was strongly challenged in the 1690's; and we find a continuous controversy between ovists and animalculists to the time of Sterne. The chief issue between the two groups was stated by one of Sterne's scientific contemporaries, whose details reveal at the same time that the homunculus of science closely resembles the homunculus of Sterne's novel:

But though Reason and Experience do now convince us, that all and every the most minute Part of every Animal, though ever so small, do really exist even to a single Artery, Vein, Nerve, Fibre; and all its Fluids were also in Motion, and circulated in the same, long before Generation: Yet whether this same Bud of Being, this *Minim* of Nature, this *Primordium Animalis,* this Principle of Body, this *Punctum vitae,* this *Stamen, Semen, Animalculum, Homunculus,* or *Manakin* in Miniature, was previously lodged in *Semine Masculino,* or in the *Ovum,* or Egg of the Female (for in one or the other it must needs be) is still Matter of Doubt and Dispute among Philosophers and Anatomists.[16]

---

ories of Sexual Generation (Oxford, 1930); Arthur W. Meyer, *The Rise of Embryology* (Stanford and London, 1939); Joseph Needham, *A History of Embryology* (2d ed.; New York, 1959). Cole and Needham include invaluable bibliographies. Good contemporary accounts of the ovist-animalculist controversy may be found in Dr. Daniel Turner's *The Force of the Mother's Imagination upon her Foetus in Utero . . . in the Way of a Reply to Dr. Blondel's Last Book,* pp. 89–105; and particularly in John Cooke's *An Anatomical and Mechanical Essay on the Whole Animal Oeconomy* (London, 1730), I, 1–29; II, 254 ff., where all the issues, scientific and religious, are examined. See also John Harris, *Lexicon Technicum* (London, 1710), Vol. II: "Generation."

15 J. C[ooke], *The New Theory of Generation, according to the Best and Latest Discoveries in Anatomy* (London, 1762), I, 15. See also I, 125: "The famous Lewenhoek and Hartsocker were the first, who . . . set this new Hypothesis of Animalcular Generation on Foot."

16 *Ibid.,* p. 14. The shift from the ovarian to the animalculist position in the early eighteenth century is made clear by James Drake, Fellow of the Royal College of Physicians and of the Royal Society: "It is agreed on all Hands, that there are in the *Ovaries* of *Women* little *Eggs.* These *Eggs,* most *Modern Anatomists,* and the most Able till very lately, have maintain'd to be the *material* and *formal* Rudiments of the Body of the *future Man,* which the *Seed* of the *Male* did only pregnate and vivifie. . . . This Opinion was first broach'd and laid down with Strength of Reason . . . by Dr. Harvey, in his book *De Generatione Animalium.* It procur'd almost universal Assent from the Writings of that Author; and seem'd perfectly establish'd by *De Graaf,* till the *Microscopical* Observations of Mr. Lewenhook grafted somewhat upon it, and took something from it" (*Anthropologia Nova, or, A New System of Anatomy* [London, 1707], I, 332).

The school of animalculists was inspired mainly by the work of three scientists, most extensively by that of Leeuwenhoek, the famous correspondent of the Royal Society, whose use of the microscope led to the discovery of spermatozoa, the *sine qua non* of the animalculist hypothesis. The other two scientists of influence were Nicholas Hartsoeker, the first to publish an illustration of a homunculus in the male sperm, and Francois de Plantades, secretary of the Montpellier Academy of Science, writing under the pseudonym of Dalenpatius. In his *Letter* on generation, which became widely known—it was reprinted in England in the *History of the Works of the Learned* (May 1699) and referred to by Leeuwenhoek in the *Philosophical Transactions* of the Royal Society (1699)—Dalenpatius helped to spread the animalculist hypothesis beyond any real merit in his investigations. His *Letter* was accompanied by illustrations depicting "little men" fully formed in human spermatozoa, allegedly seen under the microscope. These animalcules, he maintained, he had clearly observed, with tails "four or five times the length of their bodies":

They move with extraordinary agility, and by the lashings of their tails they produce and agitate the wavelets in which they swim. Who would have believed that in them was a human body? But I have seen this thing with my own eyes. For while I was examining them all with care one appeared which was larger than the others, and sloughed off the skin in which it had been enclosed, and clearly revealed, free from covering, both its shins, its legs, its breasts, and two arms, whilst the cast skin, when pulled further up, enveloped the head after the manner of a cowl. It was impossible to distinguish sexual characteristics on account of its small size. . . .[17]

The animalculist hypothesis received enthusiastic support from microscopic science in the eighteenth century. Typical is Henry Baker,

[17] See Cole, *Early Theories*, pp. 68–69, for this translation of the Latin; see also *History of the Works of the Learned*, I (May 1699), 269, for the *Letter* and the illustrations. Cole, who believes that Dalenpatius was perpetrating a hoax, says that the *Letter* was both accepted and attacked. By printing an account of the *Letter* in the *Philosophical Transactions*, XXI (August 1699), Leeuwenhoek seems to have furthered the cause of animalculism (see Cole, *Early Theories*, p. 70). It is true that Leeuwenhoek was skeptical that Dalenpatius had actually *seen* a fully formed being in the male sperm: "I put this down as a certain truth, that the shape of a Human Body is included in an Animal of the Masculine Seed, but that a Mans Reason shall dive or penetrate into this Mystery so far, that in the Anatomizing of one of these Animals of the Masculine Seed, we should be able to see or discover the intire shape of a Human Body, I cannot comprehend" ("Part of a Letter from Mr. Leuvenhook, Dated June 9th, 1699, Concerning the Animalcula in Semine Humano," in *Phil. Trans.*, XXI [August 1699], no. 255, p. 306). At another point in the same issue of the *Transactions*, Leeuwenhoek wrote: "Now if we know . . . the great Mystery that is included in the small Seed of an Apple, why might not we assert that in an Animal of the Masculine Seed of a Man, is locked up a whole Man, and that the Animals of the Seed are all descending from the first Created Man" (p. 27).

Fellow of the Royal Society and author of *The Microscope Made Easy* (1742). Like others who were fascinated by the world revealed through the microscope, Baker writes lyrically of the symmetry, beauty, and perfection found there—that whole world of nature so obviously the work of the Divine Artificer, which far surpasses the works of art, mean and rough by contrast. As one example of divine artifice, he refers to "those breathing Atoms"—the animalcules:

In them . . . we shall discover the same Organs of Body, Multiplicity of Parts, Variety of Motions, Diversity of Figures, and particular Ways of Living as in the larger Animals.—How amazingly curious must the Internal Structure of these Creatures be! The Heart, the Stomach, the Entrails, and the Brain! How minute and fine the Bones, Joints, Muscles and Tendons! How exquisitely delicate beyond all Conception the Arteries, Veins, and Nerves! What Multitudes of Vessels and Circulation must be contained within this narrow Compass! And yet, all have sufficient Room to perform their different Offices, and neither impede nor interfere with one another.[18]

Baker is of special interest because he was both a scientist and a man of letters—a poet, translator, and journalist. Well before Sterne he illustrates how literature in the period reflected embryological theory. Unlike Sterne, he makes serious use of the concept of preformation and, additionally, of the related concept of *emboitment* or encasement, in his poem, *The Universe* (1727).[19] This latter facet of embryological thought, concerned with the origin and transmission of the germ cells, had interesting implications for the actual physical transmission of original sin, and, as we shall see, for religion generally.[20] It held that all the germ cells of future generations were cre-

---

[18] *The Microscope Made Easy* (2d ed.; London, 1743), p. 298. Baker was widely read. In the 1750's, when Sir John Hill was attacking microscopic anatomy, he centered his fire to a considerable degree on Baker—that "Prince of Societarians." In 1751, Hill wrote: "We are to acknowledge Merit, great Merit indeed, in Lewenhoeck; he has the good Fortune to be one of the first People who worked at microscopical Observations, but we are to acknowledge at the same Time, That he has the Honour of having stocked the Philosophical Transactions with more Errours than any one Member of it, excepting his Successor in Peeping, Mr. *Baker*" (*A Review of the Works of the Royal Society of London* [London, 1751], p. 156).

[19] Additional contemporary comment on the concept of *emboitment* or encasement may be found in *Father Malebranche's Treatise concerning the Search after Truth*, trans. T. Taylor (Oxford, 1695), I, 15; John Ray, *The Wisdom of God Manifest in the Works of Creation* (1691; 10th ed.; London, 1735), p. 115; Nicola Andry, *An Account of the Breeding of Worms in Human Bodies* (London, 1701), pp. 190–91. See also Cole, *Early Theories*, pp. 50 ff. and *passim*; Meyer, *Rise of Embryology*, pp. 62 ff. and *passim*. For a vigorous attack on the concept, see Patrick Blair, *Botanick Essays* (London, 1720), pp. 304 ff. Blair was a Fellow of the Royal Society.

[20] The difficulty of reconciling the concept of encasement and Christian doctrines disturbed some contemporaries. See, for example, "Mr. Locke's Reply to the Bishop

ated at one and the same time by God and were contained in Eve (according to the ovists) or in Adam (according to the animalculists). "There is no necessity to think," wrote Dr. George Cheyne, the widely known physician and a Fellow of the Royal Society, "*God almighty* is confin'd to a new Creation, in ev'ry *generation* of an Animal." Since "these *Animals* Themselves are conspicuous in all male seeds hitherto examin'd, it is plain that they must be lodg'd in the Loyns of the Original Pairs of all the *species* of *Animal.*" Or as one ardent expounder of the animalculist position said: ". . . you and I did once exist and swim together, in the real, corporeal, literal Loins of our first Parent *Adam.*"[21] The "preformed" beings waited, one generation encased in the other, "to be brought forth and disclosed to view in a certain time, and according to a certain order and economy" —so Ephraim Chambers reports, in his *Cyclopaedia: Or, An Universal Dictionary of Arts and Sciences* (1728). Thus "there is not properly any new *generation* . . . only augmentation and expansion of minute parts of the bodies of seeds; so that the whole species, to be afterwards produced, were really formed in the first, and inclosed therein. . . ."[22]

Baker and his contemporaries, for whom the microscope had demonstrated the "Arithmetick of Infinites" and "the infinite Divisibility

---

of Worcester's Answer to his Second Letter," in *Works of John Locke* (London, 1812), IV, 303 ff. See also the reference to William Wollaston, note 57 below. In 1721, James Handley, in his *Mechanical Essays on the Animal Oeconomy*, disputed both the ovarian doctrine of Harvey and the animalcular hypothesis of Leeuwenhoek because if they are "absolutely in the Right, it must cause very great Doubts to arise in every Christian's Breast, and leave him in a very great Dilemma, as to the Truth of what the Bible contains: For if Harvey's *Hypothesis* be certain, how can our Saviour . . . be called the Seed of *Abraham* and *David?* Or if Lewenhoeck's were so, How can he be called the Seed of the Woman? Both which *we* know he most certainly was" (p. 38). See the answer to Handley by John Cooke, in *An Anatomical and Mechanical Essay*, I, 8–9. At another point in this work Cooke, after stating the case for encasement, wrote: ". . . so we may be said, in the literal Sense, actually to have fell with *Adam* in his first Transgression" (I, 13).

[21] *Philosophical Principles of Religion, Natural and Revealed* (London, 1724), pp. 320–21; Cooke, *An Anatomical and Mechanical Essay*, II, 256.

[22] Vol. I: "Generation." I use the edition of 1752. Sterne apparently owned the edition of 1738 (see *A Facsimile Reproduction of a Unique Catalogue of Laurence Sterne's Library* [London, 1930], p. 10, no. 236). See also B. L. Greenberg, "Sterne and Chambers Encyclopaedia," *MLN*, LXIX (1954), 560–62. For a passing reference to the concept of "*a primitive Ovum*" that contained the seeds of all future generations, see James Augustus Blondel, *The Power of the Mother's Imagination Examin'd*, p. 141. Cf. Cheyne: "*Generation* is nothing but *Accretion*, for it is beyond all Doubt, that all *Generation* is from a preceding little *Animal* lodg'd in the Male" (*Philosophical Principles*, p. 320). See also John Denne, *The Wisdom of God in the Vegetable Creation* (London, 1730), *passim*, an interesting example of a sermon in which the prevailing theories of generation are utilized.

of Matter," had no difficulty in believing "that all Mankind might once exist *in parvo* in Adam's loins":

> Each Seed includes a Plant: that Plant, again,
> Has other Seeds, which other Plants contain:
> Those other Plants have all their Seeds, and Those
> More Plants again, successively, inclose.
>
> Thus, ev'ry single Berry that we find,
> Has, really, in itself large Forests of its Kind.
> Empire and Wealth one Acorn may dispense,
> By Fleets to sail a thousand Ages hence.
> Each Myrtle Seed includes a thousand Groves,
> Where future Bards may warble forth their Loves.
> Thus Adam's Loins contain'd his large Posterity,
> All People that have been, and all that e'er shall be.[23]

Baker himself exclaims that this is an "Amazing Thought." Yet, he adds, "we must believe/What Reason tells."[24] It is indeed an amazing thought, but it had currency among scientists and laymen, poets and theologians. Sterne could have found it in many places, for instance (with ovist coloration) in his copy of Sir Richard Blackmore's *Creation* (1712),[25] where we are told that

> ev'ry foetus bears a secret hoard,
> With sleeping, unexpanded issue stor'd;
> Which num'rous, but unquicken'd progeny
> Clasp'd and inwrap'd within each other lie:
> Engendering heats these one by one unbind,
> Stretch their small tubes, and hamper'd nerves unwind;
> And thus when time shall drain each magazine
> Crowded with men unborn, unripe, unseen,
> Nor yet of parts unfolded, no increase
> Can follow, all prolific power must cease.[26]

[23] *The Universe, A Poem intended to Restrain the Pride of Man* (London, 1727[?]), p. 23. See also *Father Malebranche's Treatise*, p. 15; J. C[ooke], *New Theory of Generation*, I, 289. Malebranche, who was widely read in the period, relates microscopic revelations of the "invisible world" to the theory of preformation. "All the Bodies of Men and of Beasts," he wrote, "which shall be born or produc'd till the *End* of the World, were possibly created from the *Beginning* of it: I would say, That the Females of the Original Creatures were for aught we know, created together, with all those of the same *Species* which have been, or shall be, begotten or created whilst the World stands" (I, 15). On the subject of "the infinite Divisibility of Matter," see John Keill, *Introduction to Natural Philosophy, or, Philosophical Lectures Read in the University of Oxford, Anno Dom. 1700* (4th ed.; London, 1745), pp. 46, 53, and John Cooke, *An Anatomical and Mechanical Essay*, I, 11–14.

[24] *The Universe*, p. 23.

[25] *Catalogue of Sterne's Library*, p. 63, no. 1660. This lists the edition of 1715.

[26] VI, ll. 289–98.

Stated in the simplest terms the animalculist hypothesis maintained that the male sperm contained the animalcule or homunculus and that the act of conception involved the female only or primarily to the extent that she provides a proper nidus. She is not, as Mr. Shandy says of Mrs. Shandy, *"the principal agent."*[27] This is precisely what the animalculists were arguing, as we may see in a typical statement by John Cooke, who described himself as a "Student of Physick and Late of the College of Edinburgh." Writing in 1730, he maintained that "as the Earth seems a Nidus for all Seeds of Vegetables, so the Ova of the Female serve for the like Use":

. . . to think otherwise would be making Woman the chief Person in the Creation, in as much as she is supposed [i.e., by the ovists] to contain her Species, both materially and formally, in her self, and needs only a little of the Spirit of the Male Sperm to set those Animalcula in Motion; so that instead of God's giving Woman for a Help-mate to Man towards Procreation, he is thus made Womans Help-mate; and so hath the least share in this Action; whereas by Nature he was designed the chief Agent in it, and that from his Loins should proceed all Mankind . . . which the Text of St. *Paul* well alludes to, when he says of *Levi*, that he was yet in the Loins of his father, when Melchisedeck met him.[28]

This idea of the restricted function of the mother, in opposition to the ovist viewpoint, had profound implications reaching beyond the field of science, for example, into the realm of property rights. It is of more than passing interest that when James Boswell's father wished to entail the family estate on heirs general (i.e., both males and females), Boswell, who wished the entail to apply only to male heirs, thought he might rely on "the opinion of some distinguished naturalists"

that our species is transmitted through males only, the female being all along no more than a *nidus*, or nurse, as Mother Earth is to plants of every sort; which notion seems to be confirmed by that text of Scripture, "He was yet *in the loins of his* Father when Melchisedeck met him" (Heb. vii, 10); and consequently, that a man's grandson by a daughter, instead of being his *surest* descendant, as is vulgarly said, has, in reality, no connection whatever with his blood.[29]

27 V, xxxi, 391.

28 Cooke, *An Anatomical and Mechanical Essay*, I, 5. The animalculist view, stated by Cooke and reflected in Walter Shandy's remark that Mrs. Shandy is not "the principal agent," has ancient roots in Egypt and Greece. It was used by Aeschylus in *Eumenides*. Orestes, who revenged his father by killing Clytemnestra, is charged with matricide. Apollo, in defending Orestes, rejects this charge by maintaining, in effect, that the mother is not actually blood kin to her son, that she serves only as the nidus (ll. 637 ff. and note 2, in *Aeschylus* [Loeb Classical Library ed.], pp. 334–37). Euripides uses the same argument in his *Orestes* (ll. 552 ff.).

29 *Life of Johnson,* ed. G. B. Hill, rev. L. F. Powell (Oxford, 1934), II, 414, n. 2. In the third decade of the eighteenth century a lively controversy broke out over the influence

Boswell's qualification, that this opinion was held by "some distinguished naturalists," hints at the controversial aspect of embryological thought and of the unwillingness of many contemporaries to press the animalculist viewpoint to its extreme. A report to the Royal Society in 1693, often quoted in the eighteenth century as a compromise, illustrates the cautious attitude. The author of the report, Dr. George Garden, glances at the discoveries of Harvey, Malpighi, and de Graaf, and the inferences drawn from them—that "the Rudiments of each Animal were originally in the respective Females"—to suggest that Leeuwenhoek's discovery of "an infinite number of *Animalcula in semine*" has cast doubt on "the Propagation of all Animals *ex ovo*." He therefore offers as probabilities: "1. That Animals are *ex Animalculo*. 2. That these Animalcules are originally in *semine Marium & non in Foeminis*. 3. That they can never come forward, nor be formed into Animals of the respective Kind, *without the Ova in Foeminis*."[30]

An occasional animalculist might be dogmatic, as, for example, Thomas Morgan, writing in 1735: "that all Generation is from an Animalculum pre-existing *in Semine Maris*, is so evident in fact, and so well confirm'd by Experience and Observation, that I know now of no Learned Men, who in the least doubt of it."[31] Nevertheless, such compendiums as Chambers' *Cyclopaedia* (1728) and Dr. James's *Medicinal Dictionary* (1745) presented both the ovist and the animalculist view. But the point for our purposes is that the homunculus was widely known, involved in vigorous controversy, and readily available for witty treatment. He had been fully visualized and introduced at Oxford by John Keill, Savilian Professor of Astronomy and Fellow of the Royal Society, as early as 1700, in his Philosophical Lectures. The "Subtility of Nature," he told his audience, "is wonderful beyond measure"; and he appealed to them to imagine the "organized

---

of the mother's imagination on the foetus. Dr. James Blondel, one of the chief controversialists and a convinced animalculist, argued that no such influence (in the usual sense of stigmata and deformities) was possible. He defended his position by reference to the new theories of generation: "If *Leewenhoeck's* or Dr. *Gardener's* Notion be true, by what right has the Mother's Fancy any Influence upon the Body of the *Foetus*, which comes from the *Semen virile*, and which is consequently a distinct and separate *Individuum* . . ." (*The Power of the Mother's Imagination Examin'd*, p. 111; see also pp. 128–29). Both Boswell and Walter Shandy would have found this view comforting. For Dr. Daniel Turner's answer, see *The Force of the Mother's Imagination*, pp. 102 ff. See above, note 2.

30 Reprinted by William Derham; in *Miscellanea Curiosa* (3d ed.; London, 1736), I, 143.

31 Thomas Morgan, *The Mechanical Practice of Physick* (London, 1735), p. 281. The ovist position was strongly asserted by Patrick Blair in 1720, in *Botanick Essays*, pp. 302–25.

Body" of the animalcules "beheld through a Microscope, floating in the Seed of Animals":

. . . the Heart that is the Fountain of its Life, the Muscles necessary to its Motions, the Glands for the Secretion of its Fluids, the Stomach and Bowels to digest its Food. . . . But since every one of these Members is also an organical Body, they must have likewise Parts necessary to their Actions. For they consist of Fibres, Membranes, Coats, Veins, Arteries, Nerves, and an almost infinite number of fine Tubes. . . .[32]

We find the homunculus again with the lineaments unchanged six decades later, as *Tristram Shandy* was in progress, a "Bud of Being . . . *Punctum vitae* . . . *Animalculum, Homunculus*, or *Manakin* in Miniature" whose "Arteries, Veins, Nerves, Lymphatics, and Fibres did every one pre-exist long before Conception . . . and are after that . . . as it were, blown up, enlarged, expanded, extended, unravelled, and augmented."[33] Conception occurs when "some of the animalcules lodge in the ova placed in the Matrix of the female as a proper *Nidus* for them."

Thus Tristram's description of the homunculus as consisting of "skin, hair, fat, flesh, veins, arteries, ligaments, nerves, cartilage, bones, marrow, brains, glands, genitals, humours, and articulation," though clearly set in a context of humor, is less a parody than an accurate reflection of aspects of contemporary embryological speculation. Similarly, Tristram's reference to the homunculus as "so young a traveller"—"my little gentleman had got to his journey's end misera-bly spent"[34]—reflects humorously the animalculist view of the homun-culus seeking and finding "a proper *Nidus*." The image of the Shan-dean homunculus as a traveler undergoing the discomforts and fatigue of a journey tempts one to believe that Sterne had read and remem-bered the words of Patrick Blair, a Fellow of the Royal Society, who had vigorously opposed the animalcular position four decades earlier:

If [Blair wrote] *in an Animalcule of the Masculine Seed of a Man, a whole Man is lock'd up*, then the several Particles previously in the *Ovum*, are no more than the first Food to this Stranger; this new arriv'd Child (who after being fatigu'd by so long a Journey, and through so many difficult and unaccessible Roads, when all those in Company with him have been so wearied, that they were left behind and kill'd) had need of such Refreshment to rouse up his Spirits, and to make him grow up so as to become a brisk and lively Boy.[35]

[32] *An Introduction to Natural Philosophy*, p. 56.

[33] J. C[ooke], *New Theory of Generation*, I, 14, 41.

[34] I, ii, 6.

[35] *Botanick Essays*, p. 316.

Obviously Sterne saw the intrinsic comedy in such theories; and he is separated from the proponents of these views, scientists and others, by little more than the dimension of wit—from such a person, say, as Daniel de Superville, who reported in the *Philosophical Transactions* of the Royal Society (1740), that "each *Animalculum* . . . is a small Animal of the same Species with that which harbours it." It disengages itself, he adds, "from the Confinement in which it was, and in a Place where it meets with a Humour proper for its Vegetation and Expansion, it takes Root . . . swells like a Corn newly put into the Earth . . . spreads itself, its Members shape themselves . . . its Parts grow longer, and disentangle themselves. . . ."[36] Mr. Shandy himself reveals his animalcular prejudices in Book V. In conversing with Yorick concerning "the natural relation between a father and his child," he lists procreation as one means by which a father acquires jurisdiction over his offspring. To Yorick's remark that by this same means the mother has a similar claim to jurisdiction, Mr. Shandy gives the reply, already quoted, of a convinced animalculist: *"she is not the principal agent."*[37]

To anyone concerned with Sterne's reflection of contemporary embryological thought, the famous chapter (I, xx) on intra-uterine baptism is, of course, suggestive; and we do, in fact, find that here too the animalculist hypothesis serves comic purposes. It will be recalled that Sterne uses an actual instance, from the year 1733, in which a French obstetrical surgeon appealed to the Sorbonne for a theological opinion: the surgeon wished to know the validity of baptizing an unborn child, none of whose body could be made to appear.[38] Canon law and diocesan practice seemed to offer some flexibility. It was generally held, with Aquinas as authority, that a child fully retained in the mother's womb "cannot be counted among other men and thus cannot be the object of an external action in receiving through the ministry of men the sacraments necessary to salvation."[39] The surgeon asked whether a "conditional" baptism by means of a little injection-pipe (*"une petite camulle"*) might be permissible in this instance, giving his assurance that it could be done *"sans faire aucun tort à la mere."* Three learned doctors of theology at the Sorbonne, convinced that a child retained in the womb is capable of salvation or damnation,

[36] "Some Reflections on Generation and Monsters," *Phil. Trans.,* XLI (1744), 298 (no. 456, January–June 1740). De Superville was president of the College of Physicians in the Margravite of Brandenburg and a member of the Royal Society of Berlin.

[37] V, xxxi, 391.

[38] The letter of the surgeon and the response of the Doctors of Theology appeared in Henry de Deventer's *Observations importantes sur les Manuel des Accouchemens* (Paris, 1733), pp. 366–68.

[39] I, xx, 59.

approved (subject to assent by the bishop and the Pope) the surgeon's expedient—baptism conditionally *"par le moyen d'une petite canulle,"* or, as Sterne writes, "Anglicè *a squirt."* This "Reply" inspired Tristram to raise an ingenious, and similar, point, which he addressed to the very same Doctors of the Sorbonne:

. . . whether after the ceremony of marriage, and before that of consummation, the baptizing all the Homunculi at once, slap-dash, by injection, would not be a shorter and safer cut still; on condition as above, That if the Homunculi do well and come safe into the world after this, That each and every [one] of them shall be baptized again (*sous condition.*)[40]

The anonymous author of *The Clockmaker's Outcry* offered this passage in the novel as evidence that Sterne had abandoned the animalculist position of the early chapters for the ovist view that "all the *animalcula* are complete in the *ovaria* of the women."[41] But the Clockmaker's accusation is groundless. He ignored Tristram's all-important proviso, that baptism-by-injection be applied to the homunculi if "the thing can be done . . . *par le moyen d'une* petite canulle, and *sans faire aucun tort au pere."*[42] The significant word, of course, is *"pere"*—involving a fully calculated change by Sterne from the phrase of the French surgeon, *"sans faire aucun tort à la mere,"* in order to maintain consistency with the animalculist position of the opening chapters. Tristram, therefore, is still reflecting the hypothesis that "Animalcules are originally in *semine Marium & non in Foeminis."* It may be supererogation to point out that Sterne at this point in *Tristram Shandy* has put the homunculi into the context of long-continued theological debate concerning the human embryo and its relationship to the sacraments necessary for salvation. In effect, he has given to the homunculus the status of the unbaptized child in the mother's womb, whose damnation and torment, should it die, were so endlessly discussed from patristic and scholastic times to his own day. Sterne relies on his readers to be aware of certain issues implicit in his chapter on intra-uterine baptism, such matters as the precise moment the embryo was animated by a soul (thus becoming capable of salvation or damnation) and related considerations, as infant perdition and the mortal sin of abortion. A knowledge of these strengthens the impact of his profane wit. He did not miss the possibilities for Shandean humor in the weighty deliberations of the learned doctors of the Church; and, of course, as a child of the age, he had no delicacy or

[40] I, xx, 62.

[41] *The Clockmaker's Outcry*, pp. 34–35.

[42] I, xx, 62.

restraint in treating them. But perhaps the cream of the Shandean jest in this notable chapter is the idea of homuncular baptism in the male, a sacramental procedure possible only if there is validity in the animalculist hypothesis.

We have not yet exhausted all of the subtleties resident in Tristram's proposal that the sacrament of baptism be given the homunculi collectively. Certain philosophical and additional religious considerations reached into the biological controversies; and these too add an extra intellectual dimension to the proposal and increase the wit. Here we must look again at one of the provisions Tristram included in his address to the doctors of the Sorbonne: "if the HOMUNCULI do well and come safe into the world after this [i.e., after the proposed baptism-by-injection in the father] . . . each and every one of them shall be baptized again."[43] This proviso reflects a fundamental and disturbing point for both opponents and proponents of the animalcular hypothesis. What, they asked, of those homunculi who do *not* "do well and come safe into the world"? Here, clearly, was a problem involving the providence of God and the rational structure of the universe. We must recall that for the animalculist, animalcules were not merely "originally *in semine Marium*"; they were there by the tens of thousands. Henry Baker reported with amazement that "the Eye, assisted by a good *Microscope*, can distinguish plainly, in the Semen masculinum of Animals, Myriads of *Animalcules*, alive and vigorous, though so exceedingly minute, that it is computed three thousand millions of them are not equal to a Grain of Sand, whose Diameter is but the one hundredth Part of an Inch."[44] Human semen under the microscope is observed to be "plentifully stocked with Life": Mr. Leeuwenhoek had seen "more than ten thousand living Creatures . . . moving in no larger a Quantity of the Fluid Part thereof than the Bigness of a Grain of Sand."[45] Thomas Morgan, in his *Mechanical Practice of Physick* (1735), calculated precisely the size of "one of the largest of these seminal Animalcula": the "solid content of one of these little People," he wrote, "is not more than 1/12000000000 Part of a Cubick Inch."[46] Leeuwenhoek, had he been alive in the eighteenth century, might well have failed to recognize some of his discoveries, but he had indeed startled his contemporaries and later generations by maintaining that "the Milt of a single Cod-Fish contained more living *Animalcules,*

---

[43] *Ibid.*

[44] *The Microscope Made Easy*, p. 149. See also James Handley, *Mechanical Essays on the Animal Oeconomy* (London, 1721), p. 35.

[45] *The Microscope Made Easy*, p. 163.

[46] *The Mechanical Practice of Physick*, p. 282.

than there are People alive upon the Face of the Whole Earth at one and the same Time."[47] His computation of three thousand millions compressed into a space smaller than "one single Grain of coarse Sand" is mentioned again and again in the period with awe and even with reverence. Perhaps no one expressed the idea better than John Keill, in his lectures at Oxford, in 1700: "what some Philosophers have dreamed concerning Angels," he declared, "is true of these Animalcules, *viz.* that many thousands of them may dance on the Point of a small Needle."[48]

But, as indicated, this "numerosity" of animalcula, when only an occasional one functioned in the act of generation, had some dark implications. It meant shocking wastefulness, a squandering of potential lives, the apparently wanton destruction, if we may use Tristram's words at the opening of the novel, of fellow creatures who have "the claims and rights of humanity." Quoting the "minutest philosophers" (a pejorative phrase, of course), Tristram describes the homunculus as created by the same hand as others, a being who may be benefited or injured, one with all of the immunities of any member of the human race. Once again Sterne's humor is achieved without an exaggerated distortion of prevailing views. At least, Tristram's remark—"if the HOMUNCULI do well and come safe into the world"—raises the question of living beings pointlessly created and destroyed, a very sensitive matter for Sterne's contemporaries and one that prevented some from accepting the animalculist hypothesis. For the physico-theologists and rationalists generally, who felt assured that the deity had created nothing in vain, that all the handiwork of God had a proper function in His orderly and harmonious universe, the wastefulness implied in the hypothesis was wholly unacceptable. As early as 1692, John Ray, in *Three Physico-Theological Discourses,* voiced his disagreement with Leeuwenhoek because "the necessary Loss of an incredible Multitude of animalcula seems not agreeable to the Wisdom and Providence of Nature."[49] Such compendiums as those of Chambers and James repeated this cogent objection in the eighteenth century. "It would be necessary," Chambers wrote, "for 9999 parts of the animalcules to be in vain, and perish, which is contrary to the

[47] *The Microscope Made Easy,* p. 155. Leeuwenhoek's remarkable calculation fascinated later scientists if repetition is an indication. See, for example, James Keill, *The Anatomy of the Human Body Abridg'd* (1698; 12th ed.; London, 1759), p. 109; Nicola Andry, *An Account of the Breeding of Worms in Human Bodies,* p. 180; Cooke, *An Anatomical and Mechanical Essay,* I, 11–13.

[48] *Introduction to Natural Philosophy,* pp. 55–56.

[49] 1713 ed., p. 59.

economy of nature in other Things."[50] In his *Medicinal Dictionary* (1745) James offered a similar refutation:

... if 3000,000,000 Animalcules should be included in a Quantity of Male Sperm sufficient for the Production of one Animal only ... all the rest are superfluous, and created for no End, but to be immediately destroy'd: Besides, we must suppose that Providence aims very ill, if oblig'd to load her Engine so enormously, in order to be able to hit the Mark propos'd. But in all other Instances we find that the Author of Nature perpetually adapts much less compounded Means, in order to arrive at destin'd Ends.[51]

Not everyone felt that a problem existed. J. Turberville Needham, Fellow of the Royal Society, a scientist of repute in France and England and later a correspondent of Voltaire, was skeptical of the existence of the spermatic animals described by his contemporaries; and he exercised some humor at the expense of their imaginary spectacle (in his view) of millions of animalcules competing to impregnate the egg, a privilege to be accorded only one: "Happy the first of these minute Beings," he wrote, "that could take Possession of this Cell, and shut the Door against contending Millions!"[52]

The defense offered by the animalculists lacked full conviction; and they relied to a considerable degree on the argument from man's ignorance of God's intentions. Since mysteries and miracles abound in the works of nature and Providence, who is presumptuous enough to question the deity's design in creating this "numerosity" of animalcules? Daniel de Superville, whose report to the Royal Society in 1740 has already been mentioned, exemplifies the uneasy animalculist facing this critical problem: "I own," he declared

[50] *Cyclopaedia*, Vol. I: "Generation."

[51] Vol. II: "Generation."

[52] "A Summary of Some Late Observations upon the Generation ... of Animal and Vegetable Substances," *Phil. Trans.*, XLV (1748), 619 (no. 490, December 1748). For the curious mechanism involved in conception, one may turn to Nicola Andry: "A Friend of mine, a Physician of the Faculty of *Paris*, a Man of extraordinary skill in Physic, ... is of opinion, that at the opening of the Egg there is a *Valvula*, which suffers the Worm [i.e., the spermatic worm, Andry's name for the animalculum] to enter the Egg, but hinders it to come out, because in the inside it shuts upon the outside. This *Valvula* is held fast by the Tail of the Worm which lies against it, so that it cannot open them neither without nor within. This is the cause that no other Worm can enter there, and this opinion seems very probable" (*An Account of the Breeding of Worms in Human Bodies*, pp. 184–85). This notion of competitive impregnation had been ridiculed earlier than Needham, by Daniel Turner, who thought it cunning of the animalculum "after he was thrown into the *Uterus*, to find his Way through the dark entry of the *Tuba*, and thence jump upon the particular *Ovum*, that is ready furnish'd for him, where finding out the Perforation, or putting by the Valve, he is to creep in, and make all fast after him, to prevent those millions of millions of his companions, who are beleaguering his Castle from entering after him ..." (*The Force of the Mother's Imagination*, p. 104).

that the immense Number of *Animalcula* . . . in the Seminal Liquid of Man seems to oblige one to reject this Hypothesis, and particularly this Opinion, that every *Animalculum* is an *Embryo*. For it is certain, that in every Man there would be enough of them to people a vast Country, and of all that immense Quantity there are but a few that come to any thing. And so, there you have Millions of little Men, created never to exist; which seems directly contrary to the wise Intention of the Creator, who, in all Likelihood, made nothing in vain.[53]

After this statement of the difficulty inherent in the animalculist hypothesis, de Superville rests his case on "*Teleology* . . . one of those Parts of Philosophy, in which there has been but little Progress made." "Who dares presume," he asks, "so far as to pretend to penetrate into all the Designs of the Almighty, and into the divers Ends He has proposed to Himself in the Creation of the Universe?" De Superville saw a parallel in the rate of infant mortality. Why does "half of Mankind perish, before they come to the Age of one Year"? Clearly the deity might have saved himself the trouble of creating so "prodigious a Quantity of Creatures in order to precipitate them into nothing." But who can say that "creating so many Millions of Creatures has cost Him any more Pains" or that "all those *animalcula*, who do not come to the State of a Foetus, are annihilated"?[54]

The dilemma of the animalculists is revealed in de Superville's unwillingness to grant that superfluous animalcula were in fact created. Scientists were torn between the facts uncovered by the microscope, which implied in this instance a natural and divine order given to meaningless creativity, and the larger orientation of the age, which emphasized a rationally constructed universe with all parts meshed and functional. One edifying effort to solve the dilemma may be presented even though its relevance to Sterne is at best tenuous. This came from John Cooke, presenting his *New Theory of Generation*, in 1762. "It is very hard to conceive that Nature," he wrote, "is so idly luxurious of Seeds thus only to destroy them, and to make Myriads of them subservient to but a single one":

. . . all those other attending *Animalcula*, except that single one that is then conceived, evaporate away, and return back into the Atmosphere again, whence it is very likely they immediately proceeded; into the open Air, I say, the common Receptacle of all such disengaged minute sublunary Bodies; and do there circulate about with other *Semina*, where,

[53] *Phil. Trans.*, XLI (1744), 298–99 (no. 456, January–June 1740).

[54] *Ibid.*, pp. 299–300. De Superville points out that the principle of excess applies to the ovists as well: ". . . this seemingly useless Quantity of Animalcula equally affords an Argument against the Hypothesis of those, who believe the *Embryo* is in the Egg. One cannot maintain that all the Eggs in the *Ovaria* are fruitful" (p. 299).

perhaps, they do not absolutely die, but live a latent Life, in an insensible or dormant State, like Swallows in Winter . . . till [they] are received afresh into some other Male Body of the Proper Kind . . . to be afresh set in Motion, and ejected again in Coition as before, to run a fresh Chance for a lucky Conception. . . .[55]

Cooke had, in fact, offered this comforting viewpoint three decades earlier, when he gave assurances to his readers that though these animalcula come to nothing for the present, "Nature hath taken proper Care of them, and will in her own Time produce them all upon this Earth." "We need not wonder," he adds,

at their vast Number, since it is so necessary that they should be so, nor reckon them lost, since we know that provident Nature loses nothing, though we short-sighted Beings know not exactly how she manages them in that State in her secret chambers. And we know not but that we ourselves were once some of them . . . and that we underwent the like Circulation as they do. . . .[56]

Cooke's conception of widely dispersed animalcula in the air, risible as it may seem, is a traditional view with a long and respectable history in western thought. Latterly called panspermism, it maintained that all seminal elements, the primordial sperms, were formed simultaneously at creation and scattered over the universe, with each sperm or animalculum destined eventually to reach the genitals of the appropriate animal by means of air or food or water. "Equivocal generation," or the formation of monsters, was prevented by strainers in the recipient animal, which kept the primordial sperms or stamina of one species from finding their way into the wrong species. Panspermism in varied forms had exponents from the time of Virgil (*Georgics* III) to the middle of the eighteenth century; and Cooke's version may have struck contemporaries as unusual only by virtue of the speed with which his animalcula scrambled back into jostling competition for possible "lucky Conception."[57] But the historical fact seems to be that Cooke reflects the dying gasps of preformation and animalculism, as well as of panspermism. By 1750, dissenting views, which had never been silenced, appear to intensify. John Turberville Needham's vigor-

---

[55] *New Theory of Generation*, I, 85.

[56] *An Anatomical and Mechanical Essay*, II, 266, 268–69. Cf. I, 6.

[57] On the subject of panspermism, see Cole, pp. 169 ff., 208–9; Arthur W. Meyer, pp. 92 ff. For an interesting example of panspermism used in religious controversy, to prove the falsity of traducianism, see William Wollaston, *The Religion of Nature Delineated* (1722; 7th ed.; 1750), pp. 160 ff. Wollaston remarks on the "*animalcula* already formed; which being distributed about, especially in some opportune places and are *taken in* with aliment, or perhaps the very air; being separated in the bodies of the males by strainers proper to every kind, and then lodged in *their* seminal vessels. . . ."

ous attack of 1748 in scientific circles was followed in 1750 by Sir John Hill's satiric treatment of preformation and panspermism in a work amusingly called *Lucina sine concubitu*. Here the reader finds a machine invented to intercept the floating animalcula in the west wind, the *west* wind because Virgil's mares in *Georgics* III had snuffed the west wind and were impregnated; and Hill writes of the captive animalcula that "these small, original, unexpected minims of Existence" are revealed as "little Men and Women, exact in all their Limbs and Lineaments, and ready to offer themselves Candidates for Life, whenever they should happen to be . . . conveyed down into the Vessels of Generation."[58] Crudely interpreted and distorted, panspermism, with its hypothesis of the ubiquity of sperms—aliment, air, and water alive with them—offered embarrassing prospects if a wandering and unseemly animalculum found refuge without regard to the ethical and social codes of society. In the scientists themselves one senses a certain urgency to explain that the mechanism of conception does not and cannot go awry.[59] But Hill saw his opportunity; and I assume that no very great perceptiveness is required to realize from the title, *Lucina sine concubitu*, how he exploited humorously the concept of panspermism.

Thus a decade before the publication of *Tristram Shandy*, Sir John Hill, both scientist and literary man, had seen the possibilities for wit in the prevailing embryological theories, particularly in the homunculus. Indeed, it may well be that Sterne took his cue from Hill, of whom he had good reason to be aware;[60] and conceivably Tristram's remark—"The HOMUNCULUS, Sir, in how-ever low and ludicrous a light he may appear, in this age of levity, to the eye of folly or prejudice"[61]—is an allusion to *Lucina sine concubitu*. At any rate, Hill's

---

[58] Edited by Edmund Goldsmid (Edinburgh, 1885), p. 12. Hill makes a reference to both Virgil and Wollaston.

[59] Consider a serious variation of Hill's experiment of transferring a captured animalculum to a virgin, in Nicola Andry's *An Account of the Breeding of Worms in Human Bodies*: Andry presents the possible case of a married woman whose husband has died leaving behind an all too leisurely "spermatick worm," which does not enter the egg for several weeks. Thus, Andry warns, a woman may be "brought to bed without being criminal" (pp. 185–86). Isaac Watts gives a religious explanation for the perfect functioning of the reproductive mechanism: "Ever since that Week of creative Wonders God has ordered all these Creatures to fill the World with Inhabitants of their own kind, and they have obeyed him in a long Succession of almost six Thousand Years. He has granted . . . a divine Patent to each Creature for the sole Production of its own Likeness, with an utter Prohibition to all the rest" (*Philosophical Essays on Various Subjects* [London, 1733], p. 198).

[60] Wilbur L. Cross, *The Life and Times of Laurence Sterne* (New Haven, 1925), I, 202 ff.

[61] I, ii, 5.

pre-Shandean homunculus indicates that the time was ripe for Sterne.[62] Sterne's sortie into the microscopic world places him even more firmly than hitherto indicated in the tradition of preceding writers, including Swift, whose literary imagination found nourishment in science. The general resemblance to Swift, so often pointed out, is perhaps additionally demonstrated by the Shandean homunculus, but at the same time the difference becomes more evident. For Swift, the corruptions of science served as an emblem of the degeneracy of human nature and the entire environing culture; Sterne's treatment, though it has some implications for man's folly and the aberrations of the intellect, tends to be unleavened comic spectacle, all geniality, with no hint of that Juvenalian thunder characteristic of his great predecessor.

[62] I know of only one earlier instance of the comic use of animalculism, the casual mention in the *Memoirs of Scriblerus;* see the *Memoirs,* ed. Charles Kerby-Miller (New Haven, 1950), pp. 96–97, and n. 16, p. 189. A copy of the *Memoirs* is listed in the *Catalogue of Sterne's Library,* p. 93, no. 2664. Post-Shandean homunculi seem to have thrived. They appear several times in 1760, notably in two anonymous works, *Yorick's Meditations upon Various Subjects* and in what purports to be a third or supplementary volume to Sterne's novel. This latter work, attributed to John Carr, has the same title as Sterne's. In *Yorick's Meditations,* the author has brought Sterne and Shakespeare together, to demonstrate man's littleness and castigate his pride: "If imagination may trace the noble dust of Alexander, till it find it stopping a bung-whole [*sic*], why may not imagination trace that very Alexander, who conquered at Issus, Arbela, and Granicus, and who carried his presumption so far as to assume the title of son of Jupiter Ammon . . . why may not imagination trace that very Alexander, till it perceives him an homunculus in the genitalia of Philip, or, which seems rather more probable, of one of Philip's domestics . . ." (pp. 47–48; see also pp. 44–45). In the alleged third volume of *Tristram Shandy,* Walter Shandy tells Uncle Toby that "in generation the woman is but little different from being entirely passive. The disposition, figure, situation, number, activity, etc., etc., etc., of the homunculi depend on the male. It is his business to adjust all these matters" (p. 11). He tried to convince Uncle Toby that "the science of generation depends on as certain and as reasonable rules as any other" (p. 13). When Uncle Toby perceives the relationship between his cherished science of fortifications and generation, he is convinced (p. 16).

JOHNSON'S FEATHERED MAN:
"A DISSERTATION ON
THE ART OF FLYING"
CONSIDERED

IT IS WELL KNOWN that Johnson did not escape the excitement generated in his time by the possibility of human flight. He was familiar, as Professor Gwin Kolb has shown, with *Mathematical Magick: or the Wonders that may be Performed by Mechanical Geometry* (1648), by John Wilkins, the distinguished member of the Royal Society, who with Robert Hooke, the Secretary of the Royal Society, was the foremost English enthusiast of flight by man.[1] Johnson reflects particularly, as Kolb demonstrates, that part of *Mathematical Magick* entitled "Daedalus," in which the subject of human flight by wings is explored. In 1783 and 1784, when air balloons were dramatically provoking attention, Johnson was much interested, as is evident in his correspondence. For a brief time the subject occupied him almost as much as his own ill health. In a delightful and characteristic letter to Mrs. Thrale, then at Bath, he relegates to the end the unhappy news that his "complaint" is a sarcocele demanding immediate excision: "If excision should be delayed, there is danger of a

---

1. "Johnson's 'Dissertation on Flying,'" in *New Light on Dr. Johnson: Essays on the Occasion of his 250th Birthday*, ed. Frederick W. Hilles (New Haven: Yale University Press, 1959), pp. 91-106.

gangrene. You would not have me for fear of pain perish in putrescence."
The more "interesting" news comes at the opening of the letter in fuller
detail. Air balloons, he tells her, indubitably exist, and he explains the
principle by which they operate: a very light spherical case in which a
"vapour [hydrogen] lighter than the atmospherical air" is collected in
sufficient quantity to make it mount into the clouds. "It rises till it comes
to air of equal tenuity with its own, if wind or water does not spoil it on
the way. Such, Madam, is an air ballon [sic]."[2] He expressed doubt that
the invention could be useful, a skeptical attitude he repeated a year
later when he became weary of the subject. The arrival of three letters
in a single day, all on air balloons, produced a sharp reaction. "I could
have been content with one," he wrote to Sir Joshua Reynolds. "Do
not write about the ballon, whatever else you may think proper to say."[3]
To his physician, Dr. Richard Broklesby, he reaffirmed his opinion that
the invention would be of little or no use: "I had rather now find a medicine that can ease an asthma."[4]

But even more interesting is his earlier satirical glance, in the *Rambler*,
No. 199, Feb. 11, 1752, at the experiments in flying, particularly relevant because it reveals Johnson's amusement over the presumed aberrations of those natural philosophers, that is, the scientists, whose search
into the recondite ways of nature struck many contemporaries as foolish
and impractical. The essay, which is in the form of a letter from Hermeticus, gently chides the *Rambler* for his persistent emphasis upon
moral philosophy and his failure to give some attention to the wonders
of natural philosophy. To demonstrate the usefulness of natural philosophy, Hermeticus describes his untiring efforts as an *adeptus* (one skilled
in alchemy) who has perfected a device destined to increase happiness,
a magnet for detecting female incontinence. But he has also been active
in other areas of natural philosophy. He has experimented with the atha-
nor (the self-feeding fire of the alchemists), with diving engines, electric-
ity, transfusions of blood—and "I have twice dislocated my limbs, and
once fractured my skull, in essaying to fly." The implications of *Rambler*,
No. 199, will become clearer as we examine Chapter VI of *Rasselas*.

2. *The Letters of Samuel Johnson, with Mrs. Thrale's Genuine Letters to Him*, ed. R. W. Chapman
   (Oxford: At the Clarendon Press, 1952), III, 72.

3. *Ibid.*, p. 226.

4. *Ibid.*, p. 232.

That Johnson links human flight derisively to alchemical experiments and the absurdities of natural philosophy is highly significant, but for the moment the essay is of value in showing that he had formed early an opinion which remained unchanged for over three decades. Clearly he did not think man a volant animal, or that it was worth while for man to "improve" himself into one.

Chapter VI of *Rasselas*, entitled "A Dissertation on the Art of Flying," is itself ample testimony. It is a story of failure. The inventor, or, as Johnson calls him, the artist, is a devotee in theory and practice of what the eighteenth century called "artificial" flight. For a year he labors over his flying contrivance, bat-like wings "accommodated to the human form."[5] He then tries his wings and, as Rasselas had feared, he fails. A final crisp sentence concludes the incident: "His wings, which were of no use in the air, sustained him in the water, and the prince drew him to land, half dead with terrour and vexation." The symbolic resonance in the chapter, with its daedalian evocations, is apparent. The artist becomes something more than merely an artist: he is an emblem of aspiring and prideful man, and as such he reinforces a chief contention of the work as a whole, that man does not know his real nature — or his proper relationship to the world he inhabits. For it is not merely a choice of life which will bring the happiness Rasselas seeks; it is, as well, his true nature, that self-knowledge which was the desideratum of the moral philosopher and out of which emerged a comprehension of one's function or end in the cosmic scheme. In its simplest sense Chapter VI serves an obvious narrative intention by presenting one more in a sequence of opportunities lost to Rasselas in his attempts to escape from the Happy Valley. Additionally it reinforces a theme which gives the tale some of its philosophic substance, the theme of man's delusive hopes, the discrepancy between human pretensions and human achievement; and in this respect its resemblance to *The Vanity of Human Wishes* is obvious. But "A Dissertation on the Art of Flying" has other dimensions and richer implications which would have been apparent to contemporary readers, who would have read it in the light of one of the great organizing principles of eighteenth-century thought, the controversy be-

5. On the subject of human flight by wings, see Marjorie Hope Nicolson, *Voyages to the Moon*, 1948, particularly Ch. IV, "Wanton Wings." I am much indebted to this brilliant study, which is indispensable to anyone concerned with the subject of flight in literature.

tween the moral philosophers and the natural philosophers, or in our terms the conflicting values of the humanist and the scientist. Essentially Chapter VI is an affirmation, negatively arrived at, that man, not nature, is the proper study of mankind.

An acceptable epigraph to "A Dissertation on the Art of Flying"— and indeed to the work as a whole— might well be the remark Rasselas makes in another connection: "my business is with man" (Ch. XXX). It is a remark which suggests Johnson's affinity with the moral philosophers and, in a very general sense, the kind of work *Rasselas* is, an ethical enquiry into the nature of man and his *summum bonum*, in substance a traditional disquisition dressed up in narrative form but just the same recognizably an "essay" on man such as any moral philosopher might write. And such as Pope did write. If we are permitted a little latitude, we may with validity think of *Rasselas* as Johnson's *Essay on Man*. If Pope can ask "Why has not Man a microscopic eye?" and reply, "For this plain reason, Man is not a Fly," we may justifiably state in similar phraseology what is implicit in "A Dissertation on the Art of Flying": why has not man a pair of wings? For this plain reason, man is not a bird. Though the rhyme is lost, the parallel is exact. As Pope did, so does Johnson "Expatiate free o'er all this scene of Man." More striking, and more significant for our purposes, is Pope's couplet, "What would this Man? Now upward will he soar, | And little less than Angel, would be more" (Epis. I, 173-74), lines which could serve as a gloss on "A Dissertation on the Art of Flying." For both Pope and Johnson, and their contemporaries, aspirations of man to qualities not part of his original endowment and to activities not proper to his nature or his state in the cosmic scheme were a form of pride. We have recourse to Pope again:

> The bliss of Man (could Pride that blessing find)
> Is not to act or think beyond Mankind;
> No pow'rs of body or of soul to share,
> But what his nature and his state can bear.
>
> (*Essay on Man*, I, 189-92)

Johnson is less explicit in *Rasselas* in stating this great truth of the moral philosopher, but essentially it is summed up in one gnomic remark by Nekayah: "he does nothing who endeavours to do more than is allowed to humanity" (Ch. XXIX), a comment that obviously applies to the artist and his attempts to fly.

Johnson's striking aphorism, like Pope's lines just quoted, embodies a commonplace of the moral philosopher of the period, who believed that man should know himself and fulfill his nature, but fulfill it without seeking to go beyond his nature, without overreaching himself. The great and respected clergyman, Isaac Barrow, called attention to the respective spheres of moral philosophy and natural philosophy and indicated how the former could be beneficial to man in coming to know himself. Moral philosophy, he asserted, suggests

> to us the dictates of reason, concerning the nature and faculties of our soul, the chief good and end of our life, the way and means of attaining happiness, the best rules and methods of practice; the distinctions between good and evil ... the rank wherein we stand in the world, and the duties proper to our relations: by rightly understanding and estimating which things we may know how to behave ourselves, justly and prudently toward our neighbours; we may learn to ... govern our actions, to conduct and wield all our practice well in prosecution of our end; so as to enjoy our being and conveniences of life in constant quiet and peace, with tranquility and satisfaction of mind.[6]

Barrow did not, of course, deny the value of natural philosophy — "the contemplation of this great theatre, or visible system presented before us." This too could enlarge the mind and generate piety, love, and reverence for God, whose "transcendent perfections and attributes of immense power, wisdom, and goodness ... shine in those his works of Nature!"[7] But the emphasis for Barrow, as for Pope and Johnson, was not here. It was on *human* nature, the realm of moral values, the study and knowledge of man. As Mr. Spectator said, "Humane Nature [is] the most useful Object of humane Reason" (No. 408, June 18, 1712).

The prestige of natural philosophy, its excessive claims, and its very real promise and accomplishments, forced the moral philosophers into a defensive posture. It is observable, for example, in John Locke's insistence that morality is capable of demonstration. "I doubt not," he wrote, that the measures of right and wrong might be made out "from self-evident propositions, by necessary consequences, as incontestable as

6. *Works*, ed. Alexander Napier (Cambridge: At the University Press, 1859), III, 446-47.
7. *Ibid.*

those in mathematics."[8] His claim for morality as being "among the sciences capable of demonstration"[9] is paralleled by his skepticism that vaunted human reason can adequately arrive at a full knowledge of the nature of things or that the study of nature can ever be as useful as the study of man. In important passages in the *Essay concerning Human Understanding* (1690), Locke assesses the respective claims of the moral philosophers and the natural philosophers: " . . . since our faculties are not fitted to penetrate into the internal fabric and real essences of bodies; but yet plainly discover to us the being of a God, and the knowledge of ourselves, enough to lead us into a full and clear discovery of our duty . . . it will become us, as rational creatures, to employ those faculties we have about what they are most adapted to. . . . For it is rational to conclude, that our proper employment lies in those inquiries, and in that sort of knowledge which is most suited to our natural capacities, and carries in it our greatest interest, i.e., the condition of our eternal state. Hence I think I may conclude, that *morality* is *the proper science and business of mankind in general*, (who are both concerned and fitted to search out their *summum bonum*)."[10] Nevertheless, he adds, "I would not therefore be thought to disesteem the study of *nature*":

> I readily agree the contemplation of [God's] works gives us occasion to admire, revere, and glorify their Author; and if rightly directed, may be of greater benefit to mankind than the monuments of exemplary charity that have . . . been raised by the founders of hospitals and alms-houses. . . . All that I would say is, that we should not be too forwardly possessed with the opinion or expectation of knowledge where it is not to be had, or by ways that will not attain it: that we should not take doubtful systems for complete sciences, nor unintelligible notions for scientifical demonstrations.[11]

"The smallest Worm insults the sage's hand; | All Gresham's vanquished by a grain of sand." So remarked Henry Jones in his poem, "*An Essay on the Weakness of Human Knowledge*," (1749). This was often granted. Still, the pervasive skeptical strains in the work of the natural philosophers did not prevent large claims in some quarters for physics, astronomy,

8. *An Essay concerning Human Understanding*, ed. A. C. Fraser (New York, Dover, 1959), II, 208, bk. IV, iii, 18.

9. *Ibid.*

10. *Ibid.* pp. 350-51, bk. IV, xii, 11.

11. *Ibid.*, pp. 351-52, bk. IV, xii, 12.

and mathematics. The exaggerated claims, along with the optimistic presumption that these sciences offered final certitude about the universe, challenged the deepest convictions of the moral philosopher. His responses are relevant for our purposes.

He attacked, for instance, the presumed certitude of mathematics, the science basic to the other sciences and the one which had attained the greatest prestige from the efforts of Newton and the Royal Society. It is in the sermons of the period, as one expects, that we find a persistent effort to show that moral philosophy endows man with a superior and more useful knowledge. The clergyman stood his ground as humanist, and often adopted the strategy of denying that mathematics did or could provide the most beneficial kind of knowledge. Typical is the attitude of Richard Marsh, in a sermon entitled *The Vanity and Danger of Modern Theories*, preached at Cambridge in 1699:

> The saying something New and Surprising, makes such Speculations [i.e., of the natural philosophers] at first to be in Vogue, and gives them a Reputation; but a little Time wears this off, and then Men find they are just as Wise as they were before. . . . Had God design'd us for so nice a Search into his World, he wou'd have given us other Senses, and not so much as can skim only the Surface, but can go no deeper. There is one thing hath advanc'd the Reputation of such Speculations, and that is, the *Mathematical* Learning with which they appear in the World. But notwithstanding this, it is not in the power of that Science to give us any clearer account of the nature of Things. . . . It is to be question'd whether we understand the most ordinary appearances in the world; the structure of the least Insect being able to baffle the greatest Philosopher. . . . Philosophy, as well as Religion, teacheth a man to be humble and modest; he that makes This his study will find his greatest Discoveries to be those of his Weakness and Ignorance.[12]

Here, interwoven with the indictment of those who claimed certitude for the natural sciences, is another chief contention of the moral philosopher, an insistence on the weakness of man's reason, his limited capacities, and the necessity that he should accept in humility his limitations, applying himself only to those things which are proper to him as a man. It is a skeptical strain whose roots are deep in classical and Christian thought. Locke reflects it in his remark that "Men have rea-

12. Pp. 5-6.

son to be well satisfied with what God hath thought fit for them, since he hath given them . . . whatsoever is necessary for the convenience of life, and information of virtue." Though man is involved in darkness, so Locke maintains, "we shall not have much reason to complain of the narrowness of our minds, if we will but employ them about what may be of use to us." "Our business here," Locke adds, "is not to know all things, but those which concern our conduct."[13] One is tempted to see in these injunctions something akin to the old religious anathemas against the prying intellect, man's prideful search into the ways of God and nature. The great difference is that the Enlightenment tended to regard "forbidden knowledge" and undue curiosity in a secular rather than in a religious light, as an excess or folly, one more example of man's pride and failure to know himself. Again we may turn to Pope for memorable statement:

> Go, wond'rous creature! mount where Science guides,
> Go, measure earth, weigh air, and state the tides;
> Instruct the planets in what orbs to run,
> Correct old Time, and regulate the Sun; . . .
> Go, teach Eternal Wisdom how to rule —
> Then drop into thyself, and be a fool!
>
> (*Essay on Man*, II, 19-30)

Ethical writers of the seventeenth and eighteenth centuries never tired of calling attention to man's failure to understand himself, his inability to recognize the discrepancy between his limitations and his overweening tendency to strive for that which was not suitable to his nature. Sir William Temple is worth citing because he illustrates the way in which the idea found its place in the controversy between the Ancients and Moderns. In his famous *Essay upon the Ancient and Modern Learning* (1690), he asks: "But what would we have unless it be other natures than God Almighty has given us?"

> We cannot comprehend the growth of a kernel or seed, the frame of an ant or bee . . . yet we will know the substance, the figure, the course, the influences of all those celestial bodies, and the end for which they were made: we pretend to give a clear account how thunder and lightning (that great artillery of God Almighty) is produced; and we cannot comprehend how the voice of man is framed. . . . Nay, we do not so much

13. *Essay*, I, 29-31, Introduction, sec. 4-6. cf. Pope, *Essay on Man*, I, 71: man's knowledge is "measur'd to his state and place."

as know what motion is, nor how a stone moves from our hand, when we throw it across the street. Of all these that most ancient and divine writer gives the best account in that short satire, *Vain man would fain be wise, when he is born like a wild ass's colt.*[14]

Thus it is that Temple can remark: "We are born to grovel upon the earth, and we would fain soar up to the skies."[15]

It is not surprising that the subject of human flight became a point of controversy between defenders of the Ancients and defenders of the Moderns. It was, after all, two of the foremost members of the Royal Society, exemplars of the New Philosophy, whose experiments with flying machines were most widely known, John Wilkins and Nathaniel Hooke; and it was the New Philosophy, with its orientation in physics and mathematics, which appeared to offer the command of nature necessary for human flight. When William Wotton, stout defender of the Moderns, penned his answer to Sir William Temple, he maintained that any determination of "who Philosophized best, *Aristotle* and *Democritus*, or Mr. *Boyle* and Mr. *Newton*" would depend upon the "*Physico-Mathematical* and *Physico-Mechanical* Parts of Knowledge,"[16] that is to say, precisely those "Parts of Knowledge" on which Wilkins and Hooke—and the artist in *Rasselas*—depended in planning their sailing chariots and winged flight. Wotton, of course, had no doubts about where the superiority resided: "it seems to me," he declared, "to be sufficiently plain, that the Ancient Knowledge in all Matters relating to *Mathematics* and *Physics*, was incomparably inferior to that of the Moderns."[17] The controversy over flight should be kept in proper perspective. It was part of a larger conflict with many ramifications; and the issue was not that the Moderns had gone farther in discovering the principles of flight as such. It was the respective achievements in mathematics and physics which were being argued, or for our purposes more precisely the science of mechanics as the eighteenth century understood the term, that is, "a mixed mathematical science which considers motion and moving powers, their nature and laws, with the effects thereof in machines, etc."—so

14. *Five Miscellaneous Essays by Sir William Temple,* ed. Samuel Holt Monk (Ann Arbor: University of Michigan Press, 1963), pp. 61-62.
15. *Ibid.,* p. 61.
16. *Reflections upon Ancient and Modern Learning* (1697), p. 82. The first edition appeared in 1692.
17. *Ibid.,* p. 372.

Ephraim Chambers defines it in his *Cyclopaedia, or A Universal Dictionary of the Arts and Sciences* (1728). We must recall at this point that the artist in "A Dissertation on the Art of Flying" is described as "a man eminent for his knowledge of the mechanick powers, who had contrived many engines, both of use and recreation."

The conviction that human flight would some day be feasible as a result of progress among the Moderns is observable in Joseph Glanvill, one of the more able defenders of the New Philosophy. He had no doubt that posterity would attain as practical realities some of the things which at the moment seemed beyond the capabilities of man. "It may be," he wrote, "some Ages hence a voyage to the Southern unknown Tracts, yea possibly the *Moon*, will not be more strange than one to *America*. To them, that come after us, it may be as ordinary to buy a *pair* of *Wings* to fly into remotest *Regions*; as now a *pair* of *Boots* to ride a *Journey*."[18] To Thomas Baker, eager to defend divine revelation and ethical knowledge, this claim seemed both preposterous and, in some vague way, ominous. It was part and parcel of the excessive claims for natural philosophy. "A Philosopher's business," he granted, "is to trace Nature in her inward Recesses and latent Motions." But when the philosopher [i.e., the scientist] looks deep into nature and observes it in all of its "Windings and Mazes," he meets only with mortification. He is "forced to confess, that the ways of Nature, like those of God, are past Man's finding out."[19] And Baker, whose *Reflections upon Learning* (1699) reached a fifth edition by 1714, had only contempt for "the Vanity of some few Men, who have been so *Planet-struck*, as to dream of the Possibility of a Voyage to the Moon, and to talk of making Wings to fly thither, as they would be buying a pair of Boots to take a Journey."[20] The motives of those who rejected human flight varied. Different in tone, method, and intention, is the indictment in *The Memoirs of Martinus Scriblerus* (1741). Here Arbuthnot, Pope, Swift, and their fellow wits seized upon the follies and corruptions of contemporary learning for comic exposé. The Great Scriblerus, the Philosopher of Ultimate Causes, we are told, had squared the circle, found out the palpability of colors, calculated how

18. *Scepsis Scientifica*, 1665, p. 134.

19. *Reflections upon Learning, wherein is shown the Insufficiency thereof in its several Particulars* (1714), p. 90.

20. *Ibid.*, p. 99.

much the inhabitants of the moon eat for supper, propounded new theories of the Deluge, compiled a complete digest of the laws of nature, measured the quantity of real matter in the universe, and made a contribution to resolving the grand phenomena of nature. Among his various projects are perpetual motion and flying engines. The humor is broad, but it points up clearly the contemporary attitude in literary circles by linking flight with a number of other projects considered visionary, foolish, and impractical.[21]

A more detailed and more illuminating discussion of volant man appeared in the Boyle Lectures of 1711-1712, delivered by William Derham, a Canon of Windsor and a Fellow of the Royal Society. In the sixteen sermons which constituted the Lectures for that year Derham made a survey of all the works of creation in order to demonstrate that every aspect of creation is wisely designed to function perfectly in a universe whose harmony and rationality give complete assurance of the existence of God. In the part of his physico-theology devoted to a survey of man, Derham concludes that man shows "admirable Marks of the Divine Design and Art." Everything relating to man is "contrived, and made up in the very best Manner; his Body fitted up with the utmost Foresight, Art, and Care." The size of man, his posture, skin, teeth, feet, muscles, nerves, the placing of the various organs—all are perfectly designed and adapted so as to function in a manner consistent with the divine intention for man and his place in the cosmic scheme. Thus man has an obligation to recognize this fact, to come to know his nature, and to acquiesce gratefully in what he is—and what he is not, a winged animal, for example: "we lie under all the Obligations of Duty and Gratitude, to be thankful and obedient to, and to set forth the Glories of our great Creator, and noble Benefactor." For Derham then, and for other physico-theologists, as for Locke and Pope, it was axiomatic that man had been "endow'd exactly with such Faculties, Power, and Dispositions as the various Necessities and Occasions of the World require from such a Creature."[22] In the light of this indisputable truth Derham examines the "Inventive power of the Soul." He observes that God has

21. See *Memoirs of the Extraordinary Life, Works, and Discoveries of Martinus Scriblerus*, ed. Charles Kerby-Miller (New Haven: Yale University Press for Wellesley College, 1950), pp. 166 ff.
22. *Physico-Theology: Or, A Demonstration of the Being and Attributes of God, from His Works of Creation*, 12th ed. (1754), pp. 312 ff.

permitted man to invent and discover all "Things of great, and absolutely necessary Use" — the many things in the arts and sciences, in agriculture, in labor, things to support daily existence, and things to divert and please. On the other hand, "Things of little Use, or very dangerous Use, are rarely and slowly discover'd, or still utterly undiscover'd." There "perhaps will always remain Exercises of the Wit and Invention of Men." In this category Derham lists the squaring of the circle, finding of the longitude, perpetual motion, and the art of flying.[23]

Derham stresses the inutility of human flight, but he also emphasizes what might be called the moral argument against it, something that even the enthusiastic John Wilkins felt impelled to counter. This was the view that corrupt man ought not to possess a device so potentially destructive to peace and order. Johnson's artist in Chapter VI similarly recognizes the dangers. He extracts a promise of secrecy from Rasselas on precisely these grounds. To Rasselas's protest that "All skill ought to be exerted for the universal good," the artist replies:

> If men were all virtuous . . . I should, with great alacrity teach them all to fly. But what would be the security of the good, if the bad could, at pleasure, invade them from the sky? Against an army sailing through the clouds, neither walls, nor mountains, nor seas, could afford any security. A flight of northern savages might hover in the wind, and light, at once, with irresistible violence, upon the capital of a fruitful region, that was rolling under them. Even this valley . . . might be violated by the sudden descent of some of the naked nations, that swarm on the coast of the southern sea.

It is little wonder that John Wilkins complained: "If all those Inventions that are liable to abuse, should therefore be concealed, there is not any Art or Science which might be lawfully profest."[24] In a paragraph which Johnson may well have known, Derham granted that the art of flying could in some instances be of use to the geographer and the philosopher, yet he too felt strongly the force of the moral argument: " . . . [it] might prove of dangerous and fatal Consequence: As for Instance, by putting it in Man's Power to discover the Secrets of Nations and Families more than is consistent with the Peace of the World, for man to know; by

23. *Ibid.*, pp. 264-68.
24. See "Mercury: or the Secret and Swift Messenger," p. 90, in *The Mathematical and Philosophical Works* (1708).

giving ill Men greater Opportunities to do Mischief, which it would not be in the Power of Others to prevent."[25]

At the risk of tedium I wish to cite one more work useful in defining the climate of opinion out of which Chapter VI of *Rasselas* emerged, a work Johnson knew and commended. This was the *Spectacle de la nature, Or, Nature Displayed* (1733), by Noel Antoine Pluche, sufficiently popular in England to be translated three different times and appear in several editions before the publication of *Rasselas* in 1759. In a "dialogue" carried on between a prior, a count, a countess, and a chevalier the subject of human flight is explored. The chevalier, the only one of the four to approve, has a vision of the benefits likely to accrue, as knowledge extended, labor eased, and commerce advanced. His chief opponent is the prior, who argues that the "Art of Flying would be the greatest Calamity that could happen to Society." Whatever advantages it offered would not "countervail the Disorders that would be induced," an argument supported by the Count, who maintains that if men were capable of flight "no Avenue could be made inaccessible to Vengeance and inordinate Desires": "The Habitations of Mankind would be so many Theatres of Murder and Robbery. What Precautions could we take against an Enemy who would have it in his Power to surprise us both by Day and Night? How should we preserve our Money, and Furniture, and our Fruits from the Avidity of a Sett of Plunderers, furnished . . . with good Wings to carry off their Booty, and elude our Pursuit?" To this the prior adds another argument; the art of flying would "intirely change the Face of Nature," by which he means that the social order or customary way of life would be radically changed: " . . . we should be compelled to abandon our Cities and the Country, and to bury ourselves in subterranean Caves, or to imitate Eagles and other Birds of Prey; we should retire, like them, to inaccessible Rocks and craggy Mountains, from whence we should from Time to Time sally down upon the Fruits and Animals that accommodate our Necessities. . . ." The prospect makes the Countess tremble, but she is reassured by the Count, who confidently asserts that the art of flying "is an absolute Impossibility; Nature herself has formed an Obstacle against it, that is in some Measure made invincible, by the exceeding Disproportion between the Weight

25. *Physico-Theology*, p. 268.

of the Air, and the human Body." It is, he says, "as much forbidden to Man as the perpetual Motion."[26]

By the middle of the eighteenth century a whole cluster of ideas related to human flight, ethical, scientific, religious, and social, had crystallized and been assimilated into the thinking of interested and informed contemporaries. The experiments in flight and the claims and theories of the New Science gave special significance and urgency to this amorphous body of thought and brought some of the ideas into the controversy between the Ancients and the Moderns. Likewise some of the ideas found their way into the works of the ethical writers who, under challenge from science, were compelled to reexamine and restate their views. "A Dissertation on the Art of Flying" in *Rasselas* reflects the intellectual ferment. A contemporary reader would have realized at once that the artist represented the New Science, that he is a Modern versed in physics and mathematics. He visualizes human flight by adapting to human use what nature or God had provided for another species, a pair of wings. He speaks the language of natural philosophy — such phrases as the body's gravity, the density of matter, the earth's attraction — and obviously he believes that human inventiveness can overcome the obstacles. Implicit in his remarks is the view of the New Science that progress in modern times has given man the knowledge to control nature, or at the least the promise of doing so. To a contemporary less favorably disposed toward current theories the artist would have been seen as the embodiment of the excessive optimism, even the brazen assurance, of the natural philosophers who, in Johnson's phraseology, were attempting to do more than is given to humanity.

Like others who were enthusiastic about the art of flying, the artist suggests that it will serve the philosopher and the geographer by extending knowledge and the understanding of man and nature. But despite his enthusiasm, he voices the conventional fear, that men are not sufficiently virtuous to be trusted with an invention so easily abused. On the other hand, Rasselas voices the conventional skepticism, based partly on scientific grounds (human flight is impossible because of the tenuity of the air and the muscular structure of man), partly on the larger philosophical or religious grounds: "Every animal has his element assigned

26. See Pt. II, Dialogue X, pp. 30-33.

him; birds have the air, and man and beasts the earth." This remark
by Rasselas reaffirms by implication an old conviction, that nature or
God had made a fair and equal distribution of faculties and powers
among the various species of living things. "Every Thing has a Nature
suited to its End," Thomas Burnet had said in his Boyle Lectures of 1724-
1725.[27] Had Nature been a step-mother to man? Why was he not given
"the strength of bulls, the fur of bears"? In the *Essay on Man* Pope asked
this question, which had been considered in ancient times by Lucretius,
Pliny, and Seneca — and after them by countless theologians and others.
Inevitably the discussions came to include wings: "he were no better
than a mad man that should aske, why man should not fly as well as
the bird, and swim as well as the fish, and run as fast as the hart" — so
remarked Bishop Joseph Hall.[28] Similarly in Shaftesbury's *The Moralists*
(1709) a debate arises over the point, why should man be "any thing
less than a consummation of all advantages and privileges which Nature
can afford." Why is man born naked, more subject to disease, possessed
of fewer bodily advantages than "mere brutes"? Why does he not have
"wings also for the air, fins for the water, and so on — that he might take
possession of each element, and reign in all?" "Methinks," says the "antagonist" of Nature in the dialogue, "it had been wonderfully obliging
in Nature to have allowed [man] wings."[29] As already suggested, the

27. Thomas Burnet, "A Demonstration of True Religion," in *A Defence of Natural and Revealed Religion: Being An Abridgment of the Sermons Preached at the Lectures founded by the Honble Robert Boyle, Esq.*, 3d ed. (1765), III, 459.

28. *The Works of the Right Reverend Joseph Hall, D.D.*, ed. Philip Wynter (Oxford: At the University Press, 1863), VIII, 41. Hall discusses the problem of "Equal Distribution," that is, the justice with which God has distributed faculties and powers among the many species of living things, in Soliloquy, No. XXII. Writers of theodicies and theologians generally discussed the matter. Hall opens his Soliloquy·thus: "It was a most idle question which the philosophers are said to have proposed to Barnabas, the colleague of St. Paul: 'Why a small gnat should have six legs, and wings beside; whereas the elephant, the greatest of beasts, hath but four legs, and no wings.' What pity it is that those wise masters were not of the counsel of the Almighty when he was pleased to give a being to his crea- tures! they would surely have devised to make a winged elephant and a corpulent gnat; a feathered man, and a speaking beast. Vain fools! they had not learned to know and adore that infinite Wisdom wherein all things were made." Hall's answer to those who were blind to divine wisdom and mercy in the distribution of gifts is that man is correctly endowed, and, above all, he has been given reason. Cf. Pope's lines: "Who finds not Providence all good and wise, | Alike in what it gives and what it denies?" *Essay on Man*, I, 205-6.

29. *Characteristics of Men, Manners, Opinions, Times*, ed. John M. Robertson, with an Intro- duction by Stanley Grean (Indianapolis: Bobbs-Merrill, 1964), II, 72 ff. The problem of "equal distribution" is argued at length in *The Moralist*, Pt. II, sec. iv.

answer to these questions, at least the part of the answer relevant to present purposes, is that complaining man fails to understand that "all Creatures have their Ends assign'd, | Proportion'd to their Nature, and their Kind."[30] It is an affront to Providence that man should aspire to be other than he is — and, of course, it is the sin of pride.

Significantly in the two instances in *Rasselas* concerned with science Johnson calls attention to the limits of man's knowledge and capacities, and even more strongly to the dangers of man's failure to recognize his limitations. The learned astronomer of Chapters XL-XLIV, who has passed his time "in the attainment of sciences . . . but remotely useful to mankind," is the more extreme example. He has lapsed into melancholy and madness, a scientist who is a complete failure in what Hume called "Moral philosophy, or the science of human nature."[31] In the *Enquiry concerning Human Understanding* (1748), Hume seems to envision just such a person being admonished by Nature: "Indulge your passion for science, says she, but let your science be human, and such as may have a direct reference to action and society. Abstruse thought and profound researches I prohibit, and will severely punish, by the pensive melancholy which they introduce, by the endless uncertainty in which they involve you, and by the cold reception which your pretended discoveries shall meet with, when communicated. Be a philosopher; but, amidst all your philosophy, be still a man."[32]

The artist with his wings and his "knowledge of the mechanick powers" is a less extreme case than that of the learned astronomer, but his mortification as he attempts to study and conquer nature drives home the same truth: he would do better to study himself, or man as reflected in himself. Ephraim Chambers gives us a useful brief definition of moral philosophy: "A science whose object is to . . . teach and instruct us how to find that felicity which is agreeable to human nature."[33] Perhaps we

---

30. John Pomfret, "Upon the Divine Attributes. A Pindaric Essay," stanza 4. Cf. Pope's *Essay on Man*, Twickenham ed., edited Maynard Mack, Epis. I, 180-186, particularly Mack's notes to lines 173-176.

31. See *An Enquiry concerning Human Understanding*, in *Essays Moral, Political, and Literary*, ed. T. H. Green and T. H. Grose (London: Longmans, Green, 1875), II, 3.

32. *Ibid.*, 6.

33. See "Moral Philosophy," in Ephraim Chambers, *Cyclopaedia: Or, An Universal Dictionary of Arts and Sciences*, 5th ed. (1743). A later edition (1786) added: "Moral *philosophy* is the same with what we otherwise call Ethics, sometimes Morality."

are not wide of the mark if, speaking broadly, we see in *Rasselas* a student of *this* science, a kind of philosophic traveler seeking, as did the Chinese philosopher in Goldsmith's *Citizen of the World*, the wisdom which has happiness as its chief object. In *Tom Jones* we find Fielding proclaiming at the opening of the novel that human nature is to be the bill of fare; and he uses as an epigraph a remark that Horace had applied to Ulysses: "*Mores hominum multorum vidit et urbes.*"[34] It has a certain appropriateness for Johnson's philosophic tale as well. The incidents are chosen so as to exhibit human nature in its varied manifestations, all for the benefit of Rasselas, who hopes to find "that felicity which is agreeable to human nature." For the deeply pious Johnson the *true* felicity existed only in the austere Christian sense which he expressed to Boswell: "There is but one solid basis of happiness; and that is the reasonable hope of a happy futurity."[35] It is this wisdom which is embodied in the remark of the Princess at the conclusion of the discussion about the nature of the soul (Chapter XLVIII): "To me . . . the choice of life is become less important: I hope hereafter to think only on the choice of eternity." *Contemptus mundi*: well, not quite, but still something vaguely related to that old theme. As for "A Dissertation on the Art of Flying," with its reverberations of the conflicting claims of the scientists and the ethical writers to define the nature and state of man with respect to the universe, it should be viewed as one aspect of Johnson's larger strategy of indicating what man is not, what he may not be, and what will not contribute to his happiness. We cannot do better in conclusion than to take a clue from John Wilkins, as he turns back in time to the fourth century A.D., to Eusebius, Bishop of Caesarea in Palestine, who stated the crux of the matter as it came down traditionally. Eusebius, Wilkins tells us,

> speaking with what necessity every thing is confined by the Laws of Nature, and the Decrees of Providence, so that nothing can go out of that way unto which naturally it is designed; as a Fish cannot reside on Land, nor a Man in the Water, or aloft in the Air . . . unless his Brain be a little crazed with the Humour of Melancholy; whereupon he advises, that we should not in any Particular, endeavour to transgress the

34. *Ars Poetica*, 141.
35. *Letters*, 3 July, 1778, II, 251.

Bounds of Nature . . . and since we are destitute of Wings, not to imitate the Flight of Birds.[36]

It is, then, not too fanciful to see an affinity between Johnson's artist and the subtle philosopher who sought to confound Barnabas, the Cypriote missionary companion of Paul, when he was zealously proclaiming the divinity of Christ in Alexandria. The story is found in the Pseudo-Clementine literature of the third century A. D.[37] A learned caviller interrupted Barnabas with a question casting doubt on the justice with which God had distributed qualities among created beings. Why, he wished to know, should the small gnat have six legs *and* wings, whereas the elephant, the greatest of beasts, had been created with only four legs and *no* wings? Bishop Joseph Hall, of the generation preceding John Wilkins on the Anglican episcopal bench, "soliloquized" over this incident and expressed his scorn for such vain and philosophic cavillers who could wish that the deity had devised a winged elephant, a corpulent gnat, a speaking beast, and — of course — "a feathered man."[38] In a secular context, and in his fashion, Johnson's artist is in the tradition of this tribe of heterodox men who could not be content with man's god-given endowments. They would have man something more than the deity has made him. The experiments in flight in Johnson's day gave a new vitality to this ancient cavil, as is evident from the "feathered man" in *Rasselas*.

36. "Daedalus," p. 115, in *The Mathematical and Philosophical Works* (1708).
37. See "The Recognitions of Clement," Bk. I, ch. viii, and "The Clementine Homilies," Homily I, ch. x, in *The Ante-Nicene Fathers*, ed. Alexander Roberts and James Donaldson (Buffalo, N.Y.: Christian Literature Co., 1886), VIII, 79, 225.
38. See the quotation from Bishop Hall, note no. 28. Hall took the story of Barnabas and the philosophic caviller from the Pseudo-Clementine literature.

POPE'S BELINDA,
THE GENERAL EMPORIE OF THE WORLD,
AND THE WONDROUS WORM

Pope's heroine in *The Rape of the Lock* has deservedly been the object of extensive attention from the critics. From John Dennis in 1714 to the present, no small part of the commentary on the poem has been concerned with the character of Belinda. To Dennis, unlike certain more recent commentators, she was no goddess. As Edward Hooker remarked, Dennis by temperament and nature was incapable of understanding or enjoying "the exquisite trifling of the *Rape*."[1] He was similarly incapable of appreciating Belinda's charm. Perhaps no one has been so severe in judgment of this beguiling young woman, who becomes for him a "ramp and a Tomrigg," an "*artificial dawbing Jilt*," an "errant *Suburbian*," and, among other things, a "Lady of the Lake," a fine flow of slangy denunciation which we can understand without recourse to precise definition.[2] In our day Belinda has her detractors but in more benign terms, ranging from Hugo Reichard, who maintains that she is a coquette, to Aubrey Williams, who delicately suggests that she is a hypocrite. For Williams, too, Belinda undergoes "a kind of 'fall' in the poem; her 'perfection' is shattered, and she does lose her 'chastity,' in so far as chastity can be understood, however teasingly, as a condition of the spirit." And then there is the well-known essay by Cleanth Brooks, who is as sensible of the sexual aspects as Den-

---

[1] *The Critical Works of John Dennis*, ed. E. N. Hooker (Baltimore, 1943), II, 513–14.
[2] *Ibid.*, II, 334, 335.

nis but with a considerable difference. Fully aware of the subtleties and ambiguities of the poem, Brooks finds that Belinda is engaged in a "sexual war" with the Baron under recognizable social conventions, an encounter, however, that in no respect reduces her charm. Finally, we may mention the apotheosis of Belinda by Rebecca Parkin, who maintains that she is "a kind of sun goddess" with an Olympian pedigree.[3]

But there is another aspect of Belinda and of the poem which, so far as I am aware, has received little or no attention: Belinda as (if I may be allowed recourse to Shakesperian phraseology) the glass of fashion, Belinda who takes some coloration from her economic milieu. Although Pope has been very sparing in depicting her attire, who can read what he does say, both of her and the social ambiance, without visualizing her as "the observed of all observers," a fashionably attired young woman whose dress matches her charm in taste and costliness? We may begin most profitably with the cosmetic rites, Belinda at the toilet table, where "awful Beauty puts on all its Arms."

> The busy Sylphs surround their darling Care;
> These set the Head, and those divide the Hair,
> Some fold the Sleeve, while others plait the Gown;
> And *Betty*'s prais'd for Labours not her own.[4]
>
> (i. 145–48)

As the cosmetic rites proceed, we should not miss one useful fact: as the sylphs enhance Belinda's beauty by means of gems, combs, perfume, patches, and belladonna, they also play a role in her attire. In this brief and shining vignette of luxury and indulgence, as in earlier lines, Pope has set Belinda down in a world of glitter and fine feathers; his suggestiveness is such that we easily form an impression not only of Belinda's physical beauty but as

[3] See Hugo M. Reichard, "The Love Affair in Pope's *Rape of the Lock*," *PMLA*, 69 (1954), 887–902; Aubrey Williams, "The 'Fall' of China and *The Rape of the Lock*," *PQ*, 41 (1962), 412–25; Cleanth Brooks, "The Case of Miss Arabella Fermor: A Re-Examination," *Sewanee Review*, 51 (1943), 505–24 (also in his *The Well Wrought Urn*, 1947); Rebecca P. Parkin, "Mythopoeic Activity in the *Rape of the Lock*," *ELH*, 21 (1954), 30–38. The essays by Williams and Brooks are reprinted in *Essential Articles for the Study of Alexander Pope*, ed. Maynard Mack (1964).

[4] All quotations from *The Rape of the Lock* are from *The Rape of the Lock and Other Poems*, ed. Geoffrey Tillotson, Twickenham Edition (London, 1940), Vol. ii.

well of her stylishness. A fine lady (in the eighteenth-century sense of the phrase) in fine clothes, she undoubtedly is. If this is granted, I should like to examine (at the risk of pretentiousness) one or two aspects of the poem which have economic implications and which relate interestingly to the economic milieu from which it emerged, implications which a twentieth-century reader may conceivably miss but which Pope's contemporaries, sensitive to mercantilist doctrines, may have perceived. As I relate Belinda to certain economic ideas of the times, I am, in effect, presenting a gloss on some lines in the poem.

The lines (i, 121–48) concerned with Belinda at the toilette reflect an ideal which possessed the minds of many English economic writers and others in the seventeenth and eighteenth centuries, an ideal which at the same time generated apprehension in the minds of moralists. Pope writes: "Unnumber'd Treasures ope at once, and here / The various Off'rings of the World appear." Belinda is decked "with the glitt'ring Spoil," gems from India, perfumes from Arabia, combs of tortoise and ivory from Africa—or, as Pope says in Canto v, "all that Land and Sea afford" (l. 11). The mere mention of these objects of the toilette would have provoked a pleasing mercantile image in the minds of many contemporary readers: they testify to the vast expansion of England's trade in the seventeenth century and to the search for exotic commodities in remote lands. Belinda and her kind were the wealthy consumers whose demands gave an impetus to the merchants trading in all parts of the known world. They are referred to briefly by John Gay in his poem *Rural Sports* (1713): "So the gay lady with expensive care / Borrows the pride of land, of sea, and air" (ll. 135–36). But for sheer pleasure in the spectacle of the lady of fashion, the Belindas of the day, I have found nothing to surpass Addison's remarks in *Spectator*, No. 69 (19 May 1711). Here she becomes an illustration of England's greatness as a trading nation and testimony to the universality of its commerce. Addison writes:

The single Dress of a Woman of Quality is often the Product of an hundred Climates. The Muff and the Fan come together from the different Ends of the Earth. The Scarf is sent from the Torrid Zone, and the Tippet from beneath the Pole. The Brocade Petticoat rises out of the Mines of *Peru*, and the Diamond Necklace out of the Bowels of *Indostan*.

Earlier, in *Tatler*, No. 116 (5 Jan. 1709–10), Addison touched on the same theme, again visualizing a world explored and exploited for the purpose of adorning womankind. Mr. Bickerstaff tells us that he considers

woman as a beautiful romantic animal, that may be adorned with furs and feathers, pearls and diamonds, ores and silks. The lynx shall cast its skin at her feet to make her a tippet; the peacock, parrot, and swan, shall *pay contributions* to her muff; the sea shall be searched for shells, and the rocks for gems; and every part of nature furnish out its share towards the embellishment of a creature that is the most consummate work of it.

Addison's purpose in *Spectator*, No. 69, is primarily to eulogize the merchant, particularly Sir Andrew Freeport and others engaged in foreign trade, whose activities have organized the commercial world in such a fashion that an Englishman may have everything at his doorstep, no matter how remote its origin:

Traffick [i.e., trade] gives us a great Variety of what is Useful, and at the same time supplies us with every thing that is Convenient and Ornamental. Nor is it the least part of this our Happiness, that whilst we enjoy the remotest Products of the North and South, we are free from those Extremities of Weather which give them Birth; That our Eyes are refreshed with the green Fields of *Britain*, at the same time that our Palates are feasted with Fruits that rise between the Tropicks.

The theme is not a new one. It appears often in the poetry and prose of the seventeenth century and earlier, particularly in economic tracts stressing foreign trade or calling attention to the importance of the sea, providentially granted to England for her special exploitation. In *A Panegyrick to the Lord Protector* (1655), Edmund Waller illustrates in a few lines how the theme was assimilated into verse:

> So what our earth, and what our heav'n denies,
> Our ever-constant friend, the sea, supplies.

> The taste of hot Arabia's spice we know,
> Free from the scorching sun, that makes it grow:
> Without the worm, in Persian silks we shine;
> And without planting, drink of ev'ry wine.[5]

[5] *A Panegyric to My Lord Protector, of the Present Greatness, and Joint Interest, of his Highness, and the Nation* (London, 1655), Stanzas 14 and 15.

Now this paean to the sea and its enrichment of English life is not merely materialistic. It reflects a romantic vision, a larger conception widely prevalent in the century and later. We may turn once again to Addison for its expression. Mr. Spectator writes:

Our ships are laden with the Harvest of every Climate: Our Tables are stored with Spices, and Oils, and Wines: Our Rooms are filled with Pyramids of *China*, and adorned with the Workmanship of *Japan:* Our Morning's-Draught comes to us from the remotest Corners of the Earth: We repair our Bodies by the Drugs of *America*, and repose our selves under *Indian* Canopies. My Friend, Sir Andrew, calls the Vineyards of *France* our Gardens; the Spice-Islands our Hot-Beds; the *Persians* our Silk-Weavers, and the *Chinese* our Potters.[6]

Thus it is that Mr. Spectator confesses to a secret satisfaction and vanity that the merchants of the Royal Exchange are making London "a kind of *Emporium* for the whole Earth."

In spirit and substance these words are very much akin to those in *Windsor Forest* (1713), where Pope presents a vision of "golden days" for Albion once the Peace of Utrecht is approved. It is a shining vision uttered by Father Thames, who prophesies a new age of amity, wealth, and greatness fostered by British commerce, an enriching and unifying force: "Unbounded Thames shall flow for all mankind" (l. 398):

> Thy trees, fair *Windsor*, now shall leave their Woods,
> And half thy Forests rush into my Floods,
> Bear *Britain*'s Thunder, and her Cross display,
> To the bright Regions of the rising Day;
> Tempt Icy Seas, where scarce the Waters roll,
> Where clearer Flames glow round the frozen Pole;
> Or under Southern Skies exalt their Sails,
> Led by new Stars, and borne by spicy Gales!
> For me the Balm shall bleed, and Amber flow,
> The Coral redden, and the Ruby glow,

[6] Donald F. Bond, *The Spectator: Edited with an Introduction and Notes* (Oxford, 1965), No. 69, I, 295–96. In 1674 John Evelyn, in *Navigation and Commerce: Their Original and Progress*, anticipated Addison's passage: "Thus Asia refreshes us with spices, recreates us with perfumes, cures us with drugs, and adorns us with jewels; Africa sends us ivory and gold; America, silver, sugar, and cotton; France, Spain, and Italy, give us wine, oyl, and silk; Russia warms us in furs; Sweden supplies us with copper; Denmark and the Northern tracts, with masts and material for shipping." *The Miscellaneous Writings of John Evelyn, Esq., F.R.S.*, ed. William Upcott (London, 1825), p. 362.

The Pearly Shell its lucid Globe infold,
And *Phoebus* warm the ripening Ore to Gold.

(ll. 385–396)

In these lines and others, mingled with the millennial and saturnian strains, Pope too shows the influence of the prevalent vision of England as a world emporium, the center of a universal trade carried on by "universal merchants" (in eighteenth-century phraseology), such as Sir Andrew Freeport, of whom Mr. Spectator says, "there is not a Point in the Compass but blows home a Ship in which he is an Owner" (No. 2, 2 March 1711). Britain was "Nature's annointed empress of the deep." So Edward Young expresses it, in his *Reflections on the Publick Situation of this Kingdom* (1745),[7] echoing a view which had firm roots in the preceding century, stated typically by James Whiston, an obscure economic writer, in 1696: "God and Nature [have] designed this *Island* for the Grand *Market* of the Universe." England, Whiston adds, has all the potentialities for becoming "the General Emporie of the World."[8] At the risk of tedium I cite one more poetical expression of this theme because it has a special relevance to Pope. When he was completing *Windsor Forest* in November 1712, he was disturbed to find that some of his lines were similar to those in Thomas Tickell's *On the Prospect of Peace*, recently published. The lines from Tickell's poem are relevant to my purpose, reflecting, as they do, the conception of England as "the General *Emporie* of the World" and a land where its citizens could have "the remotest Products of the North and South" while free from "the Extremities of Weather which give them Birth" (*Spectator*, No. 69). Tickell writes:

> Fearless the merchant now pursues his gain,
> And roams securely o'er the boundless main.
> Now o'er his head the polar bear he spies,
> And freezing spangles of the Lapland skies;
> Now swells his canvass to the sultry line,
> With glitt'ring spoil where Indian grottoes shine.

[7] *The Poetical Works of Edward Young* (Boston, 1894), II, 204.
[8] *The Causes of our Present Calamities in reference to the Trade of the Nation fully Discovered* (London, 1695–96), p. 2.

Where fumes of incense glad the southern seas,
And wafted citron scents the balmy breeze.[9]

Now it may be true, as Cecil A. Moore has maintained, that in these poems we have instances of Whig panegyric;[10] but it is simply not accurate to hold that others, men of Tory persuasion, did not praise commerce or engage in it. In Tickell's poem, in *Spectator*, No. 69, in other works praising the glories of maritime commerce, something more than a partisan or factional view emerged. As I have indicated, what we do in fact have is a delectable vision of England's greatness and glory, a vision of splendor and magnificence shared by Englishmen of all persuasions. It was nourished by England's expanding trade and wealth; and it was often expressed in rapturous language, with examples and parallels drawn from antiquity and the Bible. The symbols of mercantile greatness in the past—the Phoenicians and the Carthaginians, Ophir and Tarshish, Solomon and ivory and apes and peacocks— biblical passages from Ezekiel, Revelation, and Kings, in which commerce and merchants are celebrated, these are mentioned again and again in the economic writings of the seventeenth and eighteenth centuries. But not only there. In the homiletic literature as well England is praised with extraordinary frequency as "the Mart of Nations" and "the great Empory of the World." London's resemblance to the ancient city of Tyre is a constant refrain. Tyre, too, had achieved its greatness and magnificence by a universal trade, Tyre "whose merchants are princes, whose traffickers are the honorable of the earth" (Isaiah 23:8, a text often used to demonstrate the antiquity and dignity of trade). Consider, as typical, these words from a sermon by a well-known divine, published in 1698:

That Antient flourishing City seated in the *Phoenician Sea* was deservedly reckon'd the Greatest Mart and Empory of that part of the Universe: Thither was brought the Riches of *Asia, Europe*, and *Africa*. In this also Britain resembles her, and was justly stiled by *Charles the Great* the Store-House and Granary of the Western World.

[9] For the lines as Pope quoted them in his letter to Caryll, see *The Correspondence of Alexander Pope*, ed. George Sherburn (Oxford, 1956), I, 157. Thomas Tickell, *A Poem on the Prospect of Peace* (London, 1713), p. 9.
[10] "Whig Panegyric Verse: A Phase of Sentimentalism," in *Backgrounds of English Literature, 1700–1760* (Minneapolis, 1953), pp. 104–44.

The Great City of this our Isle may be call'd the Mart of Nations, as Tyre is, Isai. xxiii.3 . . . .[11]

London as Tyre—one more instance must suffice, a sermon published in the year of Pope's death, a characteristic one but of special interest because it displays in homiletic literature what may be called the mercantile zest or hunger, the feeling for material objects exemplified in Defoe when he writes "the trading style." Alexander Catcott's sermon, *The Antiquity and Honourableness of the Practice of Merchandize* (1744), was preached before the Worshipful Society of Merchants of the City of Bristol, who doubtless liked what they heard. It presents Tyre "as a queen among the nations," raised to that eminence by its commerce. Tyre

furnished all the western parts [of the world] with the commodities of *Arabia, Africa, Persia,* and *India*. . . . Its fleets brought into *Tyre* all the useful and rare commodities of the then known world . . . silver, iron, tin, lead, brass, slaves, horses, mules, ivory, ebony, emeralds, purple, embroidery, fine linen, coral, wheat, pannag [balsam], honey, oil, balm, wine, white wool, bright iron [steel], cassia, calamus, precious cloaths, lambs, rams, goats, spices, precious stones, gold, blue cloaths and rich apparel . . . .

Hence it became the mother of navigation, the center of trade, and the "common mart of all the nations of the universe."[12] It was not necessary for Catcott to draw the parallel between Tyre and London: the theme had long been a hackneyed one. And none of his auditors would have missed the point: it was London which had become, in biblical phrase, the "crowning city," and it was England which now sat "as a queen among the nations."

I return now to the relevant lines depicting Belinda and her maid at the toilette:

> Unnumber'd Treasures ope at once, and here
> The various Off'rings of the World appear;
> From each she nicely culls with curious Toil,
> And decks the Goddess with the glitt'ring Spoil.

[11] John Edwards, "That Decay of Trade and Commerce, and Consequently of Wealth, is the Natural Product and Just Penalty of Vice in a Nation," in *Sermons on Special Occasions and Subjects* (London, 1698), p. 156.

[12] Pp. 5–7. Catcott and the other clergymen who drew the parallel between Tyre and London pointed out, of course, that Tyre was an object lesson for Londoners, that despite its wealth and magnificence Tyre fell as a result of pride and sin.

This Casket *India*'s glowing Gems unlocks,
And all *Arabia* breathes from yonder Box.
The Tortoise here and Elephant unite,
Transform'd to *Combs*, the speckled and the white.

(i. 129–136)

In the background of these lines, this brief vignette of luxury, is
the conception of England as "the great Empory of the World."
If, as I believe, this idea was deeply implanted in the consciousness
of Pope and his contemporaries, a literate reader of the poem would
have found a dimension in the passage not immediately evident to
a reader in the twentieth century. By subtle insinuation Belinda's
gems from India, her perfume from Arabia, and her ivory from
Africa would generate in a contemporary reader responses appeal-
ing to the geographical imagination and related to the romantic
image of an England made magnificent by maritime activity. I
would certainly hesitate to suggest that Pope has deliberately made
Belinda a kind of economic symbol, but she and the objects of the
toilette may well have had symbolic overtones. She, and others like
her, were the beginning and end, the stimulus to "the adventurous
merchant" whose ships roamed "securely o'er the boundless main"
from Lapland to "the sultry line"; and they were the final recipients
of the exotic products, "the glitt'ring Spoil" from Indian grottoes,
from the frozen north and the southern seas.

For them the Gold is dug on Guinea's Coast,
And sparkling Gems the farthest Indies boast,
For them Arabia breathes its spicy Gale,
And fearless Seamen kill the Greenland Whale.
For them the Murex yields its purple Dye,
And orient Pearls in sea-bred Oisters lye;
For them, in clouded Shell, the Tortoise shines,
And huge *Behemoth* his vast Trunk resigns;
For them, in various Plumes, the Birds are gay,
And *Sables* bleed, the savage Hunter's Prey!
For them the *Merchant*, wide to ev'ry Gale,
Trusts all his Hopes and stretches ev'ry Sail,
For them, O'er all the World, he dares to roam,
And safe conveys its gather'd Riches home.[13]

[13] [James Ralph], *Clarinda, Or the Fair Libertine: A Poem in Four Cantos*
(London, 1729), pp. 37–38.

In this mercantile flight or progress we witness the poetic imagination playing with the theme I have been discussing; and as the
theme found expression in Pope's day and earlier, it embodied an
element of awe and wonder at the spectacle of a world, infinitely
complex, organized to enhance the beauty of a Belinda, of ships
roaming the world:

> Now visit Russia's Snows and Guinea's Soil.
> Hence in Hesperia's Silks the Britons shine,
> Wear India's Gems and drink Burgundia's Wine.[14]

In the passage depicting Belinda at the toilette we see that Pope
has assimilated this theme, so vibrant and meaningful in his time.
Both the diction and the substance of the relevant lines are traditional; they are part and parcel of a well-developed convention in
economic writings and in literature.

At this point we must give our attention to Belinda's petticoat,
whose importance is portentously announced by her guardian sylph:

> To Fifty chosen *Sylphs*, of special Note,
> We trust th'important Charge, the *Petticoat*:
> Oft have we known that sev'nfold Fence to fail,
> Tho' stiff with Hoops, and arm'd with Ribs of Whale.
> (ii, 118–20)

If Ariel considers this garment so important, we have some warrant for taking it seriously, with a different intention, of course. I
am still concerned to gloss certain lines in the poem in terms of
prevalent economic thought and to indicate reverberations or lay-
ers of meaning likely in contemporary responses to the poem, particularly in an atmosphere suffused by mercantilist doctrine. The
hoop petticoat is too much to cope with fully in the compass of this
essay. Any student of eighteenth-century literature will be aware
of the attention it received for half a century or more, in the essay,
in poetry, and in the drama. It was celebrated facetiously by Mr.
Bickerstaff, by Mr. Spectator, by Henry Fielding, and by such
minor authors as John Durant Breval, in *The Art of Dress* (1717)
and Francis Chute, *The Petticoat: An Heroi-Comical Poem* (1716).
In the year that Pope was writing *The Rape of the Lock* there ap-

---

[14] Sir Richard Blackmore, "The Nature of Man" (1711), in *A Collection of
Poems* (London, 1718), p. 224.

peared anonymously a poem titled *The Farthingale Reviv'd . . . A Panegyric on . . . the Invention of the Hoop Petticoat* (1711).[15] Had Pope been more considerate of a later generation, he would have been more detailed in describing Belinda's petticoat. As it is, I cannot establish beyond all doubt the kind she wore. She had a choice of the dome-shaped or the oval hoop (the "orbicular," as it was called in *Guardian*, No. 114, 22 July 1713). The oblong hoop was probably too late for Belinda; but we are on somewhat safer ground with the inner petticoats, which served as structural supports for the outer. These might be made of silk or satin, paduasoy or chintz, gingham or mohair, or any of various Indian silks. It is well to keep in mind that the gown consisted of a bodice and skirt joined together, with the skirt open in front to reveal the petticoat, which was not thought of as an undergarment but as an essential part of the dress.[16] Thus petticoats were often of the richest material. We may reasonably assume, I think, that Belinda's petticoat was of the most fashionable and costly kind, of silk in some form, as brocade (perhaps her "new Brocade" mentioned in Canto II, 1. 107), or damask, or tabby, or lutestring, or satin. As an indication of the expensiveness of such a garment, we have recourse to Richard Steele's list of "absolute Necessaries for a fine Lady." Among the objects are "A Mantua and Petticoat of *French* Brocade, 26 Yards, at three pounds *per* Yard" (£78), and less expensive but still costly, "A *French* or *Italian* Silk quilted Petticoat, one Yard and a quarter deep, and six Yards wide" (£10).[17]

Now here we may view Belinda in a climate of economic

[15] The quality of the verse is apparent in these characteristic lines:
> Ev'n Boots and Spurs have grac'd Heroick Verse;
> *Butler* his Knight's whole Suit did well rehearse,
> King *Harry's* Codpiece stands upon record,
> And every Age will Precedents afford.

> Then on my Muse, and sing in Epick Strain,
> The Petticoat—thou shalt not sing in vain;
> The Petticoat will sure reward thy Pain.
> Will all this Skill its secret Virtues tell;
> A Petticoat shou'd still be handl'd well.

[16] See C. Willett, and Phillis Cunnington, *Handbook of English Costume in the Eighteenth Century* (London, 1957), p. 106 and passim.

[17] *The Spinster: in Defence of the Woollen Manufactures, No. I* (1719), in *Tracts and Pamphlets by Richard Steele*, ed. Rae Blanchard (Baltimore, 1944), p. 552.

opinion markedly different from the romantic one discussed earlier, from a more austere mercantilist atmosphere less tolerant of her indulgences. From this vantage the lady of fashion was frequently the object of criticism, a danger to the national economy. In the mercantile philosophy perhaps the most cogent doctrine was that a nation should have a favorable balance of trade. As a corollary, national frugality was deemed a virtue. Any action that caused bullion to flow out of the country was held to be harmful, particularly the importation of luxuries. Though there were arguments to the contrary from the apologists of the great trading companies, many of the more stringent economic writers complained often of the fashionable lady who insisted on dressing herself in calicoes, linens, velvets, laces, damasks, brocades, and satins imported from around the world, all at the expense of England's great staple, wool:

> Our own manufacks out of fashion,
> No country of wool was ever so dull:
> 'Tis a test of the brains of the nation
> To neglect their own works,
> Employ pagans and Turks,
> And let foreign trumpery o'er spread 'em.[18]

Perhaps the most objectionable of all the "foreign trumpery" was silk, an economic evil of the first order because of the large amount imported, both raw and wrought, and because imported silk hindered the endeavors to establish a flourishing domestic silk industry. Furthermore, it was particularly galling to many economic writers that England should depend so heavily on its great trade rival, France, for silk, though silk was also imported from Italy, India, and Persia, even from Holland and elsewhere. Belinda, I suggest, is an economic sinner (in mercantilist terms), and in the light of the French trade unusually so. When Samuel Fortrey, addressing himself to Charles II in 1663, examined England's trade with France, he found that England

transported out of *France* into *England*, great quantities of velvets plain and wrought, sattins plain and wrought, cloth of gold and silver, Armoysins and other merchandise of silk . . . made at *Lions,* and . . . valued to be yearly worth one hundred and fifty thousand pounds.

[18] *The Weavers' Complaint Against the Callico Madams* (1719), quoted in *A Calendar of British Taste from 1600 to 1800,* ed. E. F. Carritt (London, 1948), p. 183.

In silk, stuffs, taffeties, poudesoys, armoysins, clothes of gold and silver, tabbies, plain and wrought, silk-ribbands and other such like stuffs as are made at *Tours*, valued to be worth above three hundred thousand pounds a year.[19]

We may pass over the cost to England of such French products as buttons of silk, cabinets, watches, perfumes, gloves, feathers, fans, hoods, gilt looking-glasses, bracelets, and "such like mercery," all listed by Fortrey and some doubtless relevant to Belinda. But one of his categories of imports must be mentioned: "In pins, needles, box-combs, tortoise-shell combs, and such like, [imported] for about twenty thousand pounds a year."[20] These, we recall, are among the objects on Belinda's toilet-table. Little wonder that Fortrey complains that "foreign commodities are grown into so great esteem amongst us, as we wholly undervalue and neglect the use of our own, whereby that great expence of treasure, that is yearly wasted . . . redounds chiefly to the profit of strangers, and to the ruine of his Majesties Subjects."[21]

Many economic tracts in the seventeenth and eighteenth centuries echoed Fortrey's complaint,[22] and his tract itself was reprinted in 1673, 1713, and 1714. One of the more illuminating treatises, doubtfully assigned to Sir William Petyt, was entitled *Britannia Languens, or A Discourse of Trade* (1680). It was much concerned with the way in which the English merchant and shopkeeper might "avoid Trading in Foreign Consumptive Goods." The author, like Fortrey, reveals a special bitterness over England's excessive importation of silk and the women who are responsible:

The *English* formerly wore or used little Silk in City or Countrey, only Persons of Quality pretended to it; but as our National Gaudery hath

---

[19] *England's Interest and Improvement, Consisting in the Increase of the Store and Trade of this Kingdom* (1673), in *Early English Tracts on Commerce*, ed. J. R. McCulloch (Cambridge, Eng., 1952), p. 232.

[20] Ibid., p. 233. In *Tatler*, No. 149 (1 Sept. 1713), ascribed to John Gay, we find him telling us that "as Horace advises that all new-minted words should have a Greek derivation to give them an indisputable authority, so I would counsel all our improvers of fashion always to take the hint from France, which may as properly be called the fountain of dress, as Greece was of literature."

[21] Fortrey, p. 231.

[22] See, for example, *The General Remarks on Trade*, Nos. 222 and 223 (25–28, 28–30 July 1707), a London newspaper written by Charles Povey, who repeats Fortrey's figures on the annual loss to England from such importations as fans, girdles, masks, looking glasses, feathers, pins, needles, tortoise-shell combs, and other mercery ware.

increased, it grew more and more into Mode; and is now become the common Wear . . . and our *Women*, who generally govern in this Case, must have *Foreign Silks*; for these have got the Name. . . . Of the same humour are their Gallants, and such as they can influence. . . . Our ordinary People, especially the Female, will be in Silk, more or less, if they can. . . . Whence hath followed a vastly *greater Importation, and home-Consumption of the dear Silk-Manufactures* from *Venice, Florence, Genoa, France*, and *Persia*, and of late from *Holland*. . . . This our Affectation and Use of foreign Silks having apparently much increased . . . must produce a great Odds in the Ballance, and besides hath much contracted the *home-vent* of our *Woollen Stuffs and Cloths*, and *Beggered our own Silk-Weavers*.[23]

It seems clear that we have, from the vantage of certain economic writers of the period, not merely Italianate and Frenchified men but Italianate and Frenchified women as well. Belinda's "new brocade" and her petticoat, and of course the objects on the toilet table, must be suspect. Thus Belinda and the ladies of fashion would appear to have some relationship to the contemporary controversy over the importing of silk—and to the many discussions concerning the development of a domestic silk industry.

To consider Belinda in relation to the silkworm has its risible aspects, I am the first to agree. " 'Twere to consider too curiously to consider so," as Horatio said to Hamlet in a quite different context. But then we must recall Hamlet's reply: "No, faith, not a jot." At least we may recognize that the neoclassical bee has a companion in the neoclassical silkworm. The "apotheosis" of the silkworm in economic and scientific writings of the seventeenth and eighteenth centuries occasionally found its way into literature. One can take as a point of departure a writer greatly admired in England, Du Bartas, whose *Divine Weeks* (1578) was much translated—and in which the silkworm was referred to as "this wond'rous Worm":

> Which soon transforms the fresh and tender leaves
> Of Thisbe's pale tree, to those tender sleaves
> (On oral clues) of soft, smooth silken flax,
> Which more for us, than for her self she makes.
> O precious Fleece!

[23] *Britannia Languens, or A Discourse of Trade: Shewing the Grounds and Reasons of the Increase and Decay of Land-Rents, National Wealth, and Strength* (1680), in McCulloch, *Early English Tracts*, p. 421.

This was quoted by Pope's contemporary, Henry Barham, a fellow of the Royal Society, in his *Essay upon the Silk-Worm* (1719).[24] But Barham thought that Du Bartas had underestimated this "Miracle in nature": "Had *Du Bartas* fully known all the virtues and rare use of this incomparable Creature, which is even a Miracle in nature, he would have enlarged his poem in a more ample manner in the praise of it, to the great honour of the Creator, *Cui Gloria. Amen.*"[25] It may be that Du Bartas prompted such effusions in verse as *The Silkewormes and Their Flies: Lively described in Verse by T.M., a Countrie Farmer and an Apprentice in Physicke. For the Great Benefit and Enriching of England* (1599). When Nicholas Geffe published *The Perfect Use of Silk-Wormes and their Benefit* in 1607, it was prefaced by laudatory verses from three poets, including Michael Drayton. Geffe, who had been attempting for seven years to persuade his countrymen to develop a domestic silk industry, pleaded for the planting of mulberry trees, the food supply of the silkworm. This, he asserted, is "the readiest and assuredest way . . . to reare up, nourish, & feed Silk-worms, ye most admirable and beautifullest cloathing creatures of this world."[26] Drayton compared Geffe to Columbus, who once offered to England the wealth now possessed by Spain. In the silkworm Geffe offers England comparable riches:

> So may thy Silk-wormes happily increase
> From sea to sea to propagate their seed,
> That plant still, nourish'd by our glorious peace,
> Whose leafe alone, the labouring Worme doth feed.

[24] Henry Barham, *An Essay Upon the Silk-Worm* (London, 1719), p. 151.
[25] Ibid.
[26] Nicholas Geffe, *The Perfect Use of Silk-Wormes, and their Benefit. With the Exact Planting and Artificiall Handling of Mulberrie Trees whereby to Nourish Them, and How to Feed the Wormes and to Winde off the Silke . . . Done out of the French Original of D'Olivier de Serres . . . into English* (London, 1607), A² recto. Geffe adds to the tract by Serres "A Discourse of His Owne, of the Meanes and Sufficiencies of England, for to have Abundance of Fine Silk, by Seeding of Silkwormes within the Same." He pleads that the English should not avoid "such a golden fleece" (p. 10). Two years after the appearance of Geffe's work James I authorized the planting of mulberry trees in what later became known as Mulberry Garden. The king had hopes of stimulating the manufacture of silk in England, but Mulberry Garden soon became a place of public entertainment, much mentioned in Restoration drama and frequented by Pepys and Evelyn, who refer to it in their diaries.

And may thy fame perpetually advance
    Rich when by thee, thy country shall be made,
Naples, Granada, Portugale, and France,
    All to sit idle, wondring at our trade.[27]

The prefatory verses by George Carr are similarly eulogistic:

The silken fleece to England thou hath brought,
    There to endure till Doomesday cut her clue,
And when thy bones, the wormes have eate to naught,
    Yet shall the wormes thy fame still fresh renue,
And thy name, thy house, thy stocke, thy line,
Be highly honored by this great designe.[28]

From Geffe, early in the seventeenth century, to Pope's day and beyond, the silkworm was anatomized, eulogized, and "moralized." In his *Antidote Against Atheism* (1653), Henry More included it among those animals useful "as an Argument of Divine Providence," and praised it also as very useful to man: it seems to have "come into the world for no other purpose, than to furnish man with more costly cloathing, and to spin away her very entrails to make him fine without."[29] Robert Hooke, the distinguished member of the Royal Society, examined this "miracle in nature" in *Micrographia,* 1665 (Obs. XLI, Sch. XXV); and his contemporary Edward Digges contributed a paper in the same year to the *Philosophical Transactions*, in which he set down his "Observations" of the Silkworm (*Abridgment*, i.12). Both of these works came a decade after Waller had included the silkworm in his poem, quoted above, to the Lord Protector. Most of the literature on the subject is, as one would expect, primarily practical, the intention being to stimulate the development of an English silk industry, in hopes of unburdening the country from the onerous expense of imported silk. As it was sometimes stated, England should domesticate or naturalize the silkworm and free itself of dependence on foreign worms. To those who thought that the mulberry tree would not flourish in England, Virginia and the American colonies offered hope. Edward Williams, in *Virgo Triumphans: Or Virginia Richly and Truly*

---

[27] Geffe, A⁴ recto.

[28] Ibid.

[29] *Antidote Against Atheism*, 2d ed. (London, 1755), Ch. viii, "The Usefulness of Animals an Argument of Divine Providence," p. 116.

Valued (1650), directed his attention to this point, arguing that England should develop Virginia as "a reservoir of riches," since the mulberry tree flourishes abundantly there. But even in those tracts where the economic motive is primary, as in Williams, the authors dwelt on the wonders of the insect, "this Mystery of the Silkworme":

there is nothing in the world more proper than this curious atome of Nature, the Silkworme: to see this untaught Artist spin out his transparent bowels, labour such a monument out of his owne intralls, as may be the shame, blush of Artists, such that Robe that Solomon in all his Glory might confess the meanness of his Apparell.[30]

Williams is lost in admiration of nature, "who hath abbreviated all the Volumes of her other Miracles into this her little, but exact Epitome, like that Artist who contracted the whole body of Iliads and Odysses into a Nutshell" (p. 34). He, too, considers the silkworm evidence of the hand of the deity in the creation.

For a hundred years at least this "curious atome of nature" engaged the attention of Englishmen; and we may bring it close to Pope by glancing at Aaron Hill, poet, dramatist, and essayist, who over a period of years was intermittently Pope's friend and enemy. As the latter he found a place in both *Peri Bathous* and *The Dunciad*. Although Hill's "Essay on the Silkworm" (1717) is later than *The Rape of the Lock*, it is useful for establishing the climate of economic opinion (I am not concerned with sources) which may have influenced the responses to the poem in Pope's day. Hill's essay reveals the continuity of views from the preceding century. Like those before him, he maintains that the mulberry tree and the silkworm can flourish in England, and like his predecessors he gives information about the habits of the insect—its manner of breeding, proper care of the eggs, feeding habits, maladies it was subject to, and methods of spinning the silk. These were the usual subjects of the tracts of the seventeenth century. But Hill has one novel point: he pleads with the fair sex to plant mulberry trees and spin their own silk. Women, he writes, ought to "do Justice to the Industry of this *busy* little Animal, to whose constant Labours they are so highly *oblig'd*, that the least they

[30] *Virgo Triumphans* (London, 1650), p. 38.

can do, in *meer Gratitude*, is to form an *Alliance* and take their neglected, poor Servant into their Protection." By this means, he continued,

the Benefit will spread with the *Practice*, when some *one* has begun and makes visible *Profit*, not to speak of the *Pleasure*, when some Lady temptingly dress'd at a Visit, and shining in the Ornaments of her own private Industry, shall be able to answer to the Commenders of her *Gown*, or her *Petticoat*—'*Tis the Silk, which my own pretty Spinners have presented me*: Then first will *Emulation*, or *Envy* produce *Imitation*: *More* every Year will fall into the Practice . . . till some happy *Charmer* will be made Immortal by *Fame*, and be admir'd in our Histories, as the *first Introducer of the Silk Manufacturer in Engand*.[31]

In certain kinds of light verse devoted to the social scene or to social customs, the conjunction of the lady of quality or fashion and the silkworm was inevitable, as in John Durant Breval's *The Art of Dress* (1717):

> For you, th'Italian Worm her Silk prepares,
> And distant *India* sends her choicest Wares;
> Some Toy from ev'ry Port the Sailor brings,
> The Sempstress labours, and the Poet sings.[32]

Or as in Soame Jenyns in *The Art of Dancing* (1729):

> For you the Silkworms fine-wrought webs display,
> And lab'ring spin their little Lives away. . . .
> For you the Sea resigns its pearly Store,
> And Earth unlocks her Mines of treasur'd Ore.[33]

Similarly we find it in James Ralph's *Clarinda, Or the Fair Libertine* (1729): "For them the Silk worm spins her silken store / For them Peru exports its silver ore."[34] In a more serious vein, R. Collins, whose poem, *Nature Display'd* (1727) is, among other things, a justification of reptiles and insects in the deity's plan for the creation, includes the silkworm:

> All these their Uses have, when given ore,
> The Viper's Broth, the Patient will restore.

[31] Hill's "Essay on the Silkworm" appeared in *Essays for the Month of January, 1717 . . . . By a Society of Gentlemen. For the Universal Benefit of the People of England* (London, 1717), Essay v, p. 7 and passim.

[32] *The Art of Dress* (London, 1717), p. 17.

[33] *The Art of Dancing, Written in the Year 1728* (London, 1729), p. 8.

[34] *Clarinda*, p. 37.

Insects, tho' small, with larger Birds may vy;
What raises Blisters, like the Spanish Fly? . . .
How does the Silk-Worm, in her Bowels bear,
And finely Spin, what finest Ladies wear.[35]

I will not resist the temptation to include a notable example of
how the "incomparable worm" crept into the greatest prose satire
of the times. In Part III of *Gulliver's Travels*, when Gulliver visits
the Grand Academy of Lagado, he walks into a room where walls
and ceiling are covered with cobwebs. Immediately a projector
warns him not to disturb the webs. The projector, Gulliver informs us, "lamented the fatal Mistake the World had been so long
in of using Silk-Worms, while we had such plenty of *domestick*
[italics mine] Insects, who infinitely excelled the former, because
they understood how to weave as well as spin. And he proposed
farther, that by employing Spiders, the Charge of dying Silks would
be wholly saved; whereof I was fully convinced when he shewed
me a vast Number of Flies most beautifully coloured, wherewith
he fed his Spiders; assuring us, that the Webs would take a Tincture
from them; and as he had them of all Hues, he hoped to fit every
Body's Fancy."[36] Thus it is that Swift, having fun at the expense
of the Royal Society, set this satiric passage in the context of the
many current discussions of the silkworms, turning the projector
into one who sought to use "domestic worms" rather than foreign
ones.

In view of the ubiquity of this insect, it is not surprising that
Richard Bradley, a fellow of the Royal Society and a widely read
popularizer of science, should remark, in his *A Philosophical Account of the Works of Nature* (1721), that "*The Silk-Worm*, at
present, carries the Day before all others of the Papilionaceous
Tribe"; and he commends the efforts of Henry Barham, then engaged with others in planting mulberry trees in Chelsea and, with
missionary zeal, endeavoring to domesticate this preeminent member of the Papilionaceous Tribe.[37] Barham is referred to earlier in
this essay. I have, I trust, amply demonstrated that the silkworm
had a strong fascination for the seventeenth and eighteenth cen-

[35] *Nature Display'd* (London, 1727), p. 73.
[36] *Prose works of Jonathan Swift,* ed. Herbert Davis (Oxford, 1941), xi, 164–65.
[37] *Philosophical Account* (London, 1721), pp. 139–40. Bradley devotes Chs.
xii and xiii to "the Papilionaceous or Butterfly Kind."

turies, not merely for merchants and statesmen who realized its potentialities for adding wealth to the nation, but as well for philosophers, clergymen, and scientists. It also caught the imagination of literary men, poets and prose writers alike, who assimilated it into their works, at times lightheartedly, at times seriously. In Pope's day the image of this "*busy* little Animal," this "curious Atome of Nature," spinning luxury "out of its owne intralls," was indeed a vivid one, peculiarly related to the fine lady; and the very idea of it—and of silk—was deeply embedded in a whole cluster of ideas, economic and ethical, touching foreign and domestic trade, "a world emporie," economic rivalry with France and Italy, the fabulous wealth of the Indies, the universal merchant, and, along with others, pride of dress and what the economic writers called "the consumptive trades."

Belinda as a consumer, the embodiment of luxury, whose ambiance is defined by the mere mention of such objects as Indian gems, Arabian perfume, ivory combs, a fluttering fan, diamond pendants in her ears, a sparkling cross, a new brocade, and the hoop petticoat, was, as I have indicated, recognizably the final point in a vast nexus of enterprises, a vast commercial expansion which stirred the imagination of Englishmen to dwell on thoughts of greatness and magnificence. And I suggest again that for many contemporary readers of the poem something would accrue to the character of Belinda, an additional dimension in their response to her and to the poem, insinuated by the economic milieu with its awesome dynamism and its vision of a world emporium. This would be an affirmative response, which very likely would be leavened by a negative one. Whenas in foreign silks Belinda goes, she could not please the austere mercantilist. Defoe would see her, if I may adapt his phraseology for my purposes, as one who has "dethroned your True-born English Broadcloth and Kerseys." Even Addison inadvertently gives us a clue in *Spectator*, No. 45 (21 April 1711), where he expresses his apprehension over the prospect of a peace treaty with France: "What an Inundation of Ribbons and Brocades will break in upon us? . . . For the Prevention of these great Evils, I could heartily wish that there was an Act of Parliament for Prohibiting the Importation of *French* Fopperies." And fripperies too, he might have added, an addition which would have evoked a sympathetic response in many of Mr. Spectator's readers. Although Addison's tone and treatment in this essay are light and amusing, the subject itself was a serious one, as we may observe from its treatment by Defoe in the *Review* two years later. Here this laureate of trade is lamenting the change in London, "the mighty alteration in the face of trade in this city" in the past three or four decades. The metropolis, as he sees it, is now given over to the dealers in "baubles and trifles" and to such products as coffee, tea, chocolate, to "the valuable Utensils of the Tea-Table," to gilded boxes, looking-glass shops, gilders of leather, toyshops, pastry cooks, periwig makers, china or earthenware men, and other "Foreign Trifles." Ironically Defoe remarks, "how gloriously is [London] supplied."[38] In this mood Defoe would look disapprovingly at Belinda and her world. But he had other moods as well, moments in which he would have acquiesced in the remark of an apologist for the East India Company, who declared that in return for bullion the Company brought in commodities "both to adorn and entertain our ladies. Are not these riches?"[39] Alexander Pope, I'm sure, thought so.

[38] *Review*, Vol. I [IX], No. 43 (8 Jan. 1713).

[39] [? Jocelyn], *An Essay on Money & Bullion* (London, 1718), p. 17. See also *Some Considerations on the Nature and Importance of the East India Trade* (1728): "Providence in its infinite goodness designed to make life as easy and as pleasurable as possible, and gave us reason to find out arts, and to make them subservient to our delight and happiness" (p. 71). In another study I have treated the lady of fashion (and Belinda, briefly) in a different economic context. This study, titled "Of Silkworms and Farthingales and the Will of God," will appear in *Studies in the Eighteenth Century: Papers Presented at the Second David Nichol Smith Seminar, Canberra, 1970,* ed. R. F. Brissenden (1971). It may be considered complementary to this present study.

OF SILKWORMS AND FARTHINGALES
AND THE WILL OF GOD

I propose to examine a phase of eighteenth-century rationalism
hitherto little known or neglected. This rationalistic strain of
thought manifests itself in a variety of literary works whose authors
used prevalent economic ideas, ideas themselves rooted in the
diffused rationalistic philosophy of the times. Since the subject is
greatly ramified I will restrict myself to one significant aspect, a
theme involving a creature both fascinating and disconcerting to
contemporaries—the lady of quality or fashion, the Clarindas and
Belindas and Celias of the reigns of Queen Anne and the first two
Georges; and I submit that this lady of fashion becomes a figure
of special interest and complexity if we view her in the context of
the economic ideas which swirled around her head. She will be seen
to play a vital part in a universe rationally designed and providentially ordered to accommodate her. Because the eighteenth
century held firmly to the Aristotelian conviction that nature does
nothing in vain, it found a rationale for the lady of fashion in
the cosmic scheme of things. And perhaps it is not untenable to
maintain that the lady of fashion, like the seas, the mountains, and
the other artifacts of nature, was herself part of that design and
harmony in the universe which truly demonstrated the existence of
a deity.

The image of the lady of fashion relevant to present purposes
emerges from two minor poems of 1729, the first of which is James
Ralph's *Clarinda, or the Fair Libertine*, where the poet writes: for
ladies of fashion

> the Silk-worm spins his silken Store,
> For them *Peru* exports its silver ore;
> For them the Gold is dug on *Guinea*'s Coast
> And sparkling Gems the farthest *Indies boast*,

SILKWORMS AND FARTHINGALES

For them *Arabia* breathes its spicy Gale,
And fearless Seamen kill the *Greenland* Whale.[1]

Here we observe the lady of fashion, not as a fully delineated character or personality but as a kind of economic abstraction, the figurative embodiment of luxurious taste and indulgence, an idealised consumer of economic goods for whose delectation the entire universe is exploited and operated as a vast mercantile enterprise. It is of this creature that John Gay had written (in *Rural Sports*, 1713):

> So the gay Lady, with Expensive Care,
> Borrows the Pride of Land, of Sea, and Air.[2]

And in a similar vein, again in 1729, Soame Jenyns, in his poem, *The Art of Dancing*, addressed the lady of fashion thus:

> For you the Silkworms, fine-wrought Webs display,
> And lab'ring spin their little Lives away;
> . . . .
> For you the Sea resigns its pearly Store
> And Earth unlocks her Mines of treasur'd Ore.[3]

But let me take a more familiar point of departure, a passage from Pt IV of *Gulliver's Travels*, in which this attractive consumer is repudiated. She is, indeed, converted into a female Yahoo. Gulliver is conversing with his master in Houyhnhnmland: 'I assured him', Gulliver says, 'that this whole Globe of Earth must be at least three Times gone round, before one of our better female *Yahoos* could get her Breakfast, or a Cup to put it in'. This remark, which comes as Gulliver is nearing the apogee of his disenchantment, is part of a long passage primarily economic in substance. The wise and rational Houyhnhnm listens to Gulliver describe

---

[1] James Ralph, *Clarinda, or the Fair Libertine. A Poem. In Four Cantos*, London, 1729, pp. 37-8.

[2] John Gay, *Rural Sports: A Poem to Mr. Pope*, 1713, in *Poetical Works of John Gay*, G. C. Faber (ed.), London, 1926, p. 658.

[3] Soame Jenyns, *The Art of Dancing. In Three Cantos*, London, 1729, pp. 8-9. See also J. D. Breval, *The Art of Dress*, 1717, dedicated to the 'Toasts of Great Britain':

For you, th' Italian Worm her Silk prepares,
And distant *India* sends her choicest Wares,
Some Toy from ev'ry Part the Sailor brings,
The Semptress labours and the Poet sings. (p. 17).

Elsewhere I hope to write (but not extensively) about the silkworm in eighteenth-century literature, that 'wondrous worm' (to use a phrase from Du Bartas) which caught the attention and stirred the imagination of poets and clergymen, of scientists and merchants and statesmen. To contemporaries the silkworm was, as Henry Barhan, F.R.S., wrote in 1719, an 'incomparable creature, which is even a miracle in nature' (*An Essay upon the Silk-Worm*, London, 1719, p. 151).

certain aspects of life in England: the unequal distribution of wealth, the fine clothes and noble houses available to the rich, the indulgence in costly meats and drinks. And here Gulliver finds that he must explain to the Houyhnhnm what these costly meats are: 'I enumerated', he says, 'as many Sorts as came into my Head, with the various Methods of dressing them, which could not be done without sending Vessels by Sea to every Part of the World, as well for Liquors to drink, as for Sauces, and innumerable other Conveniences'. It is at this point that Gulliver remarks on the extensive economic activity—encircling of the globe three times —necessary to provide one of the better female Yahoos of England with her breakfast. The comment of his master among the Houyhnhnms—that a country unable to furnish its inhabitants with food and drink must be miserable—is mild in contrast to Gulliver's own indictment of his countrymen, who, he tells us, send away the necessities in exchange for 'the Materials of Diseases, Folly, and Vice'.[4]

---

[4] *The Prose Works of Jonathan Swift*, Herbert Davis (ed.), Oxford, 1941, XI [235]-236. Hereafter cited as *Prose Works*. An interesting parallel in medical literature to Swift's attack on sauces and liquors as emblems of luxury and intemperance may be found in John Woodward, *The State of Physick, and of Diseases*, London, 1718: 'Our Error in Diet consists partly of the Nature and Sort of it: in high Seasoning, strong Sauces . . . new Modes of Cookery, brought amongst us by the Foreigners that have come over . . . for about 30 Years past. The so frequent Use of Chocolate, of Coffee, Limonade, Punch: but more especially of Tea, drank now in so great Excess, all over the Kingdom; to the Neglect of the much better and more wholsome Products of our own Country, the Misspending our Treasure, and carrying it even to the most distant and remote Parts of the World: or to the Exchange of our own usefull Manufactures, not only for Trifles, and Things of no real Use, but for such as are detrimental, and injurious. To these Sauces, and these Liquors, our vertuous, wise, stout, healthy Ancestors were Strangers. By the former, Intemperance and Excess is promoted. . . . By the Liquors, Way is made for a fresh Appetite, and new Charge; these Swilling the Indigestion, and vitious Contents of the Stomach, into the Blood . . . Hence the great Increase of the Stone, Gout, Rheumatism, Nervine and other Affections. . . . The Consequence of this great Increase of the Arts of Luxury and Intemperance, are Vice and Immorality: Irreligion, Impiety, Passion, Animosity, Contention, Faction: Neglect of Thought, Studyes, and Business, Misspending of Time, Ignorance, Stupidity, Poverty, Discontent, Sickness, Disease.' (pp. 194-5). A similar indictment in a different context is found in R. Campbell, *The London Tradesman*, London, 1747, p. 277: 'We abhor that any thing should appear at our Tables in its native Properties; all the Earth, from both the Poles, the most distant and different Climates, must be ransacked for Spices, Pickles, and Sauces, not to relish but to disguise our Food . . . This depraved Taste of spoiling wholesome Dyet, by costly and pernicious Sauces, and absurd Mixtures, does not confine itself to the Tables of the Great; but the Contagion is become epidemical; Poor and rich live as if they were of a different Species of Beings from their Ancestors, and observe a Regimen of Diet calculated not to supply the Wants of Nature, but to oppress her Faculties, disturbe her Operations, and load her with, till now, unheard of Maladies.' But cf. Thomas Fuller, *The Holy State and the Profane State* (1642), J. Nichols (ed.), 1841, p. 109: 'God is not so hard a master, but that he alloweth his Servants sauce . . . to eat with their meat'.

Characteristically Swift brings the passage to a close with a burst of Juvenalian indignation in a catalogue of the vices and follies which inevitably result from a foreign trade thus misdirected. The fundamental point of this passage in *Gulliver's Travels* needs little attention. It is a general statement of a prevalent theoretical position in mercantilist economic thought of the period, that the importation of luxuries is *not* economically desirable, the logic being that imported luxuries have an adverse effect on the balance of trade. In a compendium of mercantilist dogma published in 1713, Sir Theodore Janssen, a director of the South Sea Company, codified the prevailing view in these words: 'That the importing Commodities of mere Luxury is so much real Loss to the Nation as they amount to'.[5]

It is well known that Swift often expounded this view—in his various Irish tracts, in his correspondence, even in one of his sermons, *Causes of the Wretched Condition of Ireland*, where he maintained that the importation of luxuries is a primary cause of Ireland's impoverishment. A year or so after the publication of *Gulliver* he wrote that a people should 'import as few Incitements to Luxury, either in Cloaths, Furniture, Food, or Drink, as they possibly can live conveniently without'—a remark which restates the economic principle of the passage in *Gulliver* here under discussion.[6]

We might expect in his Irish tracts that Swift's statement of this view would be less fervid than in *Gulliver's Travels*, where he is using it for the satirical exposé of a wasteful and corrupt society and for the denunciation of man's nature; but even in the cooler context of purely economic discussion Swift does not restrain himself. The intensity with which Gulliver inveighs against foreign importations derives from Swift's appraisal of the harsh realities of Ireland's economy, to which he bore witness so frequently in pleading for economic reforms which might achieve a measure of national self-sufficiency.[7]

But this passage in *Gulliver's Travels*, which I call the Female Yahoo's Breakfast, contains more than appears on the surface. It has ramifications and implications reaching into several fields of thought; and in using the woman of quality, this better female Yahoo, to define his economic predilections Swift had ample pre-

[5] [Charles King], *The British Merchant: A Collection of Papers relating to the Trade and Commerce of Great Britain and Ireland*, 2nd ed., London, 1743, p. 5 [1st ed. 1721]. The quoted 'maxim' is from Sir Theodore Janssen's *General Maxims of Trade*, 1713.

[6] *Prose Works*, XII, p. 7.

[7] For a general discussion of Swift's economic views, see my article, 'Swift's Economic Views and Mercantilism', *ELH: A Journal of English Literary History*, Vol. X, Dec. 1943, pp. 310-35.

cedent. She was already known in one guise or another well before *Gulliver's Travels* was published; and I wish to suggest that when Swift's contemporaries found her in the *Travels* she would have been recognised as a stock figure, or even as a convention in literary works using economic themes. She would have generated a variety of emotions, by no means all of them emotions attendant on rejection, as in Swift. Furthermore, the more knowledgeable contemporaries would have realised that the female Yahoo's breakfast was indeed a complex matter, one that went beyond merely economic considerations into considerations of medicine and national health, geography and international relations, and theology. It is not merely her imported breakfast which disturbed Swift. As this better female Yahoo emerges from his writings of the 1720s her power to consume is enlarged beyond, in Swift's words, exotic liquors, such 'Indian poisons' as tea, coffee, and chocolate. There is also an array of 'unnecessary finery—muslin, laces, silks, holland, cambric, calico', characterised by Swift as 'the instruments of our ruin', imported 'to gratify the vanity and pride, and luxury of the women, and of the fops who admire them'.[8] The opening lines of Swift's poem, *The Lady's Dressing Room* (1732), are appropriate here:

> Five Hours, (and who can do it less in?)
> By haughty *Celia* spent in Dressing;
> The Goddess from her Chamber issues,
> Array'd in Lace, Brocades and Tissues.[9]

Celia in 'Lace, Brocades and Tissues' is merely a poetic version of the Irish women who so preoccupy Swift's thoughts in these years. It is to them that he often appealed, to 'vie with each other in the fineness of their native linen', assuring them that their beauty and gentility would shine no less than if they were covered with diamonds and brocade.[10] Three years after the appearance of *Gulliver's Travels* we find Swift again erupting with blazing intensity against these fine ladies. With Bishop Berkeley he believed an Irish woman arrayed in French silks and Flanders lace to be 'an enemy to the Nation'.[11] He wrote with passion of 'those detestable Extravagancies of Flanders lace . . . Italian or Indian Silks, Tea, Coffee, Chocolate, Chinaware, and . . . profusion of wines':

8 *Prose Works*, XII, pp. 63ff., 126.

9 *The Poems of Jonathan Swift*, Harold Williams (ed.), 2nd ed., Oxford, 1958, II, p. 525.

10 *Prose Works*, XII, p. 127.

11 Ibid., XI, p. 16. See George Berkeley, *The Querist*, No. 141, 1735: 'Whether a woman of fashion ought not to be declared a public enemy', in *Works*, A. A. Luce and T. C. Jessop (eds.), London and New York, 1953, VI, p. 117.

Is it not [he asked] the highest Indignity to human nature, that men should be such poltrons as to suffer the Kingdom and themselves to be undone, by the Vanity, the Folly, the Pride, and Wantonness of their Wives, who under the present Corruptions seem to be a kind of animal suffered for our sins to be sent into the world for the Destruction of Familyes, Societyes, and Kingdoms . . . who by long practice can reconcile the most pernicious forein Drugs to their health and pleasure, provided they are but expensive . . . who . . . can sleep beyond noon, revel upon Indian poisons, and spend the revenue of a moderate family to adorn a nauseous unwholesome living Carcase.[12]

Here, then, in the Irish tracts, passionately denounced, is Gulliver's better female Yahoo, a creature of indulgence, given to 'unwholesome drugs' and 'Unnecessary finery', an emblem of ruinous economic consumption. And we get a brief flashing vision of the vast machinery of foreign trade, functioning wastefully and absurdly to satisfy this demanding consumer.

I may mention in passing that Swift's pleas for national frugality would have evoked sympathetic responses in many of his contemporaries, but my concern here is to observe other writers of the period—Addison, Pope, and Defoe, among them—who have employed this economic theme and who contrast sharply with Swift. I turn first to a work not belletristic, but one in which the conception of man's nature and of society has affinities with that of Swift, Bernard Mandeville's brilliant *Fable of the Bees* (1714). Mandeville was concerned with a paradox that made his own and a later generation uneasy: how to achieve a society whose members are frugal and honest and at the same time opulent. Mandeville thought it *not* possible. A frugal and honest society, he maintained, could arise only when men practised 'Native Simplicity': 'let them never be acquainted with Strangers or Superfluities, but remove and keep them from every thing that might raise their Desires . . .'. An opulent nation, on the other hand, was based upon the refined appetites and enlarged desires of its people. Thus Mandeville tells those who want 'an opulent, knowing, and polite Nation' to value 'commerce with Foreign Countries . . . if possible get into the Sea'. 'Promote Navigation', he urges, 'cherish the Merchant, and encourage Trade in every Branch of it; this will bring Riches, and where they are, Arts and Sciences will soon follow . . .'.[13] From the vantage of national wealth (ethical considerations are something else again) Mandeville finds nothing to condemn in sending

[12] *Prose Works*, XII, p. 80.
[13] *The Fable of the Bees: Or, Private Vices, Publick Benefits*, F. B. Kaye (ed.), Oxford, 1924, I, p. 184.

a ship thrice around the world for a female Yahoo's breakfast. 'What Estates', he writes, 'have been got by Tea and Coffee!'[14] It would be a difficult Task', he asserts, 'to enumerate all the Advantages and different Benefits, that accrue to a Nation on account of Shipping and Navigation'. And Mandeville details the multitudinous web of activities and the abundance of stores necessary for building and manning even one ship: timber, tar, resin, grease, masts, nails, cables, the employment of smiths and mariners, and the maintenance of the families of those employed—all of this spreading in a widening circle of economic activity involving large numbers.[15]

Dispassionately Mandeville looks at this universal mercantile economy—the vast nexus of enterprises—to observe 'What a vast Traffick [i.e. trade] is drove, what a variety of Labour is performed in the World to the Maintenance of Thousands of Families that altogether depend on two silly if not odious Customs; the taking of Snuff and smoking of Tobacco . . .'.[16] By this logic the woman of quality becomes not 'an Enemy to the Nation' (Swift's epithet) but a public benefactor. Her *private* vices are *public* benefits. Mandeville considers the farthingale: that 'silly and capricious Invention of Hoop'd and Quilted Petticoats', he declares, has done as much as, if not more than, the Reformation for the enrichment of nations.[17] As for a fine scarlet cloth designed for a garment: 'what a Bustle is there to be made in several Parts of the World' before it can be produced, 'what Multiplicity of Trades and Artificers must be employ'd!'[18]

In a brilliant passage Mandeville evokes the mercantile complexities involved, the vast seas to be traversed, the varied climates to be endured, the fatigues and hazards to be undergone, even the ramifications involved in so obvious a matter as providing the ingredients of the dye, ingredients 'dispers'd thro' the Universe that are to meet in one Kettle': argol from the Rhine, vitriol from Hungary, saltpetre from the East Indies, cochineal from the West Indies. 'While so many Sailors are broiling in the Sun and sweltered with Heat in the *East* and *West* of us, another set of them are freezing in the *North* to fetch Potashes from Russia'.[19] All of this to satisfy the desire for a garment of scarlet cloth.

We observe then in Mandeville a fuller expression of the theme treated all too sparsely by Swift; and Mandeville gives us the details

14 Ibid., I, p. 359.
15 Ibid., I, pp. 359-60.
16 Ibid., I, p. 359.
17 Ibid., I, p. 356.
18 Ibid.
19 Ibid., I, pp. 356-8.

not supplied by Gulliver when that disillusioned traveller is dis-
approving of ships that encircle the world to bring back vanities
for indulgent female Yahoos. Indeed, Swift might have enriched
this part of the *Travels* had he been as vivid as Mandeville in
employing concrete details.

This evocation of particulars in support of the economic theme
I am discussing is vividly present in the *Spectator*. As we know,
Addison and Steele celebrate the dignity of commerce on many
occasions, most obviously in the person of Sir Andrew Freeport, a
man concerned with foreign trade, a man, we are told, of noble
and generous ideas, better company than a scholar, one whose ships
sail to every point of the compass.[20] He is the type, Addison and
Steele are convinced, responsible for England's wealth and greatness. It is therefore not surprising that Mr Spectator, visiting the
Royal Exchange, should look about him with satisfaction and
remark that there 'are not more useful members in a commonwealth than merchants'. Mr Spectator glows with satisfaction as he
considers *foreign* trade, and his rhetoric likewise glows as he comments on seaborne traffic:

> Our Ships [he says] are laden with the Harvest of every
> Climate: our Tables are stored with Spices, and Oils, and
> Wines: Our Rooms are filled with Pyramids of *China*, and
> adorned with the Workmanship of *Japan*: Our Morning's-
> Draught comes to us from the remotest Corners of the Earth:
> We repair our Bodies by the Drugs of *America*, and repose our
> selves under *Indian* Canopies. My Friend Sir Andrew calls the
> Vineyards of *France* our Gardens; the Spice-Islands our Hot-
> bed; the *Persians* our Silk-Weavers, and the *Chinese* our
> Potters.[21]

The heightened tone, the particularity, the accumulation of consumer items in the essay I am quoting, No. 69, suggest a kind of
mercantile appetite or zestfulness.

Little wonder that the Tory foxhunter depicted by Addison in
the *Freeholder*, No. 22 (5 Mar. 1716), of the landed gentry and
disdainful of foreign commerce, is out of countenance when he

[20] *Spectator*, No. 2, 2 Mar. 1711, Donald F. Bond (ed.), Oxford, 1965, Vol. I, pp.
10-11.

[21] Ibid., No. 69, 19 May 1711, Vol. I, pp. 295-6. See Edmund Waller's poetic
version of this theme in 1665:

So what our earth, and what our heav'n denies,
Our ever-constant friend, the sea supplies.
The taste of hot Arabia's spice we know,
Free from the scorching sun, that makes it grow:
Without the worm, in Persian silks we shine;
And, without planting, drink of ev'ry wine.

('A Panegyric to My Lord Protector, of the Present Greatness, and Joint
Interest, of his Highness, and the Nation', stanzas 14-15).

discovers that the punch he loves so well contains such imported items as brandy, sugar, lemon and nutmeg. The only English ingredient is water. And what of the woman of quality, Swift's 'enemy to the Nation', Gulliver's better female Yahoo, Mandeville's lady encased in a hooped petticoat, whose desires and consumer's appetite keep the vast machinery of international trade in motion? For Mr Spectator she is a vision of delight; and he envelops her along with the merchant in his swinging eloquence and orotundity.

> The single Dress of a Woman of Quality [he declares] is often the Product of an Hundred Climates. The Muff and the Fan come together from the different Ends of the Earth. The Scarf is sent from the Torrid Zone, and the Tippet from beneath the Pole. The Brocade Petticoat rises out of the Mines of *Peru*, and the Diamond Necklace out of the Bowels of *Indostan*.[22]

Far from being an object to condemn, this woman adorned with 'the Products of an Hundred Climates', is for Mr Spectator an emblem of cosmopolitanism, a citizen of the world transcending national boundaries; and as he visualises her his imagination goes winging out over oceans to far away lands, into the frozen wastes and the steaming tropics, on a mercantile progress more extended than any royal progress ever was.

If we look back for a moment to Addison in his guise as Mr Bickerstaff in the *Tatler*, we find him, like Mandeville, glancing with the eye of both economist and moralist at the quilted and hooped petticoat. With this 'monstrous invention' Addison was ready to sacrifice economic advantage for good taste and good sense in fashions. In an amusing essay (the *Tatler*, No. 116) he depicts Mr Bickerstaff as presiding over a Court of Judicature in which the hooped petticoat is the criminal defendant. Although counsel for the defendant argues that the hooped variety in contrast to the ordinary petticoat has greatly improved the woollen trade, the ropemaker's trade, and the Greenland trade, by utilising more cloth, more cordage, and more whalebone, the decision nevertheless goes against the defendant. At the same time Mr Bickerstaff hastens to declare himself a defender of luxuries and fashions which do *not* pervert nature:

> I consider woman as a beautiful romantic animal, that may be adorned with furs and feathers, pearls and diamonds, ores and silks. The lynx shall cast its skin at her feet to make her a tippet; the peacock, parrot, and swan shall *pay contributions* to her muff; the sea shall be searched for shells, and the rocks

---

22 *Spectator*, No. 69, 19 May 1711, Vol. I, p. 295.

for gems; and every part of nature furnish out its share towards the embellishment of a creature that is the most consummate work of it. All this I shall indulge them in; but as for the petticoat I have been speaking of, I neither can nor will allow it.[23]

The light tone of the essay does not obscure Addison's concern, shared by his contemporaries, over the conflicting claims of commerce and morality; but he was not inclined, either by temperament or general outlook, to view the conflict with the austerity and intensity of a Swift. Mr Bickerstaff's apostrophe to woman, just quoted, in which he maintains that the animal and physical worlds are properly exploited for the embellishment of women, reveals that Mr Bickerstaff and Mr Spectator are in no respect at odds.

Pope presents us with a more subtle insinuation into literature of the theme we are observing. In *The Rape of the Lock* (1714) we enter a world where serious economic considerations ostensibly do not intrude. It is, of course, a world catered to by the luxury trades (to use modern parlance), a world of glitter and fine feathers, a filigree world of jewels and brocades, of Indian screens and amber snuff boxes, all an appropriate context for Pope's heroine, Belinda, whose charm and gaiety are such that to place her among the economically wasteful female Yahoos seems unforgivably churlish. When 'Belinda smiled . . . all the world was gay'. And Pope envelops Belinda in such vivid and memorable lines of poetic beauty that we may miss the economic implications. Yet Belinda at the toilette table at the close of Canto I would, I believe, have arrested the attention of any contemporary reader sensitive to economic ideas. The relevant lines depict Belinda being made up by her maid, Betty, for the daily round of pleasure and social conquest. Pope describes the objects of the toilette:

> Unnumber'd Treasures ope at once, and here
> The various Off'rings of the World appear;
> From each she [Betty] nicely culls with curious Toil,
> And decks the Goddess with the glitt'ring Spoil.
> This Casket *India's* glowing Gems unlocks,
> And all *Arabia* breathes from yonder Box.
> The Tortoise here and Elephant unite,
> Transform'd to *Combs* the speckled and the white.
>
> (Canto I, ll. 129-36)

[23] *Tatler*, No. 116, 5 Jan. 1709-10, in *The British Essayists, with Prefaces, Biographical, Historical, and Critical*, Lionel Thomas Berguer (ed.), London, 1823, Vol. III, pp. 175-6.

Here, in a somewhat different guise and transmuted into poetry, we have Addison's woman of quality whose desires caused timber to be felled, hemp and resin to be imported, ships to be built, and sailors sent to remote lands, that she may be adorned. Her adornment is 'the Product of an Hundred Climates', in Addison's phrase; or as Pope himself says, Belinda was 'decked with all that Land and Sea afford' (Canto V, l. 11), with 'the various Off'rings of the World'—and a Swift or a Mandeville, visualising the ships traversing the seas, to India for gems, Arabia for perfumes, and Africa for ivory, would be aware of the mercantile complexities implied by these poetic lines. Pope calls this ritual of the toilette the 'sacred Rites of Pride' (Canto I, l. 128), a piece of overt social or ethical indictment, without any explicit economic coloration. Perhaps there is a sly, dark hint in the phrase 'glitt'ring Spoil', but I should not want to insist on the pejorative impact of even that phrase. And the submerged theme, the suggestion of a universal mercantile economy operating for the enhancement of Belinda's beauty, is in a context of such tolerance and amiability that Pope's mild rebuke tends to dissolve in the sunshine of Belinda's charm.

But consider for a moment the reaction to Belinda of a convinced mercantilist with his austere conviction that imported luxuries are an economic evil. How would he view this beguiling young lady? What would he say of her silks, spun not by *domestic* silkworms but by the *foreign* worms of Persia, France, and Italy? Of her ivory and tortoise shell from Africa? Of her sparkling gems from India? Of her Arabian perfumes transported laboriously by camel caravan across the Arabian desert and thence down the incense road to a Mediterranean port, eventually to reach London?

The answers are obvious—and painful. But we may find some relief in what was doubtless of English manufacture, the stays of her corset covered with tabby (taffeta), the one article of her underclothing likely to be domestic, and as well her stockings and her shoes. The only conclusion possible is that Belinda, economically speaking, was a menace to the welfare of her country.

I return to Addison for a moment, for suggestions of a richer, more philosophic view of this theme, a larger vision prevalent in the period and earlier which assimilated the idea of trade and the merchant into both the natural order and the divine order. The eulogists of commerce in the eighteenth century would have been untrue to their rationalistic heritage if they had failed to see the spectacle of a universal mercantile economy as an aspect of the ordered and harmonious universe in which all parts cohere and have specific functions. A clue comes, significantly, from Addison's choice of an epigraph for the *Spectator*, No. 69, a quotation from Virgil's *Georgics* of several lines (I, ll. 54-61) concerned with regional differences. Virgil points out that nature has imposed diversity in the products of the soil:

> This Ground with *Bacchus,* that with *Ceres* suits:
> That other loads the Trees with happy Fruits:
> A fourth, with Grass, unbidden, decks the Ground.
> Thus *Tmolus* is with yellow Saffron crowned.

The genius of the soil which produces this diversity is paralleled by the genius of each nation, whose products reveal the specialised and distinctive quality of its culture:

> *India,* black Ebon and white Ivory bears;
> And soft *Idume* weeps her od'rous Tears.
> Thus *Pontus* sends her Beaver Stones from far;
> And naked *Spanyards* temper Steel for War:
> *Epirus,* for the *Elean* Chariot breeds,
> (In hopes of Palms) a Race of running Steeds.
> This is the Orig'nal Contract; these the Laws
> Impos'd by Nature, and by Nature's Cause,
> On sundry Places. . . .[24]

From Virgil down through the middle ages and into the seventeeth century the idea of regional differences received more than passing comment. Its significance was observed by geographers, theologians, and poets, by writers on travel and by those interested in commerce. The readers of Du Bartas in the late sixteenth and in the seventeenth centuries found the idea elaborately set forth in *The Divine Weekes;* and it may be that the English translations of the 'Second Week' in the early seventeenth century help to disseminate the view that the entire world is an exchange, a mart, analogous to a city, such a city as London, so Joshua Sylvester, the translator of Du Bartas (1606) would have it, *'wherein dwell People of all conditions, . . . continually trafficking together and exchanging their particular commodities for benefit of the Publicke'.*[25] Consider the following lines from Du Bartas:

> *And All's but an Exchange, Where (brieflie) no Man Keeps ought as private: Trade makes all Things Common*
> So come our Sugars from *Canary* Isles:
> From *Candy,* Currance, Muskadels, and Oyles:

[24] *Spectator,* No. 69, 19 May 1711, Vol. I, pp. 292-3. Dryden's translation.
[25] Du Bartas [Guil'aume de Saluste Sieur], *Dubartas His Divine Weekes and Workes translated . . . by Joshua Sylvester,* London, 1613, p. 352.

From the *Moluques* Spices: Balsamum
From *Egypt*: Odours from *Arabia* come:
From *India*, Drugs, rich Gemmes, and Ivorie:
From *Syria*, Mummie: black-red Ebonie,
From burning *Chus*: from *Peru*, Pearl and Gold:
From *Russia* Furres (to keep the rich from cold):
From *Florence*, Silks: From *Spayn*, Fruit, Saffron, Sacks:
From *Denmark*, Amber, Cordage, Firres, and Flax:
From *France* and *Flanders*, Linnen, Wood, and Wine:
From *Holland* Hops: Horse[s] from the banks of *Rhine*.
In briefe, each Country (as pleas'd God distribute)
To the Worlds Treasure payes a Sundry Tribute.[26]

Writers of a religious cast of mind saw in this universal dispersion of products a divine intention, that widely separated peoples
would be bound together in amity, brought to cohesion and inter-
dependence by their need for one another. Bishop Joseph Hall,
whose *Quo Vadis?* (1617) is a 'Censure of Travel', nevertheless
grants that travel for purposes of trade is valid, because trade
derives from the providential ordering by which products have
been dispersed. God, he writes, 'hath made one country the granary,
another the cellar, another the orchard, another the arsenal, of
their neighbours, yea of the remotest parts'.

It is an over rigorous construction of the works of God, that
in moating our island with the ocean he meant to shut us
up from other regions: for God himself, that made the Sea,
was the Author of navigation; and hath therein taught us to
set up a wooden bridge that may reach to the very antipodes
themselves.

Thus Bishop Hall can remark that 'no parcel of earth' has been
stored by the deity as a 'private reservation', that 'Either Indies
may be searched for those treasures which God hath laid up in
them for their far distant owners', that 'a ship of merchants, that
fetches her wares from far, is the good housewife of the commonwealth'.[27] Little more than a decade later Baptist Goodall, an
obscure London merchant, stimulated by the wonders of travel

26 Ibid., p. 353.
27 *Works of the Right Reverend Joseph Hall, D.D.*, Philip Wynter (ed.), Oxford, 1863, IX, [529]. Hall writes:
  The sea and earth are the great coffers of God: the discoveries of navigation are the keys, which whoever hath received may know that he is freely
  allowed to unlock these chests of nature without any need to pick the
  wards. In *Quo Vadis*, though Hall accepts the principle of the 'divinity of
  trade,' he is concerned to write a 'just censure of travel'; and as a result
  he strongly indicts the introduction into England of foreign fashions and
  manners. These have corrupted, he asserts, the judgment and manners of
  the English. The lady of fashion draws some of his strongest criticism:
  'it were well if we knew our own fashions; better if we could keep them.
  What mischief have we amongst us that we have not borrowed? To begin

and trade to break into verse, catalogues the products of two score and more of nations ranging from the furs of Russia, the fruits of Spain, the wool and coal of England, to the pearls of China and the silks of India—with the conclusion that there is a divinity in this diversity:

> One succours other, traffic breeds affection,
> The whole is governed by the high protection,
> For winds, seas, sky and travel all agree
> To frame on earth a just conformity.[28]

Inevitably economic writers and the apologists for the great trading companies found this viewpoint congenial. Witness Charles Davenant, one of the able defenders of the East India Company, declaring in 1697 that 'the various Products of different Soiles and Countries is [sic] an Indication that Providence intended they should be helpful to each other, and mutually supply the Necessities of one another'.[29] There is, then, a long-established traditional view in the background of Mr Spectator's remark (No. 69) in 1711 that

> Nature seems to have taken a particular Care to disseminate her Blessings among the different Regions of the World, with an Eye to this mutual Intercourse and Traffick among Mankind, that the Natives of the several Parts of the Globe might

---

at our skin: who knows not whence we had the variety of our vain disguises . . .? The dresses being constant in their mutability, show us our masters. . . . Whom would it not vex, to see how that other sex hath learned to make antics and monsters of themselves? Whence came their hips to the shoulders and their breasts to the navel; but the one from some ill shaped dames of France, the other from the worse minded courtesans of Italy? Whence else learned they . . . those high washes which are so cunningly licked on . . . Whence the frizzled and powdered bushes of their borrowed excrement: as if they were ashamed of the head of God's making . . . ?' (p. 556). This kind of tirade was, of course, a commonplace in homiletic literature. For our purposes it illustrates the juxtaposition in the same work of the principle that trade is inherent in the divine plan and the view of the moralist that it can be, as a practical matter, an evil force.

[28] *The Tryall of Travell*, London, 1630, sig. c³. I have modernised the spelling. The providential conjunction of winds and sea to further trade, as observed by Goodall, is a frequent theme in the seventeenth century. A typical example from an economic tract: 'And to the end there should be a *Commerce* amongst men, it hath pleased *God* to invite as it were, one Countrey to traffique with another, by the variety of things which the one hath, and the other hath not: that so that which is wanting to the *one*, might be supplyed by the *other*, that all might have sufficient.

Which thing the very windes and seas proclaime, in giving passage to all nations: the windes blowing sometimes towards one Countrey, sometimes towards another; that so by this divine justice, every one might be supplyed in things necessary for life and maintenance' (Edward Misselden, *Free Trade, Or the Meanes to Make Trade Flourish*, 2nd ed., 1622, p. 25). Misselden finds these providential winds mentioned in Seneca and Aristotle (p. 26).

[29] [Charles Davenant], *An Essay on the East India Company. By the Author of The Essay upon Wayes and Means*, London, 1696, p. 34.

have a kind of Dependance upon one another, and be united together by their common Interest.[30]

What Gulliver gloomily repudiated, Addison sees as the working out of a natural and rational and providential nexus: 'The Food [he writes] often grows in one Country, and the Sauce in another. The Fruits of *Portugal* are corrected by the Products of the *Barbadoes*: The Infusion of a *China* Plant is sweetened with the Pith of an Indian Cane'. It is, of course, by this same logic that Addison can cheerfully observe that 'the single Dress of a Woman of Quality is often the Product of an hundred Climates'. It is by this logic as well that merchants are recognised as instruments of a universal economy, fulfilling a principle of universal mercantile amity: Merchants, Mr Spectator writes, 'knit Mankind together in a mutual Intercourse of good Offices, distribute the Gifts of Nature, find work for the Poor, add Wealth to the Rich, and Magnificence to the Great'.[31]

This principle of universal mercantile amity is aptly termed by James Thomson, in his *Castle of Indolence* (1748), 'social commerce': social commerce joins 'land to land' and unites the poles. It raises 'renowned marts' and 'without bloody Spoil', brings home from either Indies 'the gorgeous stores'.[32] Into this concept of 'social commerce' contemporaries infused a richness of feeling well illustrated by George Lillo's popular play of 1731, *The London Merchant*. Here we are told that merchandise promotes humanity, 'as it has open'd and yet keeps up an Intercourse between Nations, far remote from one another in Situation, Customs and Religion; promoting Arts, Industry, Peace and Plenty; by Mutual Benefits diffusing Mutual Love from Pole to Pole'.[33]

Defoe, as we would expect from one who with justice may be called the laureate of commerce, utilises these various strains of thought with enthusiasm. Like Addison, Defoe envisions trade in

---

[30] *Spectator*, No. 69, 19 May 1711, Vol. I, pp. 294-5.

[31] Ibid., p. 296.

[32] *The Castle of Indolence and Other Poems*, Alan Dugald McKillop (ed.), Lawrence, Kansas, 1961, Canto II, stanza 20, p. 101. See Pope's variant of 'social commerce' in *Windsor Forest* (1713), ll.385ff. written as the Treaty of Utrecht was being completed. Pope presents a shining vision of a world peaceably united by commerce, with England, of course, as the central unifying force.

[33] Act III, sc. 1. In this scene the merchant, Thorowgood, says that trade is 'founded in reason and the nature of things' and Trueman, his virtuous apprentice, responds: 'I have observ'd those countries, where trade is promoted and encouraged, do not make discoveries to destroy, but to improve mankind by love and friendship; to tame the fierce and polish the most savage; to teach them the advantages of honest traffick, by taking from them, with their own consent, their useless superfluities, and giving them, in return, what, from their ignorance in manual arts, their situation, or some other accident, they stand in need of'.

larger, philosophic terms, in the context of the principle of universal correspondence, a principle which meant for contemporaries as I have indicated, a providential and rationalistic ordering of the universe by virtue of which the very differences in nations and peoples bind all men together. The restricted and specialised products of each nation and the national character which manifests itself by demanding certain products not indigenous—these are part of the providential design. England had been *naturally* and providentially endowed with the soil and climate for grain, Norway for lumber, Poland for flax, the Moluccas for spice. '. . . every Country', Defoe writes, 'Communicates to its other corresponding Country what they want, and these [that] can spare them *vice-versa* receive from that Country again what of their Growth these want; and not a Country so barren, so useless, but something is to be found there that can be had nowhere else'.[34] This variety in nature is paralleled by the varied and differing genius of each people which makes them seek in foreign climates what they cannot find at home. Gulliver saw only folly in 'sending Vessels by Sea to every Part of the World . . . for Liquors to drink . . .'. Defoe differs sharply. He views with satisfaction the inclination of English prelates for 'those liquors which we must fetch from abroad'.

> We cloth[e] [Defoe writes], all the Islands and Continent of *America*; and they in return, furnish us with Sugars and Tobaccoes, things by Custom becoming as useful to us as our cloths is to them. . . . What a Quantity of the *Terra Firma* has been carried from *Newcastle* in coles . . . what Cavities and Chasms in the Bowels of the Earth have we made for our Tin, Lead, and Iron. . . . These we carry abroad, and with them we purchase and bring back the Woods of *Norway*, the Silks of *Italy* and *Turkey*, the Wines and Brandies of *France*, the Wines, Oil, and Fruit of *Spain*, the Druggs of *Persia*, the Spices of *India*, the Sugars of *America*, the Toys and Gaiety of *China* and *Japan*.[35]

It is this variety, Defoe says, 'both of the Produce and Manufactures of the several Countries [which] are the Foundations of Trade, and [he says significantly] I entitle Providence to it . . .'. He adds: 'The Merchant by his Correspondence reconciles that infinite Variety which . . . has by the Infinite Wisdom of Providence been scattered over the Face of the World'.[36]

Like Addison, Defoe too can envelop the merchant in super-

34 *Review*, Vol. III, No. 2, 3 Jan. 1706.
35 Ibid.
36 Ibid.

latives and rhythmic prose; and he goes well beyond Addison in full statement of the religious and rationalistic implications of the mercantile theme. In fact, in two issues of the *Review* (3 Jan. 1706 and 3 Feb. 1713) Defoe goes so far in investing the merchant, that is, the person engaged in foreign trade, with the aura of divinity that Addison seems pale and secular by contrast. 'And what [Defoe asks] if . . . I should tell you there is a kind of divinity in the origin of trade . . .?' He then proposes to demonstrate that Providence has concurred in and prepared the world for commerce, that Providence has 'adapted nature to trade'. His demonstration begins, properly, with winds, oceans, and ships. Why is it, how does it happen, that 'Floaty Bodies, by natural levity' invariably swim upon the surface of the water; that a ship, 'toss'd by the Fury of the contending Elements, and mounted on the Surface of a Rolling Body of disordered Water', is saved from 'falling into a vast Gulph of Destruction' by these same waves, 'moved by the mighty Winds', hurrying 'into the hollow Place, and catching it [the ship] in their soft Arms . . . gently raise it up again . . . and . . . launch it forward?' To Defoe this is God acting 'in the order of Nature', to make navigation possible, 'to lay the Foundation of Commerce', to preserve 'the Communication of one part of the World with another'. Then Defoe turns to the world of man and animals. He sees here a similar 'superintendency of invisible Providence', for example, in the subjection of the lower animals to men, particularly in that wise provision whereby the useful creatures are tame and submissive and the less needful ones are left wild. Thus it is, Defoe informs his reader, that your sheep, 'the tamest, quietest, submissivest Creatures in the world . . . lay their backs to the shears. . . .'[37] The logic is inescapable: England's great staple, wool, is by divine arrangement.

It is of more than passing interest that Defoe, writing of navigation and commerce in these issues of the *Review*, uses the logic of the physico-theologies, those elaborate rationalistic demonstrations (popular in the period) that in every aspect of physical creation, in each 'visible work of God', can be traced 'his Wisdom in the Composition, Order, Harmony, and Uses of every one of them'. In the cosmic order God, the 'Wise Contriver', the divine Architect, managed so that all things are 'commodiously adopted

---

[37] Ibid. I, No. 54, 3 Feb. 1713. On the idea of regional differences and the providential arrangement by which 'God [furnished] all Countreys from the first beginning with some *Staple-commodities*, for the benefit of themselves and others, for the maintaining of that entercourse between Nation and Nation, which makes them link the closer in the bonds of Amity', see Peter Heylin, *Cosmography*, 9th ed., 1703, pp. 4-5.

to their proper uses'.[38] Defoe looks at the physical properties of ships ('Floaty Bodies'), at the nature of gravitation, wind, water, and waves, and he sees that they constitute a mingled measure, providentially designed, to make navigation and commerce possible. Shortly before Defoe wrote the second of the two *Reviews* under discussion Sir Richard Blackmore had published his poem, *Creation* (1712), possibly the most elaborate contemporary physico-theology in verse. The parallels between Defoe and Blackmore are striking: Blackmore writes:

> What, but a Conscious Agent, could provide
> The spacious Hollow, where the Waves reside?
> . . .
> What other Cause the Frame could so contrive,
> That when tempestuous Winds the Ocean drive,
> They cannot break the Tye, nor disunite
> The Waves, which roll Connected in their flight?
> . . .
> This apt, this wise Contexture of the Sea,
> Makes it the Ships driv'n by the Winds obey;
> Whence hardy merchants Sail from Shoar to Shoar,
> Bring *India's* spices home, and *Guinea's* Ore.

As for Defoe, so for Blackmore the 'wise Contexture of the Sea' acts in conjunction with the providential utility of the wind:

> Of what important Use to human Kind,
> To what great Ends subservient is the Wind;
> . . .
> Without this Aid the Ship would ne'er advance
> Along the Deep, and o'er the Billow dance,
> But lye a lazy and a useless Load,
> The Forest's wasted Spoils, the Lumber of the Flood.
> Let but the Wind with an auspicious Gale
> To shove the Vessel fill the spreading Sail,
> And see, with swelling Canvas wing'd she flies,
> And with her waving Streamers sweeps the Skies!
> Th' advent'rous Merchant thus pursues his Way,
> Or to the Rise, or to the Fall of Day:
> Thus mutual Traffick sever'd Realms maintain,
> And Manufactures change to mutual Gain;
> Each others Growth and Arts they sell and buy,
> Ease their Redundance, and their Wants supply.[39]

[38] The phraseology is from John Ray's *The Wisdom of God in the Works of Creation* (1691), 10th ed., 1705, Preface, sig. B1.

[39] Richard Blackmore, *Creation, A Philosophical Poem. In Seven Books*, London, 1712, Bk I, ll. 632-50, pp. 41-2; Bk II, ll. 698-759, pp. 95-8.

In these lines and others we have Blackmore's more elaborate versification of the theme quoted earlier from the obscure merchant of the seventeenth century, Baptist Goodall:

> One succours other, traffic breeds affection,
> The whole is governed by the high protection,
> For winds, seas, sky and travel agree
> To frame on earth a just conformity.[40]

Blackmore continues his rationalistic physico-theological analysis of the wind with a typical catalogue of luxurious mercantile items:

> Ye *Britons*, who the Fruit of Commerce find,
> How is your Isle a Debtor to the Wind,
> Which thither wafts *Arabia*'s fragrant Spoils,
> Gems, Pearls and Spices from the *Indian* Isles.
> From *Persia* Silks, Wines from *Iberia*'s Shore,
> *Peruvian* Drugs, and *Guinea*'s *golden* ore?
> Delights and Wealth to fair *Augusta* flow
> From ev'ry Region whence the Winds can blow.[41]

Here it is once again, that conventional inventory of luxuries which an eighteenth-century reader must inevitably have associated with the woman of quality—the aromatic gums of Arabia, the mineral wealth of the Indies, the woven silks of Persia, delights flowing into Queen Anne's England 'From ev'ry region whence the winds can blow'. Blackmore could assume that his inventory of shining luxuries would evoke the image of the fashionable lady. For a Swift or a Pope or an Addison, and for many others, his lines would bring her imaginatively forth.

As we observe, Defoe and Blackmore are among those who provide a rationale for this lady of fashion in terms of a providential and rationalistic scheme of things with a mercantile coloration. In the realms of economic theory and physico-theological speculation, the indulged and indulgent woman of quality had her place, so to speak, by divine right. From this vantage in theory she, like the merchant who laid at her feet 'the various Off'rings of the World', is a facet of a universal economy in which she plays a significant role; and if we accept the logic we ought not, in charity and tolerance, accuse her of vanity and ostentation. Rather with Defoe and his contemporaries we should realise that when she appeared, decked in India's sparkling gems and adorned with all that land and sea afford, she was merely fulfilling the will of God.

---

40 See above, n. 28.
41 Blackmore, *Creation*, Bk II, 11, 760-7, p. 99. See my article, complementary to this, 'Pope's Belinda, the General Emporie of the World, and the Wondrous Worm', in *The South Atlantic Quarterly: Essays in Honor of Benjamin Boyce*, Vol. LXX, Spring 1971, pp. [215]-235.

LONDON OBSERVED:
THE PROGRESS OF A SIMILE

On Good Friday in 1775, as Johnson and Boswell were on their way to the service at St. Clement's Church, Boswell remarked on the "immensity of London." Johnson agreed that London was too large; but he added, so Boswell tells us, "It is nonsense to say the head is too big for the body. It would be as much too big, though the body were ever so large, that is to say, though the country were ever so extensive." London, he maintained, "has no similarity to a head connected with a body."[1] This brief remark by Johnson, with its implied similitude in which England is likened to the human body, London being the head and the rest of the country the body, is not likely to make a modern reader of Boswell's *Life* pause; and, indeed, neither Birkbeck Hill nor L. F. Powell annotates the passage, nor does any other Johnsonian or Boswellian, so far as I know, pay any attention to it. Nevertheless, this casual, slight, innocent-looking remark would have had for Johnson's more knowledgeable contemporaries rich implications and connotations not evident to our generation: in the background of the similitude was an extensive and substantial tradition, a tradition demographic in its nature and significantly related to certain economic and social aspects of the seventeenth and eighteenth centuries—and particularly touching matters of extraordinary concern to the public authorities alert to the possibilities of famine, plague, fire, and rebellion, in fact, to the economic and social health of England as a whole.

Readers of *Humphry Clinker* will recall that Matthew Bramble, that "most risible misanthrope," soon after arriving in London with his entourage, wrote to his friend, Dr. Lewis, describing in detail his impressions of the metropolis; a "misshapen and monstrous capital," he termed it, "without head or tail, members or proportion."[2] To Bramble's distress, what earlier had been open fields producing hay and corn was now "covered with streets and squares, and palaces and churches." Now, he lamented, "I am credibly informed, that in the space of seven years, eleven thousand new houses have been built in one quarter of Westminster, exclusive of what is daily added to other parts of this unwieldy metropolis." Certain improvements were visible. This he granted, but the overwhelming fact was the massive growth, the irregular and planless expansion of London farther and farther from the inner city into the surrounding countryside, a metropolis ever more complex, crowded, and unwieldy. In remarking on London's steady spread into the countryside, Bramble quotes an unnamed Irishman who wrote: "London is now gone out of town." The words, appropriately, are part of a few lines of nostalgic lament for a rural London which had disappeared. Though they belong to a period fifty years earlier, they caught Smollett's mood perfectly:

> Where's Troy, and where's the May-Pole in the *Strand?*
> Pease, Cabbages, and Turnips once grew, where
> Now stands *New-Bond* Street, and a newer Square;
> Such piles of Buildings now rise up and down,
> *London* itself seems going out of *Town.*[3]

In the letter to Dr. Lewis, Bramble introduces and sets the tone for certain pervasive strains in the novel: the indictment of luxury, the prevalent corruption of manners, the primitivistic insistence on the superiority of country to town, and England's general decline. For Matt Bramble London was lost to innocence and simplicity, the embodiment of many evils, and by virtue of its vast size and influence it posed a threat to the entire country. London, he asserts—and here the simile is fully stated—has become "an overgrown monster; which, like a dropsical head, will in time leave the body and extremities without nourishment and support."[4] The simile, London is like a dropsical head, is appropriate to Smollett the physician and as well to his spokesman, Matt Bramble, who though a layman is himself a student of human maladies and is particularly knowledgeable on the subject of dropsy.[5]

It would be pleasant to be able to say that Johnson had Smollett and Bramble's remark in mind in 1775 when he rejected as invalid the simile that London is like a head too big for the body. In 1775 *Humphry Clinker* had been published for almost four years; and though I would not wish to underestimate Johnson's tenacious memory, there is a more convincing hypothesis: Johnson, as Smollett before him, was independently resorting to a time-honored simile, a figure of speech ready at hand for imaging forth London's relationship to the rest of the country, the image of the metropolis as a head swollen at the expense of the nation at large. Both men unquestionably would have been aware that the simile originated in and continued to reflect a demographic debate or controversy which ranged in time over two or more centuries involving, among others, John Graunt,

Sir William Petty, Daniel Defoe, and Laurence Sterne. The wording of the simile varied slightly from time to time, but the image and the ideas the simile embodied had become fixed by the eighteenth century from damnable iteration in earlier economic, political, and social thought. It is evident that this figurative representation of London, sometimes as a dropsical head, sometimes as a wen or the spleen, often as a monstrous and overgrown head, came instantly, almost automatically to the mind of contemporaries as a conventionalized, short-hand descriptive phrase, apt and evocative for writers who, unlike Johnson, believed that London's massive size threatened England's welfare.

Probably the distinction of being the first to apply a medical or anatomical simile to London in this manner belongs to royalty. It was James I who asserted that London is like "the head of a rickety child, in which an extensive flux of humour drained and impoverished the extremities, and at the same time generated distemper in the overloaded part."[6] James, it seems, was merely repeating fears already voiced by his predecessor. A Royal Proclamation issued by Queen Elizabeth in 1580 expressed concern that London was expanding at the expense of "other places abroad in the Realm, where many Houses rest uninhabited, to the decay of divers auncient good Boroughes and Townes."[7] At various times in the sixteenth and seventeenth centuries the Privy Council and other authorities issued orders designed to limit or control London's increasing growth, indicating an awareness of dangers and problems posed by this expanding population, the problems, for example, of controlling large masses of people, of vagrancy and poverty, of fire and famine, and of plagues; but of all the disruptions implicit in the simile the one which caused most concern is economic in nature. When Sir Thomas Roe, who had served as a privy counsellor and as ambassador of James I to the courts of the Great Mogul, of the Grand Signior, and of Sweden, rose in the Long Parliament of 1640 to speak of the decay in England's trade and coinage, his vivid figurative depiction of London as a "fat head" enlarged at the expense of the country at large may well have had a familiar ring. "I will trouble you," he told his fellow members of Parliament, "with a consideration, very considerable in our government, whether, indeed, London doth not monopolize all trade. In my opinion, it is no good state of a body to have a fat head, thin guts, and lean members."[8] Almost a century and a half later, Smollett, the man of medicine, turns Sir Thomas Roe's "fat head" into a dropsical head.

By 1640 the *idea* that the similitude expresses was well launched; and in the following decades we can observe the *simile* itself, with its diction or mode of expression fairly well fixed, moving down the cultural stream.

With the appearance of Peter Heylin's *Cosmography* in 1652, the notion of an overgrown and dominating London conceived in terms of human anatomy or, more interestingly, in terms of a disease or malady, was given further currency. London, Heylin wrote, "is grown at last too big for the Kingdom":

> whether it may be profitable for the State, or not, may be made a question. Great Towns in the body of a State, are like the *Spleen* or *Melt* in the body natural; the monstrous growth of which impoverisheth all the rest of the Members, by drawing to it all the *animal* and *vital* spirits, which should give nourishment unto them; And in the end cracked or surcharged by its own fulness, not only sends unwholsom fumes and *vapours* unto the *head,* and heavy *pangs* unto the *heart,* but draws a *consumption* on it self. And certainly the overgrowth of great Cities is of consequence, not only in regard of famin, such multitudes of mouths not being easie to be fed: but in respect of the irreparable danger of insurrections. . . .[9]

Heylin added a medical dimension to the similitude by drawing upon contemporary physiology and the extensive interest in spleen, the English malady, as Dr. George Cheyne and others later designated it. Heylin's simile is elaborated sufficiently to let us see more fully and more vividly than heretofore precisely how contemporaries conceived the analogy between the diseased human body and the predatory metropolis, a London economically destructive and battening upon the rest of the country. But the political strain buried in the simile also emerges in Heylin's phrase, "the irreparable danger of insurrections." In the light of the political scene in 1652 and Heylin's role as an uncompromising apologist for Anglicanism, we may safely assume that he had in mind the Cromwellian and Puritan "insurrections," with London as a focal center. And considering the overwhelming interest of the seventeenth and eighteenth centuries in the spleen, the simile stated in this phraseology was perhaps inevitable. It appears again in Heylin's phraseology, a decade later, in *The Gentleman's Monitor* (1665), a courtesy book by Edward Waterhouse, the author of *An Humble Apologie for Learning and Learned Men* (1653). Waterhouse likens London's growth to the spleen in a man's body: as the diseased spleen swells, the body wastes; as London increases, the country dwindles.[10] An example of how the imagery and the figurative language could shift while the idea expressed by the simile remained unaffected is evident in a letter written in 1665 to Charles II by William Cavendish, the first Duke of Newcastle, a military hero during the Civil War, who gained added lustre at the Restoration as an author and as the husband of the talented Margaret Cavendish. "I would have your Matie have all the Armes and Amunition in your owne handes," he wrote to the king, "& first to begin with your Metropolitan Citye of London, that great Leviathan, that Monster beinge the heade, & that heade so much too bigg for the bodye of the common wealth off

Englande, soe that Master that Citye, & you Master the whole King-dome."[11]

As one would expect, it is the economic writers who used the simile with a special cogency, such political arithmeticians as John Graunt, Charles Davenant, and Sir William Petty. Graunt's book, *Natural and Political Observations upon the Bills of Mortality* (1662), is of surpassing importance in the development of English demographic science. It is an elaborate statistical study of London's population on the presumption, so Graunt contends, *"That a true* Accompt of people *is necessary for the* Government, *and* Trade *of them, and for their* peace and plenty."[12] The third edition, in 1665, was published under the auspices of the Royal Society, of which Graunt was a Fellow. In the Epistle Dedicatory to the Lord Privy Seal, Graunt writes: "For, with all humble submission to your Lordship, I conceive, that it doth not ill become a *Peer of the Parliament* or *Member of his Majesties* Council, to consider . . . That *London,* the *Metropolis* of *England,* is perhaps a Head too big for the Body, and possibly too strong; That this Head grows three times as fast as the Body unto which it belongs; that is, it doubles its People in a third part of the time."[13] Graunt gave significance and dignity to his work by conceiving of it as a study in "the Art of Governing, and the true *Politicks*"—that is, "how to preserve the Subject in *Peace* and Plenty."[14] The primacy of the economic aspect is evident in Graunt's assertion that the foundation of "true *Politicks*" is an understanding of "the Land and the hands [i.e., the people] of the Territory, to be governed according to all their intrinsick and accidental differences."[14] With the proper knowledge of "the Land and the hands" one may see

how small a part of the People work upon necessary Labours and Callings, *viz.* how many Women and Children do just nothing, only learning to spend what others get; how many [people] are meer Voluptuaries, and as it were meer Gamesters by Trade; how many live by puzzling poor people with unintelligible Notions in Divinity and Philosophy; how many by perswading credulous, delicate, and litigious Persons, that their Bodies or Estates are out of Tune, and in danger; how many by fighting as soldiers; how many by Ministries of Vice and Sin; how many by Trades of meer Pleasure, or Ornaments; and how many in a way of lazy attendance, *&c.* upon others: And on the other side, how few are employed in raising and working necessary Food and Covering; and of the speculative men, how few do study *Nature* and *Things!*[15]

This passage from Graunt is particularly informative: it enables one to see clearly how the London of the simile, when examined in its economic aspect, might well be viewed by contemporaries as a debilitated or diseased organ, because it was London primarily in which these "consumptive trades" multiplied and flourished, with the maximum impact upon the national economy. The phrase, "consumptive trades," as used by seventeenth- and eighteenth-century economic writers included what in modern parlance would be called the service trades and a variety of other economic activities not likely to improve that great desideratum of the mercantilist, a favorable balance of trade. These "nonproducers," as they might be termed, included—so we learn from William Petyt's important economic tract, *Britannia Languens* (1680)—lawyers, scriveners, physicians, small shop-keepers who deal in imported "finery and gawdery," inn-keepers, scholars, and divines, indeed so many divines that "a late Author ... thought it necessary to export *Tunns of Divines* instead of Manufactures." [16] The point made by Graunt and Petyt is that London's massive growth had created the conditions in which these wasteful professions and occupations could thrive and prosper. The result, Petyt writes, is that "the Country [i.e., the countryside] is left poorer and barer every day," whereas new buildings constantly rise in and about London. The population flows in that direction, and not only from the "higher ranks of men": it is also "the ordinary people who used heretofore to begin upon Farming or Manufacture, hearing of *mon[e]y* in London, do post from the starving Country, and apply themselves to the selling of Ale, Brandy, Tobacco, Coffee, Brokery of all sorts, letting of Lodgings in or about *London,* and such like Imployments, which too commonly end in Bawdery and the Gallows. . . ." [17] Thus, though he is concerned primarily with economic matters, Petyt assesses as well the harmful moral impact of London's unhealthy growth and the excess of "consumptive trades": when reputable and productive means of livelihood become clogged, men turn to the less reputable and "fall to *Cheating, Canting, Shifting, Perjury, Forgery, Whoredom, Sherking, Clipping, Coyning, Buffooning, Tumbling, Pimping, Pilfering, Robbery, &c. for their ordinary maintenances.*" [18]

In the final decade of the seventeenth century Charles Davenant, an able expounder of mercantilist doctrine and one of the more prolific economic writers of the period, announced his intention to examine the opinion among landed men that "the immoderate growth of [London] undoes and ruins all the Country." It may be, he wrote, "well worth the enquiry of thinking men, what truth there is in this common and received notion, that the growth of London is pernicious to England; that the kingdom is like a rickety body, with a head too big for the other members." [19] This pronouncement of 1695 was followed by a similar one in 1698; and in Davenant's tracts we glimpse the harsh economic realities which gave vibrant meaning to the simile and as well to the extensive semi-primitivistic literature which mirrors the conflict between town and country, as in Goldsmith's *The Deserted Village* and in *Humphry Clinker.* "In former Times," Davenant tells us, "the Wealth of England was far more equally dispers'd

... and the respective Counties of the Kingdom had a larger Proportion of it; the Gentry liv'd at their Seats, the Country-Towns were Populous, several of the Out-Ports had their Share of Trade, but by degrees, in the space of about Forty Years, the Number of inhabitants, the Riches, and the Traffick of the Nation, have center'd in this Great City." [20]

Clearly, to many contemporaries, the English countryside exhibited a visible decline, its labor supply seriously drained by a voracious city, its nobility and gentry seduced by a glittering metropolis, the best administrative talents—justices and others, who with their money and the quality of their lives had given a certain tone to rural England—drawn away. These left the rural scene, and left it, not despoiled, but with reduced vitality and appeal. One can observe a deepening uneasiness and awareness in thoughtful contemporaries that something economically and socially unhealthy was in progress, something which might be described in part by the phrase, the decline of the rural virtues. Its relevance to our simile is obvious. The threat to the countryside, so feelingly observed by economic writers and others who tended to make London the villain, generated a nostalgic, defensive, and protective mood in many writers, who in countless semi-primitivistic passages lavished an idealism on the countryside little related to the realities. But a widely prevailing mood was receptive to the idealized depiction of the rural scene. The myth of a pastoral golden age, even if it deluded no one, was nevertheless a pleasing delusion easily indulged. And if certain deeper social and political emotions of the age were in fact attuned to the idea of a pastoral golden age, or something akin to it, then London, the very antithesis of such an age, could appropriately be thought of, figuratively, as a diseased organ. Therefore it would seem valid to maintain that the simile received emotional and intellectual support from a prevailing climate of opinion.

But I would not wish to leave the impression that the simile and its implications were everywhere uncritically accepted or left unchallenged. Sir William Petty, along with John Graunt the most influential demographer of the seventeenth century and himself a member of the Royal Society, examined at length the matter of London's growth and size. In *Another Essay in Political Arithmetick, concerning the Growth of the City of London ... 1682,* he posed the question, "Whether it be best to lessen or enlarge the present City?" His procedure was to hypothesize "two imaginary states": one in which London would be enlarged spatially to seven times its then size with a population fixed at 4,690,000 and the rest of the country having "but two Millions 710 Thousand more"; the "other *Supposition* is, That the City of *London* is but a seventh part of its present bigness." This hypothesis granted London only 96,000 inhabitants and gave the rest of the country a population of 7,304,000. "Now," Petty writes, "the Question is, In which of these two Imaginary states, would be the most convenient, commodious, and comfortable Livings?"[21] This general or larger question he examined from the vantage of a number of particular questions: would a larger or smaller London be more effective in defending the kingdom against foreign powers, in preventing internal strife by parties or factions, in establishing peace and uniformity in religion, in the administering of justice and a fair system of taxation, in improving foreign commerce, in advancing husbandry, manufactures, and the "Arts of Delight and Ornament," in improving internal communication, in reducing begging and thieving, in propagating useful learning, in increasing the population, and in "preventing the Mischiefs of *Plague* and *Contagion.*"[22]

In these various "Particulars" it appears that Petty has set forth meticulously all of the social, economic, and political implications clustered in the simile, including some omitted by his predecessors. As he examined each particular in turn, his discussion becomes a striking demonstration of what this simple figurative expression—London is like a monstrous, overgrown head too big for the body of the nation—could mean to a contemporary. More penetratingly than earlier writers on the subject, Petty is fully aware of the complex and vital realities of English life and society implicit in the compass of this brief similitude. He concluded that in ten of the twelve particular questions examined, a London seven times its present size would in no respect impair the quality of English life, that on the contrary it would be a distinct advantage, whereas in only a single respect the less populous London would be advantageous, the prevention of plagues and contagion.

In the eighteenth century the growth of London posed continuing formidable problems and, as in the preceding century, the simile retained its usefulness over the span of a hundred years. In *The Fable of the Bees* (1714) Bernard Mandeville raises expectations by his remark that "*London* is too big for the country,"[23] but then disappoints by failing to elaborate or use the simile. On the other hand, Defoe, as one would expect from the laureate of London and commerce, does not disappoint us. No one in the period observed the metropolis with more fascination or with such zestful appreciation, including its vast size and constant growth. And no one would have been more disposed to challenge the validity of the simile, as in fact he did vigorously in *The Complete English Tradesman* (1725; 1727): "Those people are greatly mistaken," he maintains, "who pretend the growing greatness of [London] is too much for the whole country; alledging, that the nation is liver grown, and must die of a pleura; and that the city draws away the nourishment from the country, like a dropsy, which swells the body, but draws the nourishment away from the extreme parts":

But, I say, this is a mistake; even the simile itself will not hold; for this swelling the body of the city, makes it the centre of nourishment to the whole nation; and as every part of the kingdom sends up hither the best of their produce, so they carry back a return of wealth; the money flows from the city into the remotest parts, and furnishes them again to increase that produce, to improve the lands, pay rent to their landlords, taxes to their governors, and supply their families with necessaries; and this is Trade.[24]

Defoe will not have it, this notion that London can be aptly described in the language of morbidity, in the image of a diseased and swollen bodily organ unwholesomely fattening at the expense of the rest of the body.

Defoe's attack on the validity of the simile is in the context of a long chapter composed, he tells us, "for the honour of London, which rears its head so high in the trading world."[25] He proposes to show "what prime consideration and benefit this glorious city is to the whole kingdom, preferable to what any other capital city is to any other kingdom or state upon earth." He maintains, as a *general* truth, that "all collected bodies of people are a particular assistance to trade: and, therefore, to have one great and capital city in a kingdom, is of much greater advantage to it than if the same number of people dwelt in several places." To demonstrate this general truth, he examines London in two relevant aspects, first as it is a great emporium, the center of a vast commerce in both imported and exported goods, and then as it is the vital axis of the inland or home trade. In his paean to London Defoe's prose is often vibrant with detail, as in *Robinson Crusoe,* and indeed has at times a comparable sensuousness, reflecting his fascination with material things. In a work so devoted to the utilitarian, as *The Complete English Tradesman* is, a reader may be surprised to find himself occasionally immersed in a savory ambience, evoked of course by Defoe's compulsion to catalogue for effect: pimento and ginger, rum and molasses, malt from Kent, butter in firkins from Suffolk, cheese from Cheshire and red herrings from Yarmouth, raisins and oil from Messina, wine, anchovies, and capers from Leghorn, salt fish and whale fin—and these varied delicacies interlarded with less savory but still pungent objects as pitch and tar and turpentine. Defoe had a happy talent in economic discourse for making commerce, trade, shipping, exports and imports shed their abstract quality and take on a pleasing gustatorial or sensory appeal. Who can fail to feel the texture at the mere naming of such textiles as kerseys, shalloons, camelets, duroys, serges, perpetuanas, druggets, half-thicks, callamancas, duffields, dimities, and tammies? When he is writing of London's trade, Defoe's gusto is not stemmed. His language suggests fruitfulness and abundance; and indeed he seems to envision the great metropolis as cornucopian.

In substance Defoe asks the question: what would the country do if there were no London? How would the products of the land be sold? Without London, he answers, "the land must lie waste and uncultivated, the cattle run wild, and devour the country, or be starved and die; the country sends up their corn, their malt, their cattle, their fowl, their coals, their fish, all to London, and London sends back spice, sugar, wine, drugs, cotton, linen, tobacco, and all foreign necessaries . . . and above all the rest, that useful drug called money; so that still it is the capital city that is the life of the country, and keeps them all in motion."[26] In Defoe's tribute to London's opulence and magnificence, a city which, in his words, "circulates all, exports all, and at last pays for all," we have, so far as I know, the most detailed response to the economic implications of the simile, with only Sir William Petty's analysis approaching Defoe's in seriousness and completeness.

In the two or three decades following Defoe the simile continued to surface, its usefulness not diminished by time and iteration. It appeared in some of the diatribes against luxury, for example in Erasmus Jones's tract, *Luxury, Pride, and Vanity, the Bane of the British Nation,* in a fourth edition in 1735. We hear the familiar lament: London has so depleted the countryside by its "prodigious growth" and left it so wretched that "a true *Englishman* cannot look into it without a just pity and concern." The growth of "this unweildy *City*" is such that "the Head, in a very little time longer, will grow so much too big for the Body, that it must consequently tumble down at last and ruin the whole."[27] I pass by as of no special interest a similar lament in Samuel Fawconer's *An Essay on Modern Luxury* (1765)[28] to glance at *Tristram Shandy,* where the simile is assimilated into Sterne's comedy.

It will be recalled that the marriage settlement between Walter Shandy and Mrs. Shandy contained one clause granting Mrs. Shandy the right to lie in in London, something she devoutly desired, though Mr. Shandy himself fretted at the trouble and expense. Fortunately Mr. Shandy was protected from "any unfair play": a provision included at the suggestion of Uncle Toby stipulated that if Mrs. Shandy violated the indenture by compelling Mr. Shandy to take her to London "upon false cries and tokens" of pregnancy, she then forfeited the right to lie in in London and must consent to have her next child in the country.[29] As we learn from Tristram, Mrs. Shandy had indeed in the year before his birth "whistled [Mr. Shandy] up to *London*" on a false presumption or pretense of pregnancy.[30] Thereupon Mr. Shandy exercised his rights: he insisted that Mrs. Shandy honor the indenture by being delivered of Tristram in the country, even though "she begg'd and pray'd . . . upon her bare knees." As a consequence Tristram was brought into the world by the blundering Dr. Slop, whose unskilled use of the forceps was such that his nose was crushed to his face "as flat as a pancake." [31] Thus it was that Tristram was doomed, as he related, by the marriage articles "to have my nose squeez'd as flat to my face, as if the destinies had actually spun me without one." [32] Lamentable as this was, in mitigation of Mr. Shandy we learn that his insistence upon strict adherence to the indenture was not prompted by obstinancy or mere concern for his personal rights. He was, in fact, motivated by a higher political principle, a deep concern for the public good. He was well aware that political writers from the reign of Elizabeth to his own time had unanimously viewed the strong "current of men and money" towards London as a danger to civil rights. Mr. Shandy shared their concern, but was not disposed to accept the image of a "current"; he had his own favorite metaphor to describe the flow of the population to the metropolis. To him the phenomenon was more properly described as a distemper, a distemper in the body politic comparable to a distemper in the body natural. And for which Walter Shandy, of course, had a remedy: " 'Was I an absolute prince,' he would say, pulling up his breeches with both his hands as he rose from his arm-chair"—and with this proviso we learn that he would appoint able judges to examine everyone entering London from the country. Anyone without sufficient reason would be sent back "like the vagrants as they were, to the place of their legal settlements." "By this means," Mr. Shandy maintains—and here the similitude surfaces once again—"I shall take care that my metropolis totter'd not thro' its own weight;—that the head be no longer too big for the body;—that the extremes, now wasted and pin'd in, be restored to their due share of nourishment, and regain, with it, their natural strength and beauty:—I would effectually provide, That the meadows and corn-fields, of my dominions, should laugh and sing;—that good chear and hospitality flourish once more. . . ." [33]

Thus we have wittily linked the demographic principle embodied in the simile, a blundering country doctor with his newfangled forceps, a squashed nose, an eccentric philosophic-minded father, and a Shandean clause in a marriage settlement, all the quintessence of Sternian comedy and the only instance I have found in which the simile is brought down from a serious level into a context of humor and wit. The comic inventiveness and intellectual playfulness with which Sterne has invested the figure of speech is in marked contrast to the tone and manner Smollett used a few years later.[34]

NOTES

1   *Boswell's Life of Johnson*, ed. George Birkbeck Hill, rev. L. F. Powell (Oxford: Clarendon Press, 1934), II, 356. Boswell's reference to "the immensity of London" was very likely prompted by the controversies then in progress over London's size and growth, a subject treated extensively in the excellent study by D. V. Glass, *Numbering the People: The Eighteenth-Century Population Controversy and the Development of Census and Vital Statistics in Britain* (Farnborough: D. C. Heath, 1973).

2 *The Expedition of Humphry Clinker,* ed. Lewis M. Knapp (London: Oxford U. Press, 1966), p. 90: To Dr. Lewis, May 29.

3 Ibid., p. 86. The Irishman quoted by Smollett, hitherto not identified, is James Bramston. The quotation is from his poetic imitation of Horace, *The Art of Politicks,* 1729, pp. 9–10. Bramston is perhaps better known as the author of *The Man of Taste,* 1733.

4 Ibid., p. 87: To Dr. Lewis, May 29.

5 Ibid., pp. 23–25: To Dr. Lewis, April 20.

6 Quoted from Norman G. Brett-James, *The Growth of Stuart London* (London: Allen and Unwin, 1935), p. 515, n. 41.

7 Ibid, p. 69.

8 "Sir Thomas Roe's Speech in Parliament, wherein he sheweth the Cause of the Decay of Coin and Trade in this Land," 1641, reprinted in *Seventeenth-Century Economic Documents,* ed. Joan Thirsk and J. P. Cooper (Oxford: Clarendon Press, 1972), p. 45.

9 *Cosmography, in Four Books, containing the Chorography and History of the whole World and all the Principal Kingdoms, Provinces, Seas, and Isles thereof,* sixth ed. (London, 1670), p. 306. Heylin's comparison of London to the spleen is an echo of a Paul's Cross sermon of 1627, preached by John Grent, Vicar of Ashton in Warwickshire. The sermon is titled *The Burthen of Tyre.* It is a warning to London that its wealth, luxury, and pride will bring doom, the fate of Tyre as revealed in the Bible. In homiletic literature London was often denounced as a modern Tyre. Grent admonishes Londoners in words relevant to our simile: "The riches of the Country . . . take the wings of the morning, and fly into the Citie: the whole Land emptieth her treasure into your lappes, as all the Riuers doe their waters into the Sea: Looke therefore you use your abundance to Gods glory, and the advancing of goodnesse. The *Metropolitan* City is usually the spleene of the Kingdome; the bigger the spleene, the lesse and leaner all the body besides; for the ones fulnesse draweth the other to emptinesse, which if it still swell and swell, and purge not forsooth (by good workes and almes-deedes) there must be some other remedy sought; *Leeches* must be applied. You are but *Stewards* of the Riches you possesse, improue them therefore for your masters commodity, not for your owne pompe and brauery. Traffique [i.e., commerce] hath brought you foorth Wealth, take heede Wealth bring not foorth Luxury; Luxury Pride, and Pride, Vengeance. Poor *Tyre* payeth for it . . ." (pp. 8–9, 11).

10 (London, 1665), pp. 306–07.

11 S. A. Strong, ed., *A Catalogue of Letters and Other Historical Documents exhibited in the Library at Welbeck* (London: John Murray, 1903), p. 176. Newcastle's reference to London as "that greate Leviathan" suggests a Hobbesian influence. In *Leviathan,* 1651, Hobbes makes a similar point: in Part 2, ch. xxix he discusses the "infirmities" of a commonwealth and compares them to "the diseases of a naturall body." One "infirmity" of a commonwealth, he writes, "is the immoderate greatnesse of a Town, when it is able to furnish out of its own Circuit, the number, and expense of a great army." See *Leviathan,* Everyman ed., with an Introduction by A. D. Lindsay (London and New York: Dent and Dutton, n. d.), p. 177.

12 *The Economic Writings of Sir William Petty together with the Observations upon the Bills of Mortality more probably by Captain John Graunt,* ed. Charles Henry Hull (Cambridge: 1899), II, 332.

13 Ibid., II, 320–21.

14 Ibid., II, 395–96.

15 Ibid., II, 396–97.

16   William Petyt (?), *Britannia Languens, or A Discourse of Trade,* 1680, reprinted in *A Select Collection of Early English Tracts on Commerce,* ed. J. R. McCulloch (London, 1856, new issue 1952), pp. 378 ff. Petyt (1641–1707) is credited with authorship of the tract but the ascription is dubious. He was the author of several legal works. The "late Author" who thought it necessary to export *"Tunns of Divines"* instead of manufactures is a reference to John Eachard, author of the widely read *The Grounds and Occasions of the Contempt of the Clergy and Religion Enquired into,* 1670.

17   Ibid., pp. 379–80.

18   Ibid., p. 376.

19   "An Essay upon Ways and Means," 1695, in *The Political and Commercial Works of Charles D'Avenant . . . relating to the Trade and Revenue of England,* ed. Sir Charles Whitworth (London, 1771), I, 59. It is of interest that Davenant views the simile in the context of the conflict between the landed interest and the trading interest.

20   *Discourses on the Public Revenues* (London, 1698), p. 49. In *An Essay upon Ways and Means,* 1695, Davenant lists reasons why "some people are led to think the growth of London not hurtful to the nation; but, on the contrary, to believe that there is not an acre of land in the country, be it never so distant, that is not in some degree bettered by the growth, trade, and riches of that city" (see *The Political and Commercial Works of Charles D'Avenant . . . ,* ed. Sir Charles Whitworth [London, 1771], I, 59–60).

21   "Another Essay in Political Arithmetick, concerning the Growth of the City of London . . . , 1682," in *The Economic Writings of Sir William Petty . . .* ed. Charles Henry Hull (Cambridge, 1899), II, 470. In 1682 Petty estimated the population of London to be *"about Six Hundred and Seventy Thousand Souls."* England and Wales he estimated to be about 7,400,000 (see Hull, II, 456). Gregory King, whose *Natural and Political Observations upon the State and Condition of England,* 1695, is another influential demographic study, has somewhat lower estimates. He estimated that London's population in the time of Julius Caesar was four to five thousand, at the Norman Conquest about 24,000, and in 1695 about 530,000. King calculated that by the year A.D. 3500 or 3600 the population of England having reached 22,000,000 would not then be capable of any further growth because the land would not support a larger number (see the excerpts from King's *Natural and Political Observations* in *Seventeenth-Century Economic Documents,* ed. Joan Thirsk and J. P. Cooper (Oxford: Clarendon Press, 1972), pp. 772 and 775–76.

22   See *The Economic Writings of Sir William Petty . . . ,* ed. Charles Henry Hull (Cambridge, 1899), II, 470–76.

23   Bernard Mandeville, *The Fable of the Bees: Or Private Vices, Publick Benefits,* ed. F. B. Kaye (Oxford: Clarendon Press, 1924), I, 306.

24   *The Novels and Miscellaneous Works of Daniel Defoe* (Oxford: Tegg, 1841), XVIII, 68–69.

25   Ibid., For this and the paragraph generally see chs. XXXIV and XLV. Defoe's general truth, that a nation gains more from "a great and capital city" than it would if the population were more equally distributed was stated earlier by Charles Davenant in *An Essay on Ways and Means,* 1695: "That no empire was ever great, without having a great and populous City" (see *The Political and Commercial Works of Charles D'Avenant,* ed. Sir Charles Whitworth [London, 1771], I, 59 f.). Davenant cites Rome and Athens as examples. See also the discussion by James Harrington in *The Prerogatives of Popular Government,* in *The Oceana and Other Works of James Harrington, with an Account of his Life by John Toland* (London, 1771), p. 280: "That the increase of *Rome,* which was always study'd by her best citizens, should make the head too great for her body, or her power dangerous to the tribes, was never so much as imagin'd. . . ."

26   Ibid., XVIII, 77.

27 Fourth edition (London, 1735), p. 2.

28 *An Essay on Modern Luxury* (London, 1765), pp. 8–9.

29 *The Life and Opinions of Tristram Shandy, Gentleman,* ed. James Aiken Work (New York: Odyssey Press, 1940), I, xv, pp. 38–40.

30 Ibid., I, xvi, p. 41.

31 Ibid., III, xxvii, p. 214.

32 Ibid., I, xv, p. 41.

33 Ibid., I, xviii, pp. 45–46.

34 The vitality of the simile is evident from its persistence into the nineteenth and twentieth centuries. Perhaps the best-known instance of its use in the nineteenth century is by William Cobbett in *Rural Rides,* 1830: "But what is to be the fate of the great wen . . . the monster called . . . the metropolis of the Empire?" (Everyman edition, ed. James Paul Cobbett, I, 43 and *passim*). Cf. Josiah Tucker in 1783: "London . . . has been complained of, for Ages past, as a Kind of Monster, with a Head enormously large, and out of proportion to its Body." If, Tucker continues, it was looked upon 200 years ago as "no better than a Wen, or Excrescence, in the Body Politic," what must be thought of it now, so extraordinarily expanded? See *Four Letters on Important National Subjects* (London, 1783), p. 44. Finally, consider the title of a recent study: Frances Sheppard, *London, 1808–1870: The Infernal Wen* (U. of California Press, 1973).

INDEX

LIBRARY OF CONGRESS CATALOGING IN PUBLICATION DATA

Landa, Louis A   1901–
   Essays in eighteenth-century English literature.

   (Princeton series of collected essays; 3)
   Includes index.
   1.   English literature—18th century—History and
criticism—Addresses, essays, lectures.   2.   Swift,
Jonathan, 1667-1745—Criticism and interpretation—
Addresses, essays, lectures.   I.   Title.
PR442.L3   820'.9'005   80-7541
ISBN 0-691-06449-0
ISBN 0-691-01375-6 (pbk.)